T0301798

From the
Global Financial Tsunami to the Property Bubbles in Asia
The Need for a New Discipline on Macroeconomic Management

From the
Global Financial Tsunami to the Property Bubbles in Asia
The Need for a New Discipline
on Macroeconomic Management

PAUL YIP Sau-Leung
Nanyang Technological University, Singapore

 **World Scientific**

EW JERSEY · LONDON · SINGAPORE · BEIJING · SHANGHAI · HONG KONG · TAIPEI · CHENNAI · TOKYO

Published by

World Scientific Publishing Co. Pte. Ltd.

5 Toh Tuck Link, Singapore 596224

USA office: 27 Warren Street, Suite 401-402, Hackensack, NJ 07601

UK office: 57 Shelton Street, Covent Garden, London WC2H 9HE

British Library Cataloguing-in-Publication Data
A catalogue record for this book is available from the British Library.

**FROM THE GLOBAL FINANCIAL TSUNAMI TO THE
PROPERTY BUBBLES IN ASIA**
The Need for a New Discipline on Macroeconomic Management

ISBN 978-981-4623-68-1

For any available supplementary material, please visit
https://www.worldscientific.com/worldscibooks/10.1142/9323#t=suppl

Desk Editor: Sandhya Venkatesh

Typeset by Stallion Press
Email: enquiries@stallionpress.com

Printed in Singapore

To my parents,
my wife,
my son and
my daughter.

CONTENTS

PREFACE

Since early 2009, the author has written numerous policy articles explaining that the quantitative easing (QE) programs in the US and other major economies helped the global economy avoid a great depression during the global financial tsunami. Nevertheless, the policy articles also warned the high likelihood of aftershock crises such as huge cycles in exchange rates, emergent market crises during the mid or final phase of the subsequent US interest rate hike, the formation of property bubbles in many Asian economies and the eventual bursting of these property bubbles. In particular, the policy articles highlighted that a bursting of any one of these property bubbles would trigger another Asian financial crisis through the contagion effect.

As of September 2018, the prediction of the formation of huge property bubbles in some Asian economies has proved to be correct, and unfortunately there is a high likelihood that the prediction of an eventual bursting of these property bubbles will prove to be correct. In this book, the author first outlines the theoretical frameworks behind these predictions, which will in turn suggest that the expected financial crisis is due to avoidable policy mistakes in these economies. Throughout the book, the author illustrates how the theoretical frameworks could help central bankers and economic policymakers pre-empt the formation of huge property bubbles and hence the subsequent financial crisis due to the eventual bursting of these property bubbles. Institutional and individual investors would also find the theoretical frameworks extremely useful to their property, shares and other asset investment.

In Chapters 2–4, the author discusses the likelihood of a substantial correction of property prices in many Asian economies. In particular, he draws very useful and important lessons from two extreme examples: Hong Kong was one of the poorest performers in pre-empting the formation of the bubble at the seeding stage, and stopping the rapid growth of the bubble into a gigantic one at the development stage of the bubble. Singapore was the best performer that managed to stop the growth of the property bubble at the development stage, and then squeezed its small property bubble into a much safer one between mid-2013 and late 2017. That is, while Singapore also missed the best chance to pre-empt the bubble formation at the seeding stage, the Singapore government was the only Asian government that managed to use severe enough curbing measures to bring its red-hot property market out from the automatic bubble path and successfully squeezed the bubble to a smaller one. Furthermore, the well-trained monetary officials in 2018 managed to use the ninth round of curbing measures to pre-empt the redevelopment of property bubble from the new seeding stage in 2018, thus suggesting that these monetary officials had reached a higher standard when compared with their predecessors in 2009H2–2010H2. The author believes the excellent performance in Singapore and the very poor performance in Hong Kong and other Asian economies will mean a significant difference in economic damages during the second Asian financial crisis mentioned above.

In Chapter 5, the author provides further discussions on the property market and long-term housing policies in Asia. In particular, he highlights and explains that

(1) the higher inflation, GDP growth, urbanization, infrastructure and transportation improvements, as well as the absence of capital gain tax in Asia have resulted in huge capital gains of property ownership in Asia, which has in turn made property investment a traditional investment wisdom in Asia;

(2) the high wealth and income inequality in Asia would mean that the average property price has to rise to a high enough level so that a significant portion of households cannot afford to own their home while the richer households could satisfy their desire to own a large number of residential properties;

(3) there is a vicious cycle between inequality and uneven distribution of properties;

(4) because of the market structure problem and the indicator effect outlined in Chapter 1, the total quantity of housing in urban Asia is far less than the social optimal level, albeit not necessarily in the form of the *total number* of housing units but in the form of *total size* of all housing units;

(5) there are negative effects of high real property prices on business ventures and formation, innovation, economic growth and business ethic.

Thereafter, he provides further discussions on the role of affordable public flats as a long-term solution to the housing problem in Asia.

In Chapter 6, the author and Dr. Teo use a large number of simulation exercises to illustrate that

(a) the market structure problem in the Asian property markets would result in high real housing prices and a significant portion of households who cannot afford to own their homes;

(b) the high wealth (or permanent income) inequality in these economies would further increase the proportion of households who cannot afford to own their home.

Thereafter, they show that government's direct supply and sale of "affordable public flats" to eligible households could substantially mitigate the above problems. Nevertheless, there will still be a portion of households who cannot afford to buy the affordable public flats, and so provision of "low-rental flats" to this group is necessary. The simulation results also show that

(i) by providing cheaper public flats at less convenient locations, of basic quality and/or of basic size, the government could enable more households to own their homes and reduce the required subsidies to the low-rental flats;

(ii) by charging a slightly higher price for the affordable public flats and using the profit to subsidize the low-rental flats, the combined public housing scheme (i.e., affordable public flat scheme and low-rental flat scheme) would be self-budget-balanced and fiscally sustainable.

In the final chapter, the author explains why most developing economies and some advanced economies failed to select the right people in the key macroeconomic positions, and how heavy such mistakes had costed these economies. He then proposes a proper selection procedure that could help avoid these heavy costs. He also highlights the importance of setting up a new discipline on macroeconomic management. Such a step would allow further knowledge accumulation on both the theoretical side and practical side of macroeconomic management. With further development of the new discipline, many of the painful outcomes (such as asset bubbles, financial crisis, exchange rate crisis, severe recession, hyperinflation and stagnation) could be drastically reduced. Thereafter, he discusses some more lessons for macroeconomic management and hopes that this could be the first step toward the development of the new discipline.

ABOUT THE AUTHOR

Dr. Yip is currently employed as an Associate Professor in Economics at Nanyang Technological University in Singapore. He was born in China and grew up in Hong Kong. He obtained his first degree from the University of Hong Kong, and his Master and Ph.D. degrees from the London School of Economics. He gained extensive central banking, financial and commercial experience through senior positions with the Hong Kong Monetary Authority, the Bank of China and the Bank of East Asia. In addition to substantial publications in high-ranking economics, finance and management journals, he has made numerous important exchange rate and macroeconomic policy recommendations in China, Hong Kong and Singapore.

In particular, Dr. Yip is the original proponent of China's exchange rate system reform implemented in 2005, and is the one who proposed the extension of retirement age in Singapore to 65. His policy articles have also made substantial impacts on China's banking reform, choice of maintaining a trade surplus to finance outward investment, gradual squeezing of the stock market bubble before the global financial tsunami and use of ultra-expansionary fiscal policy and substantial quantitative easing to offset the impacts of the global financial tsunami. He has also published extensively on the exchange rate systems in China, Hong Kong and Singapore. Because of his contribution to China's exchange rate system reform and macroeconomic policies, his biography was included in *Who's Who in the World* and *2000 Outstanding Intellectuals of the 21st Century*.

Since the global financial tsunami and then the quantitative easing programs in the US, Dr. Yip has written a large number of policy articles warning the risk of property bubble formation in Hong Kong, Singapore and other Asian economies, which has to a certain extent helped Singapore pre-empt the rapid growth of its property bubble. Along with these warnings and policy recommendations, he has also written the following high-quality Chinese poems on the property markets in Hong Kong, China and other Asian economies:

*《悯奴》
祇怪私房价格高，平民皆为此辛劳；
一房竟是一生债，十万房奴一富豪。

《泡沫危机》
火诱飞蛾利诱民，危机盛世众难分；
唯开笔券详提点，可救一人便一人。

《哀香港之一》
佔中花怒开，泡沫暗中抬；
昨夜洪方退，今朝火又来。

《哀香港之二》
泛民建制吵昏天，绿卫红兵尽纠缠；
一朝楼价千峰下，滚滚循环治不完。

《哀香港之三》女娲是指香港特别行政长官林郑月娥
治不完兮治不完，女娲无力补崩天；
横眉怒记庸官祸，细揭沉疴二十年。

*《和星云二句》星云大师二句为: 艳红瓣下枝有刺，花开自有花落时
楼股花开藏毒刺，劝君离去莫犹疑；
莫言泡沫不须破，最是凄凉暴挫时。

In addition to the above poems on the property markets, he has also written the following Chinese poems, whose quality could make some of them be included in the outstanding list of Chinese poems since the Tang Dynasty:

*《英伦落泊》此为笔者二十多岁时写的第一首唐诗
英伦深造志非平，欲据蟾宫意气凌；
如今方知落泊好，赏尽人间冷暖情。

*《学诗有感》此为作者二十多岁时写的第二首唐诗
仄平兼用韵，语气要惊人；
若道浓情贵，淡逸更出尘。

*《泰河望舟》泰河是泰晤士河，此为作者二十多岁时感悟到经济学为经世济民之学
沧舟一叶御洪澜，漂泊江湖浩海间；
才气疏閒潇洒落，为磨经智济河山。

《贺汇改》此诗是庆贺 2005 年中国汇制改革成功
艰难汇改伏波澜，汇率微调破险关；
可变工资从此定，风波难动秀河山。

《闻故人有感》
三十年前一样同，机缘抱负定西东；
如今再看风云榜，各自开花各自春。

《駡官之南湖掷笔》
本是书生好文章，强研经济助国昌；
无奈官僚多为己，文章未就已神伤。

《赠友之志气第一》难在此读下平声，即艰难的难
飞龙受困实非虫，运蹇多年志未穷；
莫叹人生多起落，苦难才出真英雄！

《父子和诗滨海湾之父篇》
红花绿叶浅蓝天，白浪随风拍岸前；
抛开世俗凡尘虑，父子逍遥步海边。

《父子和诗滨海湾之子篇》
今日消閒到海边，红花绿叶浅蓝天；
路阔风轻邀我跑，爸爸堕后我行先。

《投资篇之婆仔数》市盈率、派息率和市净率均只涉加减乘除，被笔者戏称为婆仔数
搞清婆仔数，拣股没烦恼；
现款能捞底，满仓易套牢。

《减肥歌之自嘲篇》
南洋有个胖诗人，好食嗜吃腍上腍；
娇妻严令将肥减，见得佳餚心又痕。

《减肥歌之自大篇》
南洋有个胖诗人，既善诗词又善文；
笔引风雷惊三界，文魁中外振乾坤。

最后一首的意境不及上一首，但【笔引风雷惊三界，文魁中外振乾坤】其实是一副对联。另，有感香港一些政客的无耻，也写过如下一副对联【自古商人皆重利，从来政客多奸狡】。作者的座右铭为【研经济、读历史、习兵法、修文学、观术数（尤其是相人之术）】，数十年来一直深信经济学是 经 世 济 民 之 学。

Note: Those marked with * are the high-quality poems.

PART I
THREE IMPORTANT SETS OF THEORETICAL FRAMEWORK

CHAPTER 1

IMPORTANT THEORETICAL BACKGROUNDS FOR THE ANALYSIS OF THE ASSET BUBBLES IN ASIA

Since 2009, the author has written a large number of policy articles[1] explaining that the US quantitative easing (QE) would help the global economy avoid a great depression similar to that in the 1930s. However, the QE would also

(i)   seed the possibility of asset bubbles and then crises in economies outside the US; and

(ii) cause a huge global exchange rate cycle

in the later phase of the global economic recovery (i.e., when the US interest rate and the US dollar start to rebound substantially during the later phase of the US economic recovery).

Unfortunately, there are now clear early evidences that the above deductions would eventually realize. Therefore, the author would like to reiterate in this book that

(1)   the property bubbles formed in some Asian economies would burst during the subsequent US interest rate hike and strong rebound of the

---

[1] The articles were published in the *Hong Kong Economic Journal* between early 2009 and mid-2018. Most of the articles published between early 2009 and mid-2011 were already summarized in Yip (2011). This book will summarize the articles published between mid-2011 and mid-2018.

US dollar, and a bursting in any one of the Asian economies would trigger another round of Asian financial crisis through the contagion effect;

(2) the expected substantial US interest rate hike and rebound of US dollar would trigger another round of emergent market crisis (especially for those emerging economies with poor macroeconomic policy management and a lot of internal economic weaknesses such as huge current account deficit, asset bubbles, poor supervision of banks and poor bank asset quality); and

(3) for those economies trying to peg their currencies with the US dollar, there would be poor export and output performance in the early years of the expected strengthening of the US dollar, with the possibility of a currency attack at the later stage of the expected strong US dollar cycle.

This book will focus on the first potential event with some discussion on the second and the third potential events. To enable the readers to appreciate the high likelihood of a bursting of property bubbles and then another round of financial crisis in Asia, I will first provide the following three sets of basic theoretical frameworks in this chapter:

(a) the impacts of US's QE on the global and the Asian economies;
(b) the characteristics of the property markets in urban Asia; and
(c) the characteristics of the various stages of an asset bubble and their policy implications.

With the help of these three sets of theoretical frameworks, I will then discuss the high likelihood and then the disastrous consequences of the first potential event in Chapters 2–4. Chapters 5 and 6 will provide further discussion on the property markets and housing policies in Asia with a wider perspective. Chapter 7 will discuss how to avoid similar disasters from happening in the future.

1.1 IMPACTS OF US's QE

Let us first start with the discussion in the last chapter of Yip (2011), which summarized my policy articles on the impacts of the US's QE programs between early 2009 and mid-2011. In the chapter, I have explained that the US Quantitative Easing One (i.e., QE1) helped avoid a great depression similar to that in the 1930s. However, the chapter also noted that the US QE1 (and then the QEs in other major economies) could seed the possibility of asset bubbles in Asia and then a bursting of these asset bubbles at the later phase of the expected global economic recovery.[2] It first highlighted that the financial crisis in the US had caused significant changes in economic behaviors, such as financial deleveraging and more hoarding of cash by the banks and the general public (e.g., a rise in the banks' desired *excess-reserve-to-deposit ratio*, *e* and the general public's desired *cash-to-deposit ratio*, *k*). Some of these changes in economic behaviors had caused a significant reduction of the US's money multiplier.[3] Figure 1.1 is an extended chart reported in Yip (2011),

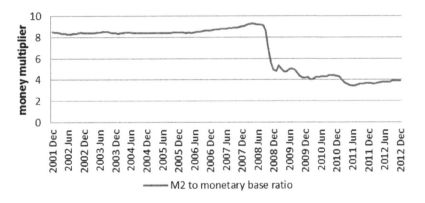

Figure 1.1: US Money Multiplier (M2/MB)

Source: Datastream.

---

[2] Since early 2009, the author has written over 30 policy articles on the formation of asset bubble in Asia as a potential aftershock crisis of the global financial tsunami. For those interested in macroeconomic management, this demonstrates that with the help of a strong theoretical background and sufficient policy insight, it is possible to anticipate the risk of an asset bubble in Asia even in January 2009 (i.e., before the end of global financial tsunami in late March 2009).

[3] For example, first consider the money multiplier formula discussed in standard textbooks such as Mishkin (2012, Chapter 15, pp. 396–397),

$$m = (k + 1)/(k + r + e),$$

which shows that the global financial tsunami has triggered a reduction of the money multiplier m by about 40–60% (i.e., from 8.5–9.5 times to 4–5 times).

From the definition of m ($\equiv M^S$/MB), one can write

$$M^S \equiv m \times \text{MB}, \tag{1}$$

where M^S is the money supply and MB is the monetary base. Thus, for any given level of MB, the 40–60% reduction in the money multiplier m would *ceteris paribus* cause a 40–60% reduction in the money supply. Such a substantial reduction in money supply would by itself be enough to trigger a great depression similar to that in the 1930s.[4] To avoid the US economy, and hence the global economy, from repeating the painful history of the great depression, identity (1) and the above discussion suggest that the Federal Reserve of the US had to offset the impacts of the 40–60% decline in m by a substantial increase in MB so as to avoid any decline in the money supply M^S. Yip (2011) also explained that during an asset inflation era, there will be changes in economic behaviors such as a decline in k and e, which will imply a rise in the money multiplier m. Meanwhile, there would also be a rise in the MB due to capital inflows and more overseas borrowings by banks to satisfy the greater demand for loans. The rise in m ànd MB will then fuel the asset inflation with greater money supply.

Thus, the above changes in economic behaviors during a crisis and an asset inflation era could cause a change in m and MB that would deepen

---

where k is the general public's desired cash-to-deposit ratio, r is the banks' required-reserve-to-deposit ratio and e is the banks' desired excess-reserve-to-deposit ratio. While the standard textbooks would assume k and e are constants, my book argued that this would be a reasonable assumption only for the normal time. During exceptional times such as a crisis or an asset inflation era, the above behavioral changes would cause a substantial rise in k and e (and hence a substantial fall in m) during a crisis, and a substantial fall in k and e (and hence a substantial rise in m) during an asset inflation era. Such a fall in m during a crisis (and a rise in m during an asset inflation era) would in turn deepen the crisis (and fuel the asset inflation during the bubble period).

[4]That is, even if one does not count the other negative developments during the crisis period, the 40–60% decline in m would by itself be enough to trigger a great depression.

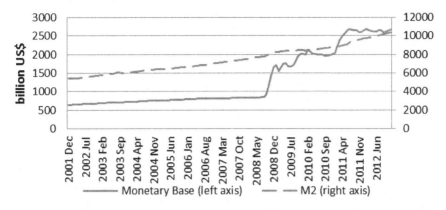

Figure 1.2: US Monetary Base and M2

Source: Datastream.

the crisis during the downturn and fuel the asset inflation during the upturn. In Chapters 2–4, I will use this result to analyze the risk and the persistence of the current property bubbles in a number of Asian economies.

Chapter 12 of Yip (2011) also noted that its discussion of a change in m due to changes in economic behaviors during a crisis and an asset inflation era is something new in the literature. Thus, it was unlikely that the Federal Reserve at that time was aware of such a discussion. Nevertheless, based on the lessons drawn from the Great Depression in the 1930s and Japan's lost (two) decades since the late 1980s, the Federal Reserve at that time was aware of the importance of avoiding a substantial fall in the money supply M^S by aggressive QE (e.g., aggressive buying of US Treasury Bonds and other eligible financial assets, which would substantially increase MB).

As shown in Fig. 1.2, the Federal Reserve's QE1 has subsequently increased the MB by 83% between end October 2008 and end March 2010, which had not only avoided any substantial fall in M^S but also resulted in a moderate increase in money supply.

Based on its theoretical discussion and the subsequent economic developments, Yip (2011) concluded that the US's QEs helped avoid a great depression in the global economy, while other policy measures such as

(i)   the Trouble Asset Relief Program (TARP),
(ii) the stress test exercise for major banks[5] and
(iii) the amendments to the over-restrictive mark-to-market rule at that time

also contributed to the end of the global financial tsunami in March–April 2009.

Nevertheless, the chapter also warned that the QE in the US could also cause a substantial rise in MB in Hong Kong, Singapore and other developing economies through the US dollar carry trade and other types of capital inflows. As these economies had not gone through that great degree of financial deleveraging and financial disintermediation such as those in the US (e.g., local banks in Singapore, Hong Kong, ASEAN and Latin America were still relatively healthy at that time), there may be no, or a much smaller, decline in the money multiplier m in these economies. Thus, a rise in their MBs due to the QE programs in the US and other major economies could result in a substantial increase in money supply in these economies. In particular, there were signs that the banking sectors in Hong Kong and Singapore were flooded with liquidity with extremely low mortgage rates. For example, the mortgage rate in Singapore was hovering around 1% during the first 2–3 years after US's QE1. Thereafter, it rose a bit but was still around the low level of 2.25% by June 2018. There were also signs that the low mortgage rates had caused substantial rise in the property prices in Hong Kong, Singapore and some other Asian economies. In the subsequent chapters, we will go into the details of these and discuss whether these would result in a formation, and then a bursting, of property bubbles in these economies. Before doing so, we need to have a brief review of the author's previous publications on (i) the characteristics of the urban property markets in Asia and (ii) the characteristics of the seeding stage, the development stage and the final stage of an asset bubble.

---

[5] Banks were given time to raise capital so as to ensure they can pass the stress test. The aims were to (i) urge the banks to raise the capital adequacy ratio and (ii) use the test as a government's endorsement of the progress made by the banks, which would raise the market confidence (and reduce the market's uncertainty) on the healthiness of the banks.

1.2 THE CHARACTERISTICS OF MAJOR URBAN PROPERTY MARKETS IN ASIA

1.2.1 Significant Differences between the Asian and Western Property Markets

Since 2007, the author has written over 30 policy articles on China's housing problems, which had a significant influence on China's housing policy.[6] While those policy articles on China's property market were incorporated in Yip (2011) with the addition of a formal theoretical framework, there were important follow-up discussions on the property markets in Hong Kong and Singapore that are worth a formal collection (with an extended theoretical framework) in this book. In these policy articles, the author extended and applied the theoretical framework in Yip (2011)[7] to (i) highlight the risk of the formation and then the bursting of property bubbles in these two economies; (ii) discuss the ineffectiveness of some standard curbing measures and (iii) provide a new view on the choice, strategy and timing of the curbing measures. Before a formal incorporation of these important policy articles in the subsequent chapters, let us first summarize and extend the theoretical framework in Yip (2011) as follows.

Yip first explained that the urban Asian property markets are very different from those in the US and other western countries such as Australia and New Zealand. For example, unlike the case in the US or Australia where there are a lot of builders building 2–3 story houses for home

---

[6] The policy articles were published as internal reports to the Chinese leaders through the Xinhua News Agency. They were also published in the various issues of the *Hong Kong Economic Journal* and the *China Securities Journal* between 2007 and 2010. Thereafter, they were incorporated into Chapters 9 and 10 of Yip (2011) under an integrated theoretical framework.

[7] In fact, part of the theoretical framework in Yip (2011) originated from the discussions of Yip (2005) on the Hong Kong and Singapore property markets. However, there were only piecemeal discussions in Yip (2005). Yip (2011) was the first one with a thorough and formal theoretical framework on China's property market. Nevertheless, this suggests the theoretical framework was most suitable not only to the property market in China but also to those in Hong Kong and Singapore.

purchasers, the limited space in the urban areas in China, Hong Kong, Singapore, Taiwan and other ASEAN economies implies that these cities have to build high-rise apartments to meet the demand for housing. As the building of such high-rise apartments involves a very high *fixed development cost* and substantial *economies of scale*, only major developers with sufficient financial strength, instead of small-sized builders,[8] could overcome the *barrier of scale*. As a result, there was insufficient competition in the property markets in these Asian cities. Worse still, these Asian developers soon, through trial-and-error or learning-by-observation, form some kind of *informal cartel* through the common adoption of some "industrial practices" or "industrial norms", such as a gross profit margin of at least 40–60% for their housing estates in China and Hong Kong (and at least 30–50% in Singapore).[9] Thus, unlike the builders in the Western world, these Asian developers do have a relatively strong market (pricing) power on their products. Yip then proceeded to explain that the supply and demand analysis used by many Asian policymakers and business economists was in fact an inappropriate and misleading model for the above Asian property markets. (*Note*: As highlighted in Yip (2014), the first-generation models and the second-generation models on housing price could be the right model on the housing market in the Western world, but not the right model for the above Asian property markets. For example, there was no discussion on the informal cartel and the indicator effect highlighted in this chapter (see Section 1.2.3 for more detailed discussions). As these are the most important characteristics of the Asian property markets, the above literature in the Western world as well as the

---

[8] It should be noted that builders in the US and Australia could be very big. However, there is sufficient competition among the builders and there does not seem to be an informal cartel in these housing markets. It should also be noted that the real price and gross profit margin of high-rise apartments in the central business districts (CBDs) of major American and Australian cities were also high relative to the real price of houses in less central areas. However, the relatively small apartment market does not seem to be able to exert a meaningful indicator effect on the relatively big housing market, i.e., the two markets seem to be relatively segmented from each other.

[9] As the Singapore government provides a lot of public housing at more reasonable price and there are more stringent regulations on private developers' marketing activities, private developers in Singapore could only charge a lower gross profit margin than those in China and Hong Kong.

supply and demand analysis could not be the right model for the Asian property markets, and could sometimes lead to misleading policy recommendations such as those discussed in the subsequent chapters. However, as most discussants on the above Asian property markets were not aware of the above two generations of models in the literature and most of the discussions were at most based on the supply and demand analysis, this book will put more emphasis in explaining why the supply and demand analysis would be the wrong model with plenty of misleading policy implications for the above Asian property markets.)

1.2.2 High Wealth and Income Inequality in Asia

The first problem of analyzing the above Asian property markets with the simple supply and demand analysis (which would lead to the dogmatic belief for free market forces in these property markets) is its implicit assumption of a fairly even wealth and income distribution. Unfortunately, the truth is that wealth and income inequality are very high in Hong Kong, China and even Singapore (e.g., their Gini coefficients for income inequality in 2016 were 0.539, 0.465 and 0.458, respectively).[10] As a result, market force will only allocate the limited supply of housing to those who are *rich* instead of those who *need* the flats. In fact, it is not uncommon that some speculators or rich people own tens or even hundreds of flats,[11] while many ordinary urban Chinese citizens are not even able to own a small one-room flat. Thus, because of the high wealth and income inequality, just relying on free market force to allocate housing in the above Asian property markets, could lead to highly undesirable results.

1.2.3 The Market Structure Problem and the Indicator Effect

The second problem is that the supply and demand analysis assumes *no barriers of entries* and developers are *price takers*. The reality is that not

---

[10] Wealth inequalities, especially those in Asia, are usually much higher than income inequalities.

[11] There was news reflecting that some investors or rich people in China, Hong Kong and Singapore own hundreds of properties.

every individual or small enterprise in urban Asia could buy a piece of land and build their own houses at a reasonable cost. This is because the scarcity of land has dictated the building of high-rise apartments instead of 2–3 storey houses in these Asian cities, and there is an economy of scale in building these high-rise apartments. In particular, property development in these Asian cities involves a very high fixed development cost such as the fixed cost in connecting the public water supply, electricity supply and sewage drainage as well as providing common areas, facilities, lifts and security for residents on the whole estate. As a result, estate development in urban Asia has to reach a certain scale (i.e., number of flats) before it is economically viable or cost-effective. Such a *barrier of scale* could only be overcome by property developers with sufficient financial strength, but not individuals or small enterprises from other industries.[12]

Meanwhile, product differentiation (e.g., in terms of location, quality and other characteristics) means that the demand curve for each housing estate will be downward sloping instead of horizontal. Worse still, as explained above, developers in China, Hong Kong and Singapore have successfully formed an *informal cartel* to keep the housing prices at high levels. The cartel is "informal" as the developers do not formally sit together to set a high or even profit-maximizing price for the whole group. However, through the "industrial practice" or "common adoption" of a high gross profit margin of at least 40–60% (or 30–50%) for each housing estate, they were able to push the average housing price to a relatively high level.[13] What I would like to supplement here is that the "industrial

---

[12]Yip (2011) did note that in China there were new entrants such as overseas developers, large state or private enterprises from other industries, and even local residents rebuilding their 2–3 story houses into 8–9 story walk-up apartments for rentals to the low-income group. However, he also noted that (i) all the new developers became part of the informal cartel by adopting the industrial practice of at least 40–60% gross profit margin for their housing estates and (ii) the number of new entrants was not sufficient to change the market structure.

[13]In the case of identical properties, the developers will be collectively maximizing their profit if the chosen gross profit margin is at the profit-maximizing level. However, the industrial practice of an adjustable range, instead of a specific level, of gross profit margin could be even more appealing for the case of product differentiation (i.e., some housing estates' profit-maximizing margin could be slightly higher while the others could be slightly lower). It is also more flexible as changes in demand or other exogenous shocks

Box 1.1: Cumulative dynamic efficiency as another barrier of entry in the Asian property market

On top of the above barrier of scale, cumulative dynamic efficiency could be another important barrier of entry in the Asian property market. That is, through past experiences of property development, experienced property developers have accumulated numerous cost savings and revenue enhancement practices or set-ups in marketing and sales, building and designs, financing, purchases and procurements, inventory managements as well as outsourcing and sub-contraction of building works. As a result, large and experienced property developers are usually more efficient than small and less-experienced developers, not to mention individuals and inexperienced small enterprises from other industries.

To see this, consider the simple case where developers could accumulate cost-saving practices and set-ups through their previous development experiences of housing estates. If so, the average cost (AC) curve would be a downward sloping curve with respect to the cumulated number of flats built by the developers.

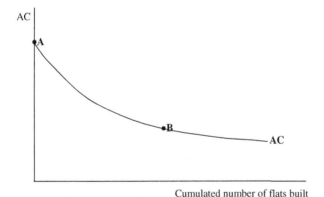

Diagram 1.1: Cumulated Dynamic Efficiency

Ceteris paribus, potential developer **A** with no property development experience would have a much higher AC than the experienced developer **B**.

Other than the cost-saving practices and set-ups, experienced developers have also accumulated highly effective revenue and marketing enhancement practices and set-ups. Thus, cumulated dynamic efficiency is an important source of the high barrier of entry in Asian property market.

range" of gross profit margin is adjustable (e.g., 40–60% during the boom years in China and 30–50% during the consolidating periods). With the wide and adjustable range, it is possible that the profit-maximizing gross profit margin of each housing estate lies within this industrial range.

Even more troublesome in the above Asian property markets is the existence of a very strong *indicator effect* from new property prices to resale property prices. Because of Chinese (and East Asian) home pur-chasers' strong preference to new properties and these developers' excel-lent marketing capacity and skill, the developers were usually able to set the prices of their new flats at a premium of about 30–50% above nearby resale flats of similar quality. As owners of resale flats tend to use the prices of new flats as important indicators or yardsticks for the assessment of the market values and selling prices of their resale flats, launches of new flats would usually be able to pull up the market prices of the nearby resale flats through the above indicator effect until the above price pre-mium narrow to, say, 15–25% (i.e., to justify the difference in age between the new and resale flats). As we will see in the subsequent chapters, the above discussion of *informal cartel* and *indicator effect* is not only realis-tic but also has significant implications on (i) the likelihood of property bubble formation; (ii) the ineffectiveness of some standard curbing meas-ures and (iii) the choice, strategy and timing of curbing measures.

The book also explained and highlighted the following:

(1)   With the high wealth and income inequality in Asia, the choice of free market for the above Asian property markets would mean that there are always some people who can own tens or even hundreds of prop-erties, while many others could not afford to own their home. Thus, it is important for the Asian governments to provide affordable public flats, such as the HDB flats in Singapore, to the lower income groups.

(2)   Asian developers are *price setters*, not price takers. That is, while one is justified to draw an independent demand curve for the above Asian property markets as there are numerous home buyers, it will be erroneous to draw an independent supply curve for the above Asian property markets.

---

would imply a rise in, or fall of, the profit-maximizing margin. This could be taken care by an adjustment of the industrial range, say, from 40–60% to 30–50%.

(3) With the *informal cartel* and *indicator effect* discussed above, developers can collectively set the prices of new properties to very high (or even profit-maximizing) levels, and extract most of the consumer surplus from buyers of new properties. Through the indicator effect, their high prices for new properties would also pull up the prices of resale properties. In other words, developers are not only able to use their market (pricing) power to set the prices of new properties to very high levels but, through the indicator effect, they also have a powerful leverage on the prices of the much bigger pool of resale properties. In the subsequent chapters, we will discuss how the developers' pricing power and the indicator effect could make it extremely difficult for the government to curb the property bubble.

(4) Worse still, developers might be able to push up the property prices to very high levels where the consumer surpluses of home buyers are not only zero, but at highly negative values. Negative consumer surpluses are possible because many home buyers have used the wrong yardstick (i.e., the market price of the property) to measure the satisfaction or utility they could derive from the property. During the property boom, these home buyers are not aware of the problem as they mistakenly believe that they can always sell the property at the current market price (which is higher than their purchasing price). However, when property price collapses, many of them would suddenly find that their purchasing price is now much higher than the collapsed market price and begin to realize that their true satisfaction derived from the property is in fact much lower than that implied by the purchasing price.

(5) The choice of free market force for the above Asian property markets would result in a gradual but sustained reduction of flat size over time. That is, during property booms, developers would have the incentives to reduce the flat size so that they can achieve a higher *price per square foot* and yet the *total quantum* of the smaller flats is still within the affordable limit of potential buyers of new properties. As the norm of acceptable flat size at any particular period will depend on the culture of the economy at that time, there is a limit in the pace for developers to reduce their flat size. Nevertheless, developers could reduce the flat size bit by bit over time. As a result, developers would still be able to reduce the average flat size by a substantial

amount over a long enough time, such as 2–3 decades. In fact, the very small flat size in Hong Kong today was due to such a process over the past 2–3 decades, and there is now an emerging tendency of a gradual but sustained shrinkage of flat size in China, Singapore and some other Asian cities.

(6) In these Asian economies, too much effort, funds and social resources have been devoted to activities related to property investment, which might only have very minor contribution to the productivity and efficiency of the economy. As property investment had turned out to be an important source of wealth accumulation in the above Asian economies (see Yip, 2011, Chapter 9 for the detailed explanation), people's attention, animal spirit and funds have been diverted away from the riskier but more growth-enhancing and efficiency-improving activities such as new product or cost-saving innovations, or taking the risk to start new business with potential positive impacts on the efficiency and productivity of the economy. Meanwhile, too much social resources have been diverted to property-related activities. For example, advertisements of launches of new private properties in Singapore (and Hong Kong) usually occupy most of the weekend advertisement pages in the newspapers. When compared with the launches of the HDB flats by the Singapore government, the far bigger scale of newspaper advertisements by the 20% share of private properties have resulted in tons of unnecessary waste of paper (or substantial recycling costs) every day. The high property price and hence the high commission have also supported an unnecessarily large number of property agents in Singapore, Hong Kong and China. More importantly, the high land price and high property price have resulted in an excessively large property loan business for the banks, thus crowding out a significant portion of loans, and hence making less loans available, for other growth-enhancing activities or businesses.

1.2.4 Role of Government Supply in Providing the Necessary Competition in the Above Asian Property Markets

Seeing that (i) China's wealth and income inequality would remain high in the foreseeable future and (ii) it was not promising to solve the above market structure problem by bringing in more private competitors (i.e., new private developers will find it beneficial to join the informal cartel by adopting the industrial practice of a high gross profit margin), the book highlighted that a more promising and effective way to deal with China's housing problem is a substantial supply of affordable public flats by the government. In particular, he recommended four types of flats with the following recommended percentages in the *new supply* for each year:

(1)   10% in low-rental flats for the lowest income group[14];
(2)   15% in economy flats (i.e., flats with zero or negligible profit to the government) for the low- to middle-low income group;
(3)   45% in sandwich-class flats (i.e., flats with reasonable profit to both the central and local governments, and yet at affordable price to the eligible citizens) for the middle-low to middle-high income group; and
(4)   30% in private flats for the middle-high to high-income group.

As the price of private flats in China was already beyond the affordability of many middle-high income earners, the author believed 70% of public housing in the new supply is necessary. He also recommended a few classes of sandwich-class flats with rising gross profit margin so that (i) the public housing scheme could cause reasonable but controllable correction of private property price (i.e., the price of private flats would at most fall to the price of the highest class of sandwich-class flats)[15] and (ii) profit from the sandwich-class flats could be used to finance other reforms (e.g., the medical reform, the education reform or the provision of low-rental flats), support other essential expenditures or reduce other tax rates.[16]

---

[14] In a mathematical model with another co-author, we have found that, for a standard income or wealth distribution, there will always be some people in the lower end of the distribution who cannot afford to buy a property even at a very low and heavily subsidized price. Thus, it is necessary to provide low-rental flats for this group of people (see Chapter 6 for a more detailed discussion).

[15] If the price correction of private flats is too much, it could trigger a financial crisis and severe recession. In fact, Yip (2011) noted that this was what happened in Hong Kong between 1997 and 2004.

[16] This is because demand for the sandwich-class flats at the recommended price will be relatively inelastic so that the profit from the sandwich-class flats is in fact one of the least distortive tax. He also highlighted that this would probably be the only tax that the taxpayers (i.e., the sandwich-class flat buyers) would be willing to queue overnight to pay the tax.

The impacts of the recommendations were substantial. For example, the Chinese government completed 17 million public flats in 2008–2012, and is planning to build another 31 million public flats between 2013 and 2017. Nevertheless, his recommendation on the sandwich-class flats was never taken seriously. Meanwhile, without any potential profit (and hence local government revenue) from the low-rental flats and the economy flats, the local governments were not particular keen to support the central government's plan of bigger public housing supply.

1.3 CHARACTERISTICS OF THE VARIOUS STAGES OF AN ASSET BUBBLE

Another set of theories important to the discussion of this book is the characteristics of the various stages of an asset bubble. While this origi-nated from the author's discussion on China's stock market bubble between 2006 and 2007,[17] this section will demonstrate that, after some appropriate adaptations and extensions, the discussion is also applicable to the property bubbles. Based on the characteristics of previous asset bubbles such as those during the Asian Financial Crisis, the author first partitioned a typical asset bubble into the following three stages: *the seed-ing stage*, *the development stage* and *the final stage*.

1.3.1 The Seeding Stage

The seeding stage usually occurs when the asset price has a chance to rebound from a trough for a few months or quarters. For example, the Chinese stock market was able to gain an *upward inertia* after a few months of sustained rise (or recovery) from its trough in mid-2005. Similarly, the property prices in Hong Kong and Singapore were able to gain an upward inertia after a few months or quarters of sustained rise or recovery from March 2009. The sustained rise in the asset price in the first few months or quarters would then create *an expectation of further rise in the asset price* (i.e., *expectation of asset inflation*). This change in expec-tation will in turn trigger many *changes in economic behaviors*, which would then fuel further rises in the asset price.

---

[17]The discussion was also incorporated in Yip (2011, Chapter 8).

For example, the expectation of asset inflation could substantially augment the individuals' and firms' demand for the asset. During that period, individuals and firms will put more and more funds into that asset investment. Thereafter, some will even increase their investments in that asset with funds originally meant for other purposes (e.g., retirement money or lifetime savings for individuals, and working capital, investment funds or other company money for firms). Many of the market participants will also increase their investment in the asset through higher leverage and borrowings. In fact, during China's stock market bubble in 2006–2007, many of the market participants had put their lifetime savings in shares while many others had substantially increased their borrowings for share investments. Managers or owners of firms had also used company money and borrowed money for share investment. Similarly, the upward inertia of property price, and hence the expectation of further rise in property price since 2009H2, had also created enormous speculative demand, investment demand and then panic demand for housing in Hong Kong and Singapore.

In addition to the above direct increase in demand for asset, there will also be changes on the monetary side. As explained in Section 1.1, during an asset inflation era (crisis), the expected change in asset price will induce changes in economic behaviors such as a fall (rise) in both the general public's desired *cash-to-deposit-ratio k* and the banks' desired *excess-reserve-to-deposit-ratio e*, which will in turn cause a rise (fall) in the money multiplier *m*. In addition, to satisfy the higher demand for loans during the asset boom, banks would also borrow funds from overseas, thus resulting in an increase in the MB. As a result, there will be both an increase in *m* and MB, and hence money supply M^S (= $m \times$ MB), which would in turn fuel and support further rises in asset price.

1.3.2 The Development Stage

Once the expectation of further rise in asset price causes the above *changes in economic behaviors*, the asset market has entered the development stage. It should be highlighted that the upward force due to such changes in economic behaviors would be enormous. For example, during China's stock market bubble in 2006–2007, tens of million people (including businessmen, employees, housewives, retirees and students) had changed from non-investors to investors of shares. Firms also used the company money and/or borrowed money for shares investment. Similarly, in Hong Kong and Singapore, the hike of property prices since March 2009 had also created enormous amount of speculative demand, investment demand and then panic demand for housing. In the subsequent chapters, I will explain that these newly created demands are in fact substantial during the current property bubbles in Hong Kong and Singapore, and a simple increase in housing supply to meet these increased demands could result in excess supply in the future.

In this development stage, there will also be the emergence of a few **vicious cycles** that would fuel the rise in asset price. For example, there would be a *vicious cycle between the rise of property prices and the rise of stock prices*. That is, rise in property prices will raise the profits and hence prices of property shares, which will raise the stock prices of other sectors through an indicator effect, a portfolio adjustment effect and other spillover effects. The rise in stock prices will in turn induce some stock investors to invest in more properties and hence support further rise in property prices. There would be a *vicious cycle between the rise of asset prices and the rise of aggregate demand*. That is, the rise in property prices and stock prices will increase consumption through the wealth effect, and increase investment through the Tobin's q effect. The rise in consumption, investment and hence aggregate demand will in turn fuel the rise in property prices and stock prices. There would also be a *vicious cycle between the rise in asset prices, capital inflows and the rise in money supply*. That is, a rise in asset prices will attract investments by foreign investors (i.e., capital inflows). Under a fixed exchange rate system or a managed floating, the capital inflows would cause a substantial rise in the MB (and hence multiple creation of money supply) unless the related central bank completely sterilizes the capital inflows. The increase in money supply would then fuel the rise in asset prices which would in turn attract more capital inflows.[18]

---

[18] Note, as illustrated by the latest experience in Hong Kong and Singapore, the two economies either did not sterilize, or could not completely sterilize, the capital inflows during the current property bubble.

Meanwhile, there will be *upward spirals* among property prices, rentals, general prices and wages, which would again fuel or support the rise in property prices. For example, higher property prices will cause higher rentals, which will increase the general price level and induce workers to ask for higher wages, and higher wages and higher general prices will allow the developers to raise the prices of new properties, which will pull up the prices of resale properties through the indicator effect.

1.3.3 The Final Stage

In the final stage, the sustained and powerful rise in the asset prices in the previous stage will cause herding behavior. That is, there will be more and more people and funds going into the asset market, which will fuel the rise in the asset prices. At this stage, standard curbing measures will not be sufficient to stop the asset prices from rising. However, when close to 100% of the potential investors have already invested close to 100% of their available funds into the asset market, the rise in the asset prices will slow down and then stop. At this time, even a very mild change can cause a fall in the asset price, trigger herding behavior in the downward direction and cause a reversal of the above vicious cycles and changes in economic behaviors until the asset price plunges to a level well below the normal equilibrium level.

1.3.4 Two Types of Bursting

Thus, once the bubble reaches the final stage, a bursting of bubble will be just a matter of time instead of whether or not. Here, there could be two types of bursting, and the eventual outcome will depend on whether there is a large enough negative shock to trigger a bursting of the bubble at the early part of the final stage. In the lucky case that there is a large enough negative shock at the early part of the final stage (i.e., before the bubble becomes too large), the bursting would only cause an economic crisis and severe recession, but not yet political and social instability. In the unlucky case that there is no large enough negative shock at the early part of the final stage, the bubble would have the chance to grow to an extremely big one. However, as explained above, when close to 100% of the potential investors have already invested close to 100% of their funds in the asset market, even a very mild negative shock is sufficient to trigger a bursting. By then, the crisis and recession could be so severe that there could be political and social instability (e.g., the ruling party would lose the election, and strong political leaders would lose people's respect and hence the moral authority for ruling).

1.3.5 Policy Implications

As the forces behind the rise in asset prices in the development stage and the final stage are extremely powerful, it implies that

(a)   it is always the best to use curbing measures to pre-empt any potential rampant asset inflation era (or asset bubble) at the seeding stage; and
(b)   if an expectation of rampant asset inflation has been formed, it will be far more difficult to curb the asset inflation (or bubble) as the expectation will cause a lot of changes in economic behaviors and create enormous speculative demand, investment demand and possibly panic demand. By then, much greater curbing measures are needed before the asset inflation could be properly controlled.

In fact, Yip (2005) was the first one to draw the above conclusions and lessons from the Asian Financial Crisis and previous asset bubbles, although it had not yet made the above classification of the three stages of asset bubble and spelt out the characteristics of these three stages. With the above conclusions and lessons drawn from previous bubbles, the author was able to warn from 2009H2 that the rebound of property prices in Hong Kong and Singapore could eventually end up as a property bubble, and the related government should pre-empt the bubble formation by implementing curbing measures at the seeding stage (i.e., in 2009H2 or early 2010).[19] Unfortunately, because of different reasons (see subsequent

---

[19] Since 2009H2, the author has kept on providing such warnings in the form of policy proposals to the related ministers in Singapore, seminars in the Monetary Authority of Singapore (MAS) and the Hong Kong Monetary Authority (HKMA), letter to the of Chief Executive of Hong Kong, policy articles in the newspapers and interviews with the TV channels.

chapters for more details), both Hong Kong and Singapore missed the best time of pre-empting the property bubbles at the seeding stage.[20] Before continuing the discussion in the subsequent chapters, the author would like to add the following lesson drawn from the asset bubbles before the Asian Financial Crisis, the Chinese stock market bubble in 2006–2007 and the current property bubble in Hong Kong and Singapore:

Expectation could be *very stubborn during the asset boom*, but *very fragile during the plunge*. For example, during the asset inflation period or the development stage of an asset bubble, even if the government introduces a lot of curbing measures, many people would still want to buy the asset. However, when the asset price starts to fall, even if the government introduces a lot of supporting measures, most market participants still want to sell the asset.

In the subsequent chapters, the author will discuss the policy implications of this lesson.

---

[20] With the same theoretical framework, the author was also able to warn from 2006Q2 that the rebound of China's share price from the trough at that time could eventually end up as a stock market bubble. Unfortunately, the Chinese government at that time did not have the knowledge to appreciate the importance of the lessons that the author had drawn from previous asset bubbles. In particular, it did not have sufficient confidence or conviction on (and hence fail to act in response to) the author's warning that (i) once there is an expectation of further rise in asset price, the chance of a bubble formation will be much higher than normal circumstances and (ii) it will be least costly to pre-empt the potential bubble at the seeding stage. Fortunately, with an internal report in September 2007 through the Xinhua News Agency (also published in a major newspaper in Hong Kong), the author managed to convince the Chinese leaders to curb the stock market bubble. Nevertheless, the curbing at such a late stage did involve a relatively heavy, albeit not too disastrous, economic cost (see Yip, 2011, Chapter 8 for more details).

PART II

THE ASIAN PROPERTY MARKETS SINCE THE GLOBAL FINANCIAL TSUNAMI

CHAPTER 2

THE FORMATION OF PROPERTY BUBBLES IN SOME ASIAN ECONOMIES SINCE THE GLOBAL FINANCIAL TSUNAMI

This chapter will briefly review the hike in property prices in some Asian economies since US's quantitative easings (Qes). In general, because of Singapore's and Hong Kong's well-developed financial sectors and free capital mobility, they are the two Asian economies that were the first and the most affected by the QEs. That is, although the QEs had also caused capital inflows and lower interest rates in the other Asian economies, the relative effect on them were much slower and smaller than those on Singapore and Hong Kong. On top of that, the very high (or close-to-one) ratio of the number of urban properties to the number of rural properties in Hong Kong and Singapore would also mean that their property prices would be most affected by the low interest rates and capital inflows caused by the QEs. As a result, the rises in the property prices in Singapore and Hong Kong during the first two years after the US's QE1 were among the highest in Asia.

Nevertheless, government curbing measures could also play an important role on the hike of property prices. As will be discussed in the subsequent sections and Chapters 3 and 4, Singapore's third-to-eighth rounds of curbing measures between 2011 and 2013 had contributed to a significant difference in the subsequent rises in property prices between

Singapore and Hong Kong.[1] In Section 2.3.3, the author will also explain why the rise in property prices in Malaysia was initially much more moderate than that in Singapore. Nevertheless, because of the difference in government curbing measures, the cumulated rises in property prices in Kuala Lumpur and other major Malaysian cities have already surpassed that of Singapore. Similarly, the absence of strong enough curbing measures in India and many other Asian economies have contributed to much higher cumulated rises of their urban property prices than that recorded in Singapore. In fact, the cumulated rises in property prices in these economies suggest that Hong Kong and India are among the top candidates that would be most vulnerable to a major correction of property prices during the mid or final phase of the US interest rate hike amid the economic recovery (with possibly an overheating phase) from the global financial tsunami. More importantly, the collapse of property prices in any one of these Asian economies would, through the contagion effect, trigger a severe correction of property prices in the other Asian economies which would in turn trigger another Asian financial crisis. Thus, even for economies with only moderate rises in property prices, they would still be vulnerable to a substantial fall of property prices and other asset prices.

2.1 THE FORMATION OF A HUGE PROPERTY BUBBLE IN HONG KONG

Because of Hong Kong's free capital mobility and its currency peg with the US dollar, the QEs in the US resulted in ample liquidity in Hong Kong's banking system with exceptionally low mortgage rates.

As shown in Figure 2.1, the HIBOR-based mortgage rate[2] for newly approved loans was in the exceptionally low range of 0.77–1.03% between January 2009 and October 2010. Even after a moderate rise between

---

[1] The first round of curbing in Singapore was implemented in September 2009. However, as will be discussed in Chapter 3, it was the later rounds (especially, the fifth, seventh and the eighth rounds) of curbing that had reasonable effects on the property prices.

[2] Before the QEs in the US, most of the mortgage rate in Hong Kong was best lending rate-based (BLR-based). The interbank rate-based (i.e., HIBOR-based) mortgage was still small in 2008. However, HIBOR-based mortgage rate started to grow rapidly in Hong Kong since the QE1 in the US. By 2010Q2, the majority of mortgage rates in Hong Kong were HIBOR-based.

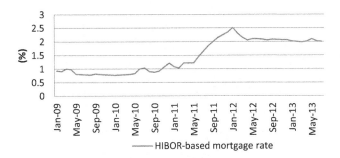

Figure 2.1:   Hong Kong's Mortgage Rate

Source: Hong Kong Monetary Authority (HKMA) staff estimates, Half-Yearly Monetary and Financial Stability Report, September 2013 and March 2014, HKMA.[3]

mid-2011 and early 2012, the mortgage rate in 2013 was still hovering around the exceptionally low level of 2%.[4]

The low mortgage rate and the ample liquidity in Hong Kong's banking system in turn triggered a sustained rebound of the property prices and then the formation of a huge property bubble in Hong Kong (see Chapter 4 for the detailed discussion). As shown in Figure 2.2 and Table 2.1, the cumulated rise in residential property price was 244% between March 2009 and April 2018. In addition, according to the housing affordability measures published by the HKMA, housing affordability in Hong Kong was at a highly vulnerable level. For example, the price-to-income ratio in 2017Q4 was at 16.4, surpassing the 14.6 recorded at the peak of the gigantic property bubble in 1997.[5]

---

[3] Because of free competition on mortgage rates and hence different mortgage rates offered by different banks, there is no longer any official publication on Hong Kong's mortgage rate. Nevertheless, because of the impacts of the extremely low mortgage rates in 2009–2013, the HKMA did provide its staff estimates on Hong Kong's mortgage rate in the above publications.

[4] A check on the latest mortgage rates offered by major Hong Kong banks confirmed that the mortgage rates in Hong Kong in early 2018 were still around 2%, even though there were signs that the mortgage rates would, sooner or later, rise with the subsequent US interest rate hike.

[5] The HKMA published the following two affordability measures based on the following hypothetical cases:

  (i) The price-to-income ratio measures the average price of a typical 50 square-meter flat relative to the median income of households living in private housing; and

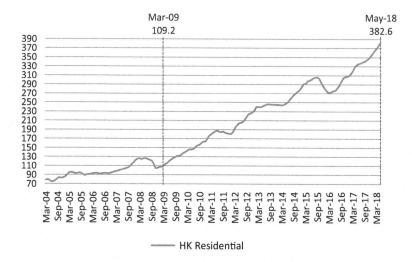

Figure 2.2:   HK Residential Property Price Index

Source: CEIC.

Similarly, as shown in Table 2.1, the cumulated rise of non-residential property price indices in Hong Kong during the same period were also gigantic at 258%, 250% and 341% for office, retail premises and flatted factories, respectively.

Worse still, other asset prices, such as the prices of car park and taxi licenses, also surged substantially and were generally believed to be substantially overvalued.[6] When all these asset prices plunged with the collapse of residential property prices, the damage would be enormous.

(ii) The income-gearing ratio compares the mortgage payment for a typical flat of 50 square meters (under a 20-year mortgage scheme with a 70% loan-to-value ratio) with the median income of households living in private housing. Note that the gearing ratio is not the actual debt-servicing ratio, as the actual mortgage span could be more or less than 20-year and the actual loan-to-value ratio should be less than 70%.

The income-gearing ratio also rose to 74.1% in 2017Q4, which is significantly higher than the long-term average of about 50%. Nevertheless, as the mortgage rate in 2017Q4 is still much lower than that in 1997 and could rise substantially in the subsequent years, the author believes the price-to-income ratio would be a much better measure for the comparison of the size of the current property bubble and that of the 1997 bubble.

[6] In Hong Kong, many car parks and taxi licenses are privately owned and tradable among citizens. There are quite a lot of Hong Kong citizens speculating heavily in these assets.

Table 2.1: Cumulated Rises in Hong Kong
Property Price Indices Between March 2009
and April 2018

Residential	244% (14.6% p.a.)
Office	258% (15.1% p.a.)
Retail	250% (14.8% p.a.)
Flatted Factories	341% (17.7% p.a.)

Source: CEIC.

In Chapter 4, the author will first discuss the likelihood, and then the probable timing, of a bursting of Hong Kong's property bubble. He will also discuss the proposed curbing during the seeding stage of the bubble and the bubble-squeezing strategy during the development stage of the bubble. If seriously implemented, these measures could help avoid the rapid growth of the property bubble and, hence, the expected disaster of an eventual bursting of the gigantic bubble. Unfortunately, as explained in the same chapter, the author was eventually disappointed with the related government officials' lack of knowledge and courage to take up responsibility. In particular, he believes that the then Financial Secretary (Mr. John Tsang Chun Wah) and the Chief Executive of the HKMA (Mr. Norman Chan Tak Lum) should be responsible for the formation, and then the unavoidable bursting, of the huge property bubble at that time. By making such a discussion known to the readers as well as citizens in Hong Kong and other developing economies, the author hopes that they will, in the future (say, after the disastrous bursting of Hong Kong's property bubble), be more aware of the great importance of selecting the right experts to monitor their own economies.

2.2 THE SURGE IN PROPERTY PRICES IN SINGAPORE

Similar to the case in Hong Kong, Singapore's choice to be an international financial center means that it has to opt for free capital mobility. Although Singapore's exchange rate system is different from that of Hong Kong and the Monetary Authority of Singapore (MAS) did

Figure 2.3   Singapore's NEER

target a higher exchange rate appreciation after the US's QE1, there is a limit on the amount of appreciation that Singapore could opt for. For example, as shown in Figure 2.3, the MAS has already allowed an appreciation of its nominal effective exchange rate (NEER) by 11% between December 2009 and December 2012. Further appreciation of Singapore's NEER could severely hamper its export, output and employment.

Thus, unlike the case of the 1997–1998 Asian financial crisis during which Singapore could use exchange rate depreciation to mitigate the adverse impacts of the crisis and hence achieved a far much better macro-economic management performance than that in Hong Kong (see Yip, 2005 for the detailed discussion), Singapore's ability to target its exchange rate did not give it much advantage in offsetting the gigantic impacts of the US's QEs. That is, targeting too much exchange rate appreciation would imply too huge a cost in terms of losses in export, output and employment (see Box 2.1 for Singapore's choice of exchange rate policy for its internal balance).

As a result, the QEs in the US also resulted in ample liquidity in Singapore's banking system with extremely low mortgage rates. For example, the mortgage rates were hovering around 1% during the first 2–3 years after US's QE1. Thereafter, it rose a bit but was still around the low level of 2.25% by June 2018. Thus, similar to the case in Hong Kong, the

---

Box 2.1: Singapore's choice of exchange rate policy for its internal balance

As explained in Yip (2005), with a high export content in its production and a high import content in its consumption, Singapore has opted for the use of exchange rate policy for the fine-tuning of its internal balance. According to the doctrine of Impossible Trinity, its choice of free capital mobility and exchange rate policy for internal balance would mean that it has no independent monetary policy (i.e., its interest rate would be affected by the US interest rate and the expected appreciation of the Singapore dollar).

US's QEs and hence the low mortgage rate and the ample liquidity for property loans triggered a sustained rebound of Singapore's property prices and then the formation of a property bubble in Singapore. Nevertheless, because the Singapore government was more willing to curb its property market and there was a much higher proportion of affordable public flats in Singapore (i.e., 80% of the total), the property bubble in Singapore was much smaller than that in Hong Kong (see Chapters 3 and 4 for the detailed discussion). As shown in Figure 2.4, the rise in Singapore's private property price index in the first six quarters after 2009Q1 was as sharp as that in Hong Kong. Nevertheless, there was a significant difference in rate of property price hike since 2011Q1. In particular, because of the relatively severe fifth and seventh rounds of curbing measures in Singapore, the rise of Singapore's private property price index started to decline from the very high 25.1% in the first year after 2009Q1 toward the relatively low 1.1% during the year between 2012Q4 and 2013Q4. As a result, the cumulated rise in residential property prices in Singapore between 2009Q1 and 2013Q4 were 53% for private properties and 48% for resale HDB flats,[7] which were much smaller than the

---

[7]As the local minimum of the Singapore's private property price index occurred at 2009Q2, most comments would usually report the cumulated rise since 2009Q2. According to this criterion, the cumulated rise in Singapore's property prices between 2009Q2 and 2013Q4 were 61% for private properties and 44% for resale HDB flats. Nevertheless, in order to have a fair comparison with the cumulated rises in other Asian property markets, the author believes it would be better to compare the cumulated rises between 2009Q1 and 2013Q4.

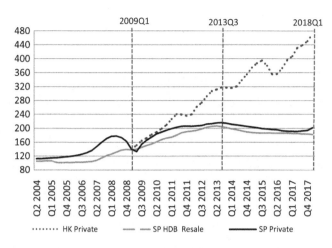

Figure 2.4:   SP Residential Property Price Indices

Note: The Hong Kong private residential price index is rebased so that its starting point in 2009Q1 is the same as that of Singapore's private residential property price index.

Source: CEIC.

127% cumulated rise recorded in Hong Kong between 2009Q1 and 2013Q4.[8]

More importantly, because of the Total Debt Servicing Ratio (TDSR) measure in the eighth round of curbing, the index peaked in 2013Q3, and then exhibited a moderate decline by 3.6% per annum between 2013Q3 and 2016Q3. Thereafter, it went through a bottoming process with very small changes between 2016Q3 and 2017Q3. As a result, the cumulated rise in residential price indices in Singapore between 2009Q1 and 2018Q1 were 44.1% for private properties and 31.6% for resale HDB flats. Even if we take into account of the 16% appreciation of the Singapore dollar vis-à-vis the US dollar, the 67% and 53% cumulated rises in US dollar terms were still much smaller than the 239% (or 235% in US dollar term) cumulated rise recorded in Hong Kong during the same period.

As will be discussed in the subsequent part of this chapter and in Chapter 3, Singapore was the only Asian economy which managed to use

---

[8] As Singapore's property price indices are released on the quarterly basis while those in Hong Kong are released on a monthly basis, the Hong Kong quarterly indices reported here are computed by taking the average of the indices during the three months within the quarter. For example, the indices for 2009Q1 are the average of the indices in January, February and March in 2009.

severe enough curbing measures to bring its property market out from the development stage of a property bubble and then gradually squeezed its property bubble to a safe enough size. (Nevertheless, after the gradual decline and bottoming process in the property price indices between 2013Q3 and 2017Q3, there was a rebound of the private property price index between 2017Q4 and 2018Q2. If left unattended, such a rebound could result in an upward inertia of property prices and then an expectation of further rise in property prices. If so, according to the theoretical framework in Chapter 1, this could again bring the Singapore property market back on a bubble path. We will come back to such a discussion in Chapter 3.)

Similarly, the cumulated rises in Singapore's non-residential property price indices were far smaller than the corresponding rises in Hong Kong. As shown in Table 2.2, the corresponding rises for offices, shop space and flatted factories in Singapore were, respectively, 37%, 2% and 70%, which are much smaller than the 253%, 249% and 338% recorded in Hong Kong.

In addition, because of a different choice of system, there were also no corresponding speculation and hence bubble in the car parks and taxi-licenses in Singapore, even though there was a certain rise in the Certificate of Entitlement (CoE) for car ownership (see Box 2.2 for the detailed discussion).

In Chapter 3, the author will explain that, because of Singapore government's curbing effort and other factors, Singapore's property bubble would not be large enough to have a bursting by itself (say, during the subsequent interest rate hike in the US). Nevertheless, it would still be vulnerable to the contagion effect of a collapse in property price in any neighboring economy or any economy with similar economic characteristics (e.g., Hong Kong).

Table 2.2: Cumulated and Per Annum Rises in Property Price Indices Between 2009Q1 and 2018Q1

	Hong Kong	Singapore
Residential (private)	244% (14.5% p.a.)	44% (4.1% p.a.)
(HDB resale)		32% (3.1% p.a.)
Office	258% (15.0% p.a.)	37% (3.6% p.a.)
Retail	250% (14.9% p.a.)	2% (0.3% p.a.)
Flatted Factories	341% (17.8% p.a.)	70% (6.1% p.a.)

Source: CEIC.

Box 2.2:   The differences in the car parking, taxi license and CoE systems between Hong Kong and Singapore

The binding factor that limits the number of cars in Hong Kong is the car parking fees, while the binding factor in Singapore is the CoE, which is only valid for 10 years. During the asset bubble period, speculation on the freely tradable car parks and taxi licenses in Hong Kong pushed the price of these assets toward a huge bubble. Unlike the case of Hong Kong where many residential car parks are detachable from the flats and are freely tradable, most of the car parks in Singapore are not separately tradable (i.e., the car parks are either individually included in the private landed properties, collectively included in the whole condominium estates or owned by the government for the HDB housing estates). As a result, there is no transaction, and hence no speculation, on the car parks in Singapore. For the case of taxi in Singapore, all taxi owners have to bid for a CoE before the taxi is allowed to operate. As the CoE is only valid for 10 years, the value of the CoE will decline by 10% every year; so there is little incentive for speculators or investors to use the CoE as a long-term asset investment. As a result, there is also no huge bubble in the price of CoE in Singapore.

2.3 THE RISE IN PROPERTY PRICES IN SOME OTHER ASIAN ECONOMIES

In this section, the author will review the trend and cumulated rises in property prices in some other Asian economies. With the help of the theoretical discussion in Chapter 1, one can judge whether the particular property market is at the seeding stage, development stage or final stage of a property bubble. This would in turn provide important information on the direction of that market's property price in the subsequent quarters. Together with the information on the cumulated rise of that market's property price since 2009Q1, one can extract valuable information on the vulnerability of a major correction of property prices in that economy.[9]

---

[9] Because of limitation of data availability, the author does not have the official affordability measures on residential properties and the official rental yields on both the residential and non-residential properties in these economies. As a result, the analysis here could at most be suggestive. Additional data on the affordability measures and rental yields could provide further support of, or a different view from, the analysis here.

2.3.1 India

Similar to the case of Hong Kong, the cumulated rises in property prices since 2009Q1 were huge in major Indian cities. As shown in Figure 2.5, the cumulated rise in property prices between 2009Q1 and 2017Q4 was 307% for Mumbai (Bombay) and Delhi, and 243% for all major Indian cities. Taking into account the depreciation of the Indian rupee vis-a-vis the US dollar during the same period, this would mean 223% and 172% cumulated rises in US dollar term. Such gigantic cumulated rises also meant very rapid and non-sustainable per annum rises of 17.4% (14.3% in US dollar term) for Mumbai and Delhi and 15.2% (12.1% in the US dollar term) for all major Indian cities over the prolonged 8.75 years between 2009Q1 and 2017Q4!

With the huge cumulated rises in property prices, there is a high risk that the urban property market in India could experience a major correction in the future, say, during the later phase of the interest rate hike in the US or during another emergent market crisis triggered by the US interest rate hike. (*Postscript*: At the time of writing the first draft of this book, there was not yet any emergent market crisis. Nevertheless, by 2018Q2, there were a few medium-size emergent market crisis happening in Turkey, Brazil, Argentian

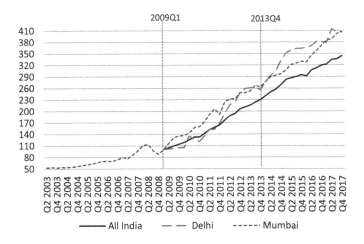

Figure 2.5: Indian Property Price Indices

Note: The "All India" index is defined as the population-weighted average of the indices for the following major cities: Mumbai, Delhi, Bangalore, Ahmedabad, Lucknow, Kolkata, Chennai, Jaipur and Kanpur.

Source: CEIC and Reserve Bank of India.

Box 2.3:   An application of the theoretical framework outlined in Section 1.3 to the case of India

To demonstrate the usefulness of the theoretical framework outlined in Section 1.3, the author would like to reproduce the following first draft comment written before this final draft:

> *Figure 2.5 and the theoretical discussion in Chapter 1 also suggest the Indian property market in 2013Q4 should be at the development stage of a property bubble. Neither were there severe curbing measures such as those adopted in Singapore. According to the characteristics of the development stage of asset bubble outlined in Chapter 1, Indian property prices would probably surge beyond the 2013Q4 level in the subsequent quarters.*

As shown in the extended part of Figure 2.5, the above discussion was eventually proved to be right. Together with the subsequent discussion on the property bubbles in other economies, this suggests that policymakers could in the future use the theoretical framework outlined in Section 1.3 to evaluate the subsequent development at the various stages of a property bubble, and use it to design appropriate curbing measures to pre-empt or contain a potential property bubble.

---

and India. It should however be noted that there could be more serious crises during the later phase of the US interest rate hike.) Furthermore, if we take into account of the less good market fundamentals in India (e.g., India has a large current account deficit while both Singapore and Hong Kong have a current account surplus; India's banks and financial structure could also be weaker than those in Singapore and Hong Kong), one should be very alert to the potential damages of a major correction of Indian property prices.

With the weak market fundamentals mentioned above, the author believes India is one of the top candidates that would eventually experience a disastrous plunge in its property prices and other asset prices. The only remaining question is whether it would be India, Hong Kong or another developing economy that turns out to be the one that triggers another Asian financial crisis by being the first one to have a collapse in its asset prices.

2.3.2 Taiwan

For the case of Taiwan, the cumulated rises in property prices in the major cities were also substantial and dangerous. As predicted by the theoretical discussion in Chapter 1, the few rounds of curbing measures before June

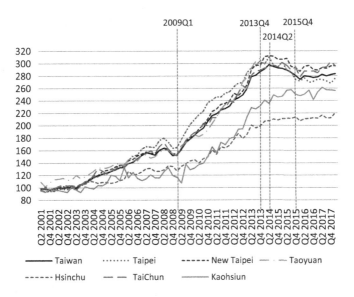

Figure 2.6:   Taiwan Property Price Indices

Source: CEIC.

2014 were too mild when compared with the substantial upward driving forces during the seeding stage and the development stage of the property bubble. As a result, the rises in Taiwan's property prices between 2009Q1 and 2014Q2 were rapid and substantial. For example, as shown in Figure 2.6, the cumulated rise in the property price index between 2009Q1 and 2014Q2 was 94.9% for the major cities in Taiwan, implying a rapid and persistent 17% per annum rise for these 4.25 years.

Fortunately, the curbing measures since 26 June 2014 were powerful enough to cause a moderate consolidation of the property price indices in Taipei, New Taipei, Taoyuan and Taichun, and a slower rise in Hsinchu and Kaoshiun. As a result, the cumulated rise in the overall property price index between 2009Q1 and 2018Q1 moderated a bit to 85.4% in local currency term (or 117% in US dollar term). While this is smaller than the gigantic cumulated rises recorded in Hong Kong (244%) and India (172% in US dollar term), it is still a substantial and sharp rise (e.g., 8.0% rise per annum when compared with the 4.1% per annum rise and 44% cumulated rise in Singapore during the same period), suggesting that Taiwan will be highly vulnerable to the contagion effect of a plunge in property prices in Hong Kong, India or other Asian economies.

2.3.3 Malaysia

As predicted at the beginning of the chapter, the rises in Malaysia's property price indices were much slower than that of Singapore's private property price index during the first 1–2 years after 2009Q1. For example, as shown in Table 2.3 (and Figure 2.7), the rises in property price indices during the first year after 2009Q1 were 5.6% for Malaysia and 7.7% for its capital (Kuala Lumpur), which were far smaller than the 25.1% recorded in Singapore. Even for the second year after 2009Q1, the rises in Malaysia (9.5%) and Kuala Lumpur (10.8%) were still smaller than the 13.8% in Singapore.

Table 2.3: Per Annum Rises in Property Prices in Malaysia

	First year after 2009Q1	Second year after 2009Q1	2011Q1–2013Q3	2013Q3–2017Q4
Malaysia	5.2% p.a.	9.5% p.a.	12.7% p.a.	6.8% p.a.
Kuala Lumpur	7.7% p.a.	10.8% p.a.	14.9% p.a.	7.2% p.a.
Singapore (private)	25.1% p.a.	13.8% p.a.	3.4% p.a.	−2.5% p.a.

Source: CEIC.

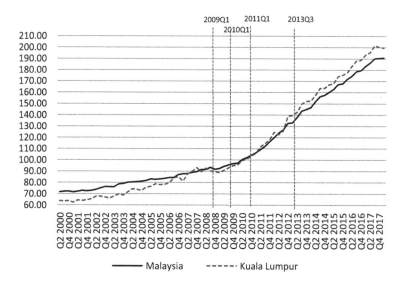

Figure 2.7: Malaysia Property Price Indices

Source: CEIC.

Nevertheless, because of differences in subsequent developments in both Singapore and Malaysia, the above trend started to reverse from 2011. On Singapore's side, after many rounds of relatively severe curbing measures, the rise in Singapore's private property price index started to fall from the initially high 25.1% to 13.8% and then to 3.4% per annum in 2011Q1–2013Q3 and −2.5% per annum in 2013Q3–2017Q4. On Malaysia's side, because of

(i)   lack of strong enough curbing measures in Malaysia
(ii) the curbing measures in Singapore having induced many Singaporean developers to expand their property developments in Malaysia and many Singaporean investors to buy properties in Malaysia,

Malaysia's (and Kuala Lumpur's) property price index continues to accelerate from 5.6% (7.7%) per annum in the first year after 2009Q1 to 9.5% (10.8%) per annum in the second year after 2009Q1 and then to 11.9% (14.1%) per annum in 2011Q1–2013Q3 before it slows down a bit to 6.8% (7.2%) per annum in 2013Q3–2017Q4. As a result, the cumulated rises in the property price indices between 2009Q1 and 2018Q1 were 107% for Malaysia and 125% for Kuala Lumpur. Even if we take into account of the depreciation of the ringgit vis-à-vis the US dollar during the same period, the cumulated rise in US dollar term were 95% for Malaysia and 112% for Kuala Lumpur. Thus, because of the difference in the quality of curbing measures, the cumulated rise in Malaysia's property price indices had well exceeded the 44% (or 67% in US dollar term) for private properties and 32% (or 53% in US dollar term) for resale HDB flats in Singapore (see Box 2.4).

Box 2.4: Another application of the theoretical framework outlined in Section 1.3 to the case of Malaysia

Again, to demonstrate the usefulness of the theoretical framework outlined in Section 1.3, the author would like to reproduce the following first draft comment written before this final draft:

> *As a result, the cumulated rises in the property price indices between 2009Q1 and 2013Q4 were 52% for Malaysia and 76% for Kuala Lumpur.*[10] *Thus, by 2013Q4,*

(Continued)

---

[10]The corresponding cumulated rises for high-rise apartments were even higher at 121% for Malaysia and 134% for Kuala Lumpur.

Box 2.4: *(Continued)*

the cumulated rise in Malaysia's property price indices were either close to, or had already exceeded, the 53% recorded in Singapore. Furthermore, with the adoption of the relatively severe curbing measure (i.e., the Total Debt Servicing Ratio, TDSR) in Singapore since June 2013, Singapore's property prices had peaked in 2013Q3 and started to exhibited a moderate decline from 2013Q4 (see Chapter 3 for further details). On the other hand, the curbing measures in Malaysia were too mild when compared with the upward forces due to the changes in economic behaviors and vicious cycles during the development stage of the property bubble (see Chapter 1 for the details).[11] Given that the Malaysian government would probably not be able to recognize the importance of implementing strong enough curbing measures to stop the bubble from growing to a bigger one, there is a high likelihood that Malaysia's property prices could surge up to more dangerous levels. In other words, it is highly likely that Malaysia property market would sooner or later be more vulnerable to a major correction than that of Singapore.

As shown in the extended part of Figure 2.7, the above discussion was eventually proved to be right. Together with the discussion on the property bubbles in other economies, this suggests that policymakers could in the future use the theoretical framework outlined in Section 1.3 to evaluate the subsequent development at the various stages of a property bubble, and use it to design appropriate curbing measures to pre-empt or contain a potential property bubble.

2.3.4 INDONESIA

Unlike the case of Hong Kong and Singapore whose property prices were the first and the most affected by the QEs in the US, there were two major differences in the pattern of the rise in residential property prices in Indonesia. Firstly, only the property prices of the first- and second-tier

---

[11] In 2014Q1, Malaysia did introduce an additional buyer stamp duty for foreign property investors. However, as could be predicted by the theoretical discussion in Chapter 1 (and the discussion in Chapters 3 and 4 on Singapore's and Hong Kong's slightly earlier experiences during the development stage of their property bubble), the curbing measures had only caused a very mild (−0.08%) and very temporary softening of the property price index in Kuala Lumpur. From 2014Q2 onwards, developers were able to use their price setting power and hoarding power to push for another surge in Kuala Lumpur's property prices. For the case of "All Malaysia", there was not even any softening of the property price index in 2014Q1.

Table 2.4:   Property Price Indices in Major Cities in Indonesia

	2009Q1–2012Q3 cumulated (p.a.)	2012Q3–2018Q1 cumulated (p.a.)	2009Q1–2018Q1 cumulated (p.a.)
Surabaya	12.4% (3.2% p.a.)	72.0% (10.4% p.a.)	93.2% (7.4% p.a.)
Monado	13.7% (3.5% p.a.)	73.5% (10.5% p.a.)	97.2% (7.6% p.a.)
Makassar	21.9% (5.4% p.a.)	65.1% (9.5% p.a.)	101.4% (7.9% p.a.)
Bandung	13.4% (3.4% p.a.)	43.3% (6.8% p.a.)	62.7% (5.4% p.a.)
Medan	13.6% (3.5% p.a.)	35.7% (5.7% p.a.)	54.2% (4.8% p.a.)
Jabodetakbek-Banten	15.0% (3.8% p.a.)	34.3% (5.5% p.a.)	54.5% (4.8% p.a.)
Palembang	12.8% (3.3% p.a.)	33.4% (5.4% p.a.)	50.5% (4.5% p.a.)
Bandar Lampung	7.0% (1.8% p.a.)	22.9% (3.8% p.a.)	31.5% (3.0% p.a.)
Banjarmasin	6.9% (1.8% p.a.)	29.7% (4.8% p.a.)	38.6% (3.6% p.a.)
Denpasar	10.8% (2.8% p.a.)	24.1% (4.0% p.a.)	37.6% (3.5% p.a.)
Semarang	5.0% (1.3% p.a.)	27.9% (4.6% p.a.)	34.3% (3.2% p.a.)
Yogyakarta	6.5% (1.7% p.a.)	11.6% (2.0% p.a.)	18.8% (1.9% p.a.)
Pandang	9.8% (2.5% p.a.)	20.5% (3.4% p.a.)	32.2% (3.1% p.a.)
Pontianak	8.3% (2.1% p.a.)	12.5% (2.2% p.a.)	22.3% (2.2% p.a.)

Source: CEIC

cities were eventually affected by the US's QEs. Secondly, even for those affected cities, the significant surges in property prices only started with a substantial delay (e.g., 2–3 years after 2009Q1).

For example, as shown in the lower part of Table 2.4, during the period between 2009Q1 and 2012Q3, there were only normal 1.3–2.8% per annum rises in the property price indices in the third-tier cities such as Bandar Lampung, Banjarmasin, Denpasar, Semarang, Yogyakarta, Pandang and Pontianak. Even though there was a slightly faster 2.0–4.8% per annum rise in 2012Q3–2018Q1, the cumulated rises of these property price indices during the nine years between 2009Q1 and 2018Q1 were still within the safe and acceptable range of 19–39% (i.e., 1.9–3.6% p.a.).

For major cities such as in Surabaya, Manado and Makassar, the per annum rises between 2009Q1 and 2012Q3 were still at the moderate or moderately-high rate of 3.2% p.a., 3.5% p.a. and 5.4% p.a., respectively. Nevertheless, there were a sharp surge in the per annum rises since 2012Q4 (i.e., 9.5–10.5% p.a. during the period between 2012Q3 and

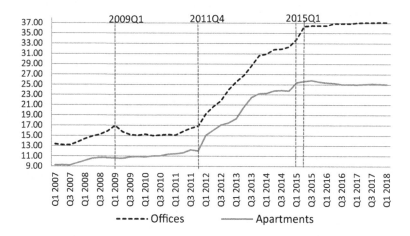

Figure 2.8:   Property Prices in Jabodebek (mill. Rh/m^2)

Source: CEIC.

2018Q1). As a result, the cumulated rises of property price indices in these cities over the whole nine years in 2019Q1–2018Q1 were at the alarming and dangerous levels of 93.2–101.4%. Taking into account of the 16% depreciation of Indonesian rupiah vis-à-vis the US dollar during the same period, the cumulated rises were 62–69% in US dollar term, which were just moderately lower than the 117% in Taiwan and the 95% in Malaysia.

For the case of Indonesia's capital (i.e., Jabodebek or Greater Jakarta),[12] Figure 2.8 shows that the rise of property index of apartments started three quarters earlier than the above three major cities (i.e., started from 2012Q1 instead of 2012Q4), and the cumulated rises between 2011Q4 and 2015Q1 was substantial and alarming (i.e., 111%). Although the average property price started to consolidate from 2015Q2, the cumulated rise during the nine years between 2009Q1 and 2018Q1 was still substantial and dangerous at 136%. Taking into account the depreciation of rupiah, this would mean a cumulated rise of 114% in US dollar term, which is similar to the 117% in Taiwan and higher than the 95% in Malaysia. In addition, the average price level for apartments (22.41 million

---

[12]As Jabodetabek-Banten includes other satellite cities as well as Jabodebek (Greater Jakarta), the rise of property prices in Jabodetabek-Banten were more moderate and may not reflect the case in Greater Jakarta well. As such, the author also collects and reports the property price indices for apartments, offices and retail premises in Greater Jakarta.

rupiahs or 1629 US dollars per square meter) was extremely high when compared with the median income in Greater Jakarta. Similarly, the average price level for offices only started its sharp surge from 2012Q1, although it peaked and started the consolidation one quarter after the average price level of apartments. As a result, the cumulated rise during the whole nine years between 2009Q1 and 2018Q1 was again at the dangerous level of 119%. Given that the average price level for offices was also at the extremely high level (35.58 million rupiahs or 2586 US dollars per square meter) when compared with the median income and other business costs in Greater Jakarta, it is obvious that there were property bubbles in Greater Jakarta's residential apartments market and offices market.

Thus, while the rises of residential property prices in the third-tier cities in Indonesia were still acceptable, there were big property bubbles in major cities such as Greater Jakarta, Surabaya, Manado and Makassar. Therefore, these cities will be the first few Asian cities that would be affected by the contagion effect of a bursting of property bubble in Hong Kong, India or another Asian city. As a bursting of the property bubbles in these major Indonesian cities would quickly trigger a fall in property prices in the other Indonesian cities (say, from slightly overvalued levels to slightly undervalued levels, or from fair levels to substantially undervalued levels) through the contagion effect, the property bubbles in Greater Jakarta and the other three major cities had substantially increased Indonesia's vulnerability to a severe collapse of property prices and the implied financial crisis during the mid or final phase of the US interest rate hike amid the US's economic recovery from the global financial tsunami.

2.3.5 Other Asian Economies

As shown in Figure 2.9, the cumulated rises in the property price indices in Thailand between 2009Q1 and 2018Q1 were 71.7% for the Condominium market (6.3% p.a.), 50.1% for the Town House market (4.5% p.a.) and 39.6% for the Detached House market (3.7% p.a.). Moreover, the cumulated rise for land cost during the same period was 74.4% (6.3% p.a.).

Taking into account the prices of these properties relative to the median income, the cumulated and per annum rises in the price indices of condominiums and town houses suggest that there is a moderately large

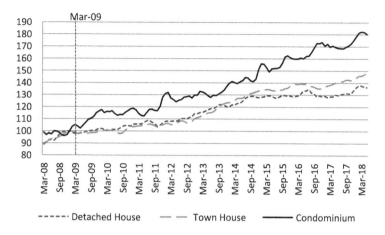

Figure 2.9:   Property Price Indices in Thailand

Source: CEIC.

bubble in the Condominium market and a small bubble in the Town House market. As the condominiums are mostly in the urban area while the detached houses are mostly in the rural area, this suggests that there could be a moderately large property bubble in the urban area. Thus, the Thailand urban property market could be vulnerable to a bursting of property bubble in Hong Kong, India or another Asian city.

The timing of the bubble formation and the subsequent consolidation in South Korea was quite different from the above Asian economies. First consider the case of Seoul (i.e., the dotted line shown in Figure 2.10), which hosts about half of the population in South Korea.[13] After the formation of a property bubble in July 1987–April 1991 and then the substantial correction in April 1991–November 1998, there was once again the formation of a big property bubble in November 1998–July 2008 and then a prolonged consolidation in July 2008–September 2013.

As predicted by the theoretical framework in Chapter 1, the sustained rebound since September 2013 has probably created an expectation of further rise in property price and is pushing the property market in Seoul into the development stage of a property bubble. (Note that the per square

---

[13] Because of that, the property price index for all major cities (i.e., the "Total" line in Figure 2.10) was actually somewhere between "Seoul" and "Six Large Cities".

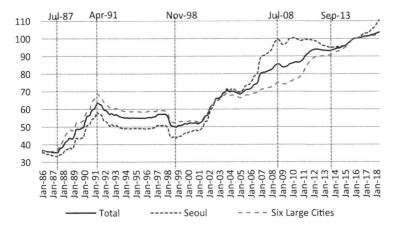

Figure 2.10:   South Korea's Property Price Index

Source: CEIC.

meter price of residential properties in Seoul during the first 1–2 years after September 2013 was still very high when compared with the median income. Thus, the Seoul property market at that time was at a seeding stage with relatively unaffordable property prices.) If the upward momentum in the development stage is left unattended, the property market will continue to be on the automatic path toward a big property bubble. Nevertheless, given that the property markets in Hong Kong, India and other Asian cities will probably burst in the foreseeable future, the contagion effect will probably cause a correction in Seoul's property market well before it could reach a gigantic bubble.

The pattern of property price indices for the other six large cities in July 1987–April 1991 and in April 1991–November 1998 was very similar to that of Seoul. However, because of the less unreasonable rise in November 1998–July 2008 when compared with that in Seoul, the property price indices in the other six large cities did not have to go through the prolonged consolidation triggered by the global financial tsunami. As such, the property price indices in the other six major cities continued to rise in both July 2008–September 2013 and September 2013–May 2018. Since the 97% cumulated rise (i.e., 7.4% p.a.) of the property price index in the other six large cities between November 1998 and May 2018 was substantial and the corresponding rise in Seoul was even more substantial at 155% (i.e., 10.3% p.a.), one can conclude that the urban property market in South Korea is highly vulnerable to a bursting of property bubble in Hong Kong, India or another Asian city.

From the policy point of view, although the timing of bubbles and consolidations in South Korea is quite different from those of other Asian economies, the pattern of these bubbles and consolidations is highly consistent with the pattern discussed in our theoretical framework outlined in Chapter 1. Thus, one can conclude that the South Korean government has so far performed badly in pre-empting or containing its property bubbles, which have in turn caused severe pain to South Korean households. The author believes future policymakers in South Korea could learn from the theoretical framework outlined in Chapter 1, and use them to pre-empt the formation of gigantic bubbles in the future.

PART III

TWO EXTREME EXAMPLES ON THE CURBING MEASURES AGAINST PROPERTY BUBBLES IN ASIA

CHAPTER 3

LESSONS FROM THE SURGE IN PROPERTY PRICES AND THE CURBING MEASURES IN SINGAPORE

In this chapter, the author will use Singapore's experience to explain how the theories in Chapter 1 could help in pre-empting a property bubble in the seeding stage and containing a property bubble in the development stage. Thereafter, he will discuss the nine rounds of curbing measures in Singapore and draw lessons from the effectiveness of these nine rounds of curbing. In particular, he will explain (i) why Singapore missed the best time to pre-empt the property bubble at the seeding stage; and (ii) how Singapore's subsequent persistent and determined effort in curbing its property bubble had eventually stopped the bubble from growing and then helped squeezing part of the bubble. The author hopes such an analysis of the earlier mistake and the subsequent success in Singapore could provide valuable lessons for pre-empting or containing property bubbles in the future.

3.1 HOW THE THEORIES COULD HELP PRE-EMPTING AND CONTAINING A PROPERTY BUBBLE: AN APPLICATION TO THE CASE OF SINGAPORE

3.1.1 It is Possible to Anticipate the Risk of a Bubble at the Seeding Stage

As explained in Chapter 2, with the very low mortgage rates and ample liquidity in the banking sector after the US's QE1, the residential property prices in Singapore and Hong Kong had the chance to make a sustained rebound from 2009Q2 (see Figures 3.1 and 4.1). While most of the policymakers and business economists were not aware of the risk of a potential bubble at the early stage (say, in 2009Q3–2010Q1), the theoretical discussion in Chapter 1 had enabled the author to judge, at the early stage, that the rebound could be the beginning of a bubble formation.[1]

That is, a sustained rebound of the property prices from the trough could result in an expectation of further rise in property prices, which would in turn result in the changes in economic behaviors outlined in Chapter 1. In particular, the expectation of further rise in property prices could create enormous speculative demand, investment demand and then panic demand. (*Note*: As will be discussed in Section 3.2.2, the increase in long-term investment demand is usually much greater than the increase in short-term speculative demand, and is usually more difficult to deal with.) Individuals and firms would also increase their leverage and borrow more money for property investment. These increases in demand, and the informal cartel discussed in Chapter 1, would allow the developers to use their collective pricing power to keep raising the price of new properties beyond the current level. Through the indicator effect discussed in Chapter 1, the rising price of the relatively small amount of new properties could keep pulling up the price of the far greater pool of resale properties. The rise in both the prices of new and resale properties would then create even more speculative demand, investment demand and panic demand, which would in turn fuel further rises of property prices toward a huge bubble.

On the monetary side, capital inflows and overseas borrowings by banks (to satisfy the higher demand for property loans and other loans) would cause a rise in the monetary base *MB*, while changes in banks' desired *excess-reserve-to-deposit-ratio e* and the general public's desired *cash-to-deposit-ratio k* would also increase the money multiplier m.[2]

---

[1] In fact, the author's first warning of the risk of an asset bubble was in the form of policy articles published in the Hong Kong Economic Journal in January 2009, which were subsequently incorporated in Yip (2011). That is, it was possible to identify the risk of an asset bubble in Asia even before the end of the global financial tsunami, if one was equipped with the theories outlined in Chapter 1.

[2] In the case of Singapore, there was a rise in the banks' loan-to-deposit ratio instead of a rise in *m*.

The increase in both m and MB would cause a substantial increase in money supply, thus providing the necessary fuel for further increase in asset prices. Thereafter, there would be

(i) a few vicious cycles (e.g., between the rise of property prices and the rise of share prices, between the rise of asset prices and the rise of aggregate demand; and among the rise in asset prices, capital inflows and the rise of money supply); and

(ii) upward spirals among property prices, rentals, prices and wages, which would further fuel the rise of property prices. Finally, herding behavior could emerge, which would further push the property prices toward a huge bubble.

It should be noted that not all rebounds from the trough would eventually end up with a bubble. However, with the lessons drawn from previous bubbles (i.e., the lessons outlined in Chapter 1), the author was able to judge at the early stage that there was a risk of bubble formation, *especially when the rebound was sustained and uninterrupted for a few months*. This is particularly the case for the property bubble, as the informal cartel and indicator effect in the urban Asian property market would (i) make it more difficult to curb the rise of property prices, and (ii) substantially augment the likelihood of a bubble formation.

3.1.2 The Best Time to Pre-empt the Bubble is the Seeding Stage

As such, the author started to provide such a warning through a public seminar in Singapore in August 2009, whose content was also summarized and reported in a major newspaper in Singapore. In September–October 2009, the Singapore government established the Strategic Economic Committee to invite policy proposals for future development strategies for Singapore. While pre-empting the property bubble was not an exact fit for the theme of development strategy, the author took the chance to write a four-page policy proposal by arguing that pre-empting the potential bubble was a necessary condition for any development strategy. The proposal was well received by the related ministers, and it was also why policymakers in Singapore were all the way more alert to the current property bubble than policymakers in Hong Kong. Nevertheless, Singapore still missed the best chance of pre-empting the bubble with strong enough curbing measures at the seeding stage. At the end of this chapter, the author will draw lessons from this experience so that policymakers can avoid similar outcomes in the future.

3.1.3 Once at the Development Stage, Waves of Severe Curbing Measures are Needed to Stop the Bubble from Growing

With further rises in property prices in 2010 and 2011, the author made further warnings and urged for more curbing measures on the property bubble through policy comments in newspapers and television interviews in Singapore. For example, in the television interviews at that time, he warned that more severe curbing measures, instead of moderate standard curbing measures, were necessary to stop the bubble from growing. He also highlighted that there existed severe enough curbing measures, such as a mortgage tax,[3] to stop the property bubble from growing. The key was that the government had to be more determined to implement more severe curbing measures, as the effect of moderate standard curbing measures would be far smaller than the effect of the changes in economic behaviors triggered by the expectation of further rise in property prices. (In fact, as explained in Yip (2005), failure to take into account the effect of the above changes in economic behaviors was the main reason for the failure of most Asian policymakers and central bankers in containing the asset bubble in the early and mid 1990s. If these policymakers were knowledgeable and determined enough to implement severe enough curbing measures at that time, the damages of the subsequent Asian Financial Crisis in 1997–98

---

[3]The mortgage tax was first proposed by the author at that time. In view that the low US interest rate and hence the low mortgage rates in Hong Kong and Singapore would result in a property bubble formation, the author recommended a tax on top of the low mortgage rates in Hong Kong and Singapore, and explained that there existed a high enough mortgage tax that could stop the property bubble formation. In the 2014 policy proposal for the Hong Kong government, the author modified this into a prepaid mortgage rate (see the details in Chapter 4).

could have been greatly mitigated, if not avoided. Thus, it is important for policymakers to avoid similar mistakes in the future.)

In May–July 2011, the author also published the arguments in the last chapter of Yip (2011) and held an internal discussion with the related staff at the Monetary Authority of Singapore (MAS). He also published a policy article in the major Chinese newspaper in Singapore, highlighting the following:

(i) The two rounds of quantitative easing in the US at that time had already caused a sustained rise in property prices in many Asian economies. If left unattended, this would cause a property bubble and then an eventual bursting of the bubble as well as the implied financial crisis. In the worst-case scenario, the financial crisis could trigger political and social instability in the related economies.

(ii) Even if Singapore managed to control the rise of its property prices, a bursting of property bubble in *any one* of its neighboring economies could still cause severe damages to the Singapore economy through the contagion effect. Thus, further effort to contain the rise in Singapore's property prices would help mitigate the future damages.

(iii) With respect to some discussants' worry of a relatively big correction of property prices due to government curbing measures at that time, the article explained that the true worry should be no meaningful correction at that time and then persistent rise of property prices toward a huge bubble in the subsequent years. By then, the eventual plunge in property prices, and hence the implied damages, would be more severe and more painful. On the other hand, even in the unlikely case that there was any meaningful correction at that time, the fall in property prices could at most be moderate to medium.[4]

After outlining the characteristics of the seeding stage, the development stage and the final stage of an asset bubble, it pointed out that the property markets in Hong Kong and Singapore had already passed the seeding stage and were at the early phase of the development stage. Thus, unless there were strong enough signs that the European Debt Crisis at

---

[4]As explained in Chapter 1, the effect of changes in economic behaviors will be greater than the effect of the curbing measures.

that time would turn out to be a full-blown crisis,[5] the related economies should seriously consider more severe curbing measures. In particular, it would be important for Singapore to use waves of more severe curbing measures to change the *expectation of further rise in property prices* into one *with no clear expectation of a rise or fall in property prices.*

3.1.4 Once on a Bubble Path, Curbing Demand Should be the Key Measure

After a brief summary on the informal cartel and the indicator effect, the article highlighted the following misleading policy implications when applying the supply and demand analysis to urban Singapore and Asian property markets at that time: *an increase in land supply for housing could curb the rise in property prices through greater supply of housing.* It then explained that the reality would be more complicated:

(i) In the most-likely scenario that the increase in land supply was not enough to meet the substantial surge in housing demand triggered by the expectation of property inflation at that time, the developers could first set the prices of new properties at a 30–50% premium of the prices of resale properties, which would pull up the price of resale properties through the indicator effect. As a result, whenever there is a launch of new private properties, *the price of the nearby resale properties would be pulled up instead of dampened* — a result that would be in sharp contrast to that implied by the supply and demand analysis.

(ii) In the less-likely scenario that the increase in land supply was large enough to meet the substantial surge in demand triggered by the expectation of property inflation at that time, it would imply severe excess supply (and hence substantial collapse of property prices and rentals) when the expectation of property inflation was reversed in the subsequent future.

---

[5]If it could be judged that the European Debt Crisis at that time would only result in a medium-scale or severe recession but not a full-blown crisis, the right policy strategy at that time should be implementing enough curbing measures to contain the rise in property prices, while letting the slowdown of the European economy to induce a more meaningful correction of Singapore's (and Hong Kong's) property prices towards less overvalued levels.

After cautioning the Singapore government that *expectation could be very stubborn during the property boom and very fragile during the downturn*, the article gave the following hypothetical example to highlight that the increase in demand (especially the increase in investment demand) triggered by the expected property inflation would be substantial, and the first scenario stated above would be the likely scenario: Even if we do not count the increase in demand by the (less-rich) 80% HDB flat owners and assume each of the (richer) 20% private property owners would, on average, demand *only* one more flat due to the expected property inflation, this would mean an increase in demand equivalent to 20% of the *total housing stock* in Singapore.[6] Such a figure would be far greater than the previous and subsequent rounds of increase in land supply. Thus, it would be not only "not surprising" but also "more than natural" that the developers would be able to keep pushing up the property prices with their pricing power (derived from the informal cartel) and the indicator effect (from new properties to resale properties).

Therefore, while a temporary increase in land supply above the long-term trend might help a bit, the appropriate policy strategy should be waves of relatively severe curbing measures to curb the exuberant demand triggered by the expectation of further rise in property prices. The article then reiterated the author's previous proposal of a mortgage tax, and suggested further reduction of the loan-to-value (LTV) ratio cap for the purchase of the second property and beyond.

3.1.5 Role of Government Supply of Affordable Public Flats During the Bubble Period

To prepare for the worst, it also suggested the government to supply more, and sufficient number of, new HDB flats to eligible Singaporeans who wish

---

[6] Note that many private property owners had actually bought quite a number of flats during the property boom while some others missed the chance to buy another one. More importantly, the focus here should be on the increase in *demand* instead of *actual purchase*. That is, those who missed the chance to buy another one did have a higher demand, although they failed to buy another one because their upward revision of expectation was slower than the actual rise in property prices. Thus, the assumption of an increase in demand equivalent to 20% of the total housing stock was reasonable, if not conservative.

to buy one. To cut the indicator effect from the prices of private properties to the prices of new HDB flats, the government should also avoid increasing the price of new HDB flats with the rise in general property prices. Instead, it should set the prices of new HDB flats at slightly lower levels so that there could be an indicator effect in the reverse direction to slow down the rise in the prices of resale HDB flats. Thus, even if the Singapore government eventually fails to stop the property bubble from growing, these actions can still mitigate the harm of the subsequent bursting to the 80% HDB flat owners. Finally, the government should consider reforming the price setting mechanism of the Design, Build and Sell Scheme (DBSS) flats and the Executive Condominiums (ECs) toward the *revised* price setting mechanism of new HDB flats,[7] as the current practice of allowing the developers to set the price of DBSS flats and ECs had not only allowed the developers to keep pushing up the price of these properties toward less affordable levels, but also helped fuel the rise in overall property prices.

3.1.6 Some Major Changes in Singapore's Bubble-fighting Strategy

The article, the book and the visit to the MAS seemed to have a lot of influence, as the Singapore government had since stopped raising the prices of new HDB flats with the rise in property prices in the market.[8]

---

[7] Both DBSS flats and ECs in Singapore are meant to fill the gap between public HDB flats and private condominiums. Because of better location (for DBSS flats) or better facilities (for ECs), their market prices are usually higher than those of HDB flats. On the other hand, because of the household income cap (e.g., S$12,000 per month at that time) for eligible applicants and the sale restrictions (e.g., 5 years to permanent residents and 10 years to foreigners), their market prices are also lower than those of private condominiums. However, one neglected but extremely important point is that the land price of DBSS flats and ECs are determined by auctioning, and the successful bidders (usually the developers) are the one who set the price of the new DBSS flats and ECs. Because of this neglected but important characteristic, developers of the DBSS flats and ECs would also have the incentive to use this price setting power to (i) charge a high (and hopefully profit maximizing) price and (ii) raise the (profit maximizing) price during the property boom.

[8] In fact, the government has set a lower price of new HDB flats with the intention to contain or slow down the rise of the price of resale HDB flats. However, as there were other factors such as the ineligibility of Singapore's permanent residents to purchase new

More importantly, while Singapore continued to increase private and public housing supply slightly above the long-term trend, the focus of its bubble-fighting strategy had since then shifted to the curbing of the exuberant demand triggered by the previous rises in property prices. In addition, the Singapore government had thereafter become daring enough to adopt severe enough measures to curb the bubble. In fact, some of these curbing measures, especially those in the fifth, the seventh and the eighth rounds, were quite innovative and powerful. In Section 3.2, the author will go into the details of these nine rounds of curbing.

3.2 LESSONS FROM THE NINE ROUNDS OF CURBING IN SINGAPORE

In this section, the author will discuss the nine rounds of curbing measures in Singapore, and draw lessons from the effectiveness of these nine rounds of curbing. In particular, he will explain why (i) the first four rounds and the sixth round of curbing failed to stop the property prices from rising; (ii) the fifth and seventh rounds of curbing had at least helped stop the bubble from growing; and (iii) the eighth round of curbing had helped squeeze part of the bubble. The author believes such an analysis of Singapore's experience will provide valuable lessons for policymakers in the future.

3.2.1 The Relative Ineffectiveness of the First Two Rounds of Curbing

As listed in Table 3.1, the first round of curbing was basically the removal of the interest absorption scheme, which should be abolished even during the normal time.

Thus, strictly speaking, this should be regarded as a return-to-normal and should not be regarded as a curbing measure. That is, the curbing measures actually started from February 2010, which is known as the second round of curbing measures. Unfortunately, the curbing measures were too mild, involving only (i) a reduction of the LTV ratio cap from 90% to 80%, and (ii) an imposition of a relatively small SSD if the buyers

---

HDB flats, the price of resale HDB flats still went up because the permanent residents' expected property inflation and hence their strong demand for resale HDB flats.

Table 3.1:   The Nine Rounds of Curbing in Singapore

14 Sep 09:	The interest absorption scheme (which allowed some deferment of principal payments) and interest-only loans were disallowed.
09 Feb 10:	LTV ceilings were lowered from 90% to 80% for all private property loans. A seller stamp duty (SSD) was introduced on all private properties sold within one year of purchase at the rate of 1% for the first S$180,000, 2% for the next S$180,000 and 3% for the remaining balance.
30 Aug 10:	The SSD was extended to sales within three years of purchase, with one-third, two-third, or full SSD rates depending on the length of the holding period. LTVs ceiling were lowered from 80% to 70% for buyers with one or more outstanding housing loans.
13 Jan 11:	The SSD was extended to sales within four years and rates raised to 16% for sales within a year, decreasing gradually thereafter to a minimum 4% for the fourth year. LTVs were lowered to 60% for individuals with one or more outstanding loans and to 50% for non-individuals.
08 Dec 11:	An additional buyer's stamp duty (ABSD) was imposed over and above the existing BSD, with a rate of 10% on foreigners and corporate entities buying any residential property, and of 3% on permanent residents buying their second or subsequent residential properties and on Singaporeans buying their third and subsequent residential properties.
06 Oct 12:	Limit all residential loan tenures to 35 years. For loans exceeding 30 years and those extending beyond the retirement age of 65, the LTV cap is reduced to (i) 40% (from 60%) for those with one or more residential loans; and (ii) 60% (from 80%) for those with none. Non-individual borrowers' LTV cap is also reduced to 40% (from 50%).
12 Jan 13:	LTV cap reduced to (i) 50% for individuals' 2nd outstanding loans; (ii) 40% for individuals' 3rd or more outstanding loans; and (iii) 20% for non-individual borrowers. Minimum cash downpayment for 2nd or more housing loans will be raised to 25% (from 10%). Mortgage Servicing Ratio (MSR) cap for loans to purchase new or resale HDB flats is reduced to 35% (from 40%) if loan is from HDB, and capped at 30% if loans is from financial institutions. PRs are now disallowed to sublet their whole HDB flat, and must sell their HDB flat within 6 months of purchasing private residential property in Singapore. Limits imposed on using CPF funds to purchase public housing with 30–59 years of remaining lease capped at private valuation limit based on ratio of remaining lease when the youngest buyer who can use CPF turns 55 year old to the lease at point of purchase. Using CPF funds to purchase public housing with <30 years of remaining lease is now not allowed.

(continued)

Table 3.1: (*continued*)

	Developers of future EC sites from the GLS program can launch sale after 15 months or after completing foundation works, whichever is earlier. Maximum floor strata area of new EC units capped at 160 m². SSD imposed on industrial property: 15% if sold in the 1st year of purchase; 10% in the 2nd year and 5% in the 3rd year.
29 Jun 13:	Imposed a 60% Total Debt Servicing Ratio (TDSR) limit for all property loans by financial institutions to individuals. Under the TDSR framework, all borrowers' other outstanding debt obligations will be taken in consideration, and a 30% haircut will be applied to rental incomes and other variable incomes (e.g. bonuses, commissions and business incomes). Borrowers named on property loans are required to be mortgagees of the residential property, guarantors for loans are to be brought in as co-borrowers, income-weighted average age of joint-borrowers are to be applied to rules on loan tenure.
06 Jul 18:	Increased ABSD for Singapore citizens (0% for 1st flat, from 7% to 12% for 2nd flat, from 10% to 15% for the 3rd flat and onwards), Singapore PR (5% for 1st flat, from 10% to 15% for the 2nd flat and onwards), foreigners and non-developer entities (from 15% to 20%) and developers (form 15% to 30% for *en bloc* purchases). For 1st home loan, LTV limit reduced from 80% to 75% and remaining downpayment (Cash/CPF) increased from 15% to 20%. LTV limit for 2nd home loan reduced from 50% to 45%, and LTV limit for 3rd home loans and onwards reduced from 40% to 35%.

sell their properties within one year. As the 80% LTV cap was still high (i.e., still 5 times gearing for property buyers) and the SSD was relatively low and only limited to a year, the curbing effect was much smaller than the effect of the rise in demand due to the expectation of further rise in property prices. As a result, the very mild second round of curbing measures was not able to stop the property prices from rising (see Figure 3.1).

3.2.2 Why the Third and Fourth Rounds of Curbing were not Powerful Enough

With further rises in property prices, the government implemented the third round of curbing in August 2010 and then the fourth round of curbing in January 2011. In these two rounds, the LTV ratio cap for the second property and beyond was further reduced to 70% and then to 60%.

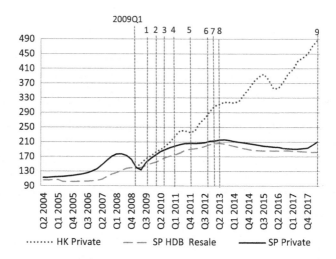

Figure 3.1:   SP Residential Property Price Indices

Note: The numbers 1, 2, 3, 4, 5, 6, 7, 8 and 9 represent the nine rounds of curbing.
Source: CEIC.

Meanwhile, the SSD was extended to 3 years with higher SSD rates, and then to four years with further rises in the SSD rates (see Table 3.1). While the two rounds, especially the fourth round, of curbing were more meaningful in terms of severity, the effect of the changes in economic behaviors grew even faster than the severity of the measures. Besides, there were loopholes and other unexpected complications in these two rounds of curbing. Some examples of these are as follows:

(i) For example, the SSD would only affect short-term speculators but not long-term investors (i.e., long-term investors would not have to pay the SSD as long as they are willing to hold the property for more than 3 or 4 years). As highlighted in Section 3.1.4, the increase in long-term investment demand would be much greater than the increase in speculative demand. Thus, the SSD failed to deter the long-term investment demand, with only moderate effect on short-term speculative demand (i.e., short-term speculators could still avoid or reduce the SSD by switching to be medium-term speculators).[9]

---

[9] If the SSD, or any other curbing measure, could change the expectation of further rise in property prices to an expectation of a fall (or no further rise) in property prices, then the

(ii) The 70% LTV cap in the third round was still not that low, and hence not that binding, for most property investors. Worst still, for those investors who had already bought properties at the early stage of the rebound, the rise in the property prices (and hence the bank valuation) of these earlier investments would enable them to *cash in* through *refinancing*. That is, these investors could take a lot of cash out by increasing the amount of mortgage loans of these earlier properties, and use this cash to support the downpayment of the new purchase. For example, in late 2010–early 2011 (i.e., just before the announcement of the fourth round of curbing measures), the author was able to anticipate the possibility of another round of curbing with lower LTV cap. He therefore rushed to buy another private property. Thereafter, he did a refinancing with one of his properties purchased in September 2009. It turned out that the total mortgage loans he could get from the refinancing was 25% higher than the initial purchasing price of the property. That is, the investment did not use up his cash. Instead, it eventually gave him more cash for more asset investments. While the author was using the cash for share investments, there were many property investors using the above loophole to obtain more cash for more property investments. The above example suggested that this loophole should be addressed if there was another potential bubble in the future. (For example, the LTV cap for the refinancing of existing mortgage could be set at a rate lower than that of new purchase, i.e., 50–60% for the former and 60–70% for the latter.)

(iii) While the 60% LTV cap in the fourth round of curbing and the higher property prices at that time had stopped some experienced and conservative long-term investors, such as the author, from making more property investments, the expectation of further rise in property prices still induced the less-experienced, or more risk-loving, investors to make more property investments. One way of dealing with the lower

---

measure would still be effective through the indirect expectation effect. Unfortunately, the market had correctly judged that the measure would not be enough to cause such a change in expectation. As a result, the measure turned out to be ineffective, which in turn justified the market's initial expectation, and made even more market participants lose their confidence in the government's ability to control the rise in property prices. In Section 3.2.3, I will further explain that even the heavy ABSD was not able to cause the above change in expectation.

LTV cap was switching to smaller size flats and/or lower-end flats such as flats in the less central area and the Executive Condominiums.[10] While such a switch would allow them to buy a flat with the original amount of cash, it also caused a faster rise in the per-square-foot price of these properties. In particular, flats of sizes less than 500 ft^2 (nicknamed as shoe-box flats in Singapore) were having a 20–50% per-square-foot price premium over a bigger flat of similar quality and location. That is, while the lower LTV cap was supposed to help cushion the banks and property investors from future collapse of property prices, the faster rise in the property prices of these types of flats had offset most of the cushioning effect on these properties. In particular, with the rapid rise in the per-square-foot price of the shoe-box flats, it would not be surprising that the net cushioning effect on the shoe-box flats was negative instead of positive.

(iv) Parallel to the switching to small-size flats, many property investors also increased the length of their mortgage tenure to 30 years and then to 35–40 years, which in turn supported higher property prices without raising the debt-service-ratio (DSR) of the property buyers. (*Note*: DSR is the ratio of total monthly debt repayments (including the mortgage installment) to the mortgagee's monthly income. As quite a number of banks have been using this ratio for mortgage loans approval, if the maximum mortgage tenure is capped at a certain value (say, 20 years), the ratio will ensure an automatic curbing mechanism against the rise in property prices. However, if the mortgage tenure is allowed to increase, as in this case and in many previous property bubbles, such an extension would disable the automatic curbing mechanism. Thus, an important lesson for the future is fixing the maximum mortgage tenure to 20 years or less, and forbidding banks from going beyond that limit during the property boom. Such a cap,

---

[10]Note, because of more MRT (Mass Rapid Transit) lines and stations built and expected to be completed, there was also a long-term fundamental support for a faster rise in the prices of outside-central-region properties near the MRT stations. Because of this major change, the author believes the old classification of the Core Central Region (CCR), the Rest of Central Region (RCR) and the Outside Central Region(OCR) would need to be changed or modified in the future (i.e., it would be very important whether the property is near the MRT stations).

and hence the home buyers' budget constraints, will help in not only pre-empting a property bubble in the future but also in containing the property prices in the normal period. In fact, the author is more inclined to further reduce the cap to (a) 20 years for the first mortgage; and (b) 10–15 years for the second mortgage and beyond.[11])

3.2.3 The Fifth Round of Curbing Had At Least Temporarily Stopped the Property Prices from Rising

Another problem with the third and fourth rounds of curbing measures was that it did not address the huge increase in investment demand by mainland Chinese[12] and other foreign investors at that time. As this had contributed significantly to the rise of property prices at that time, the Singapore government introduced a relatively innovative measure in its fifth round of curbing measures: a 10% ABSD for foreigners and corporate entities buying residential properties in Singapore. Such a 10% ABSD (on top of the close to 3% standard buyer stamp duty) had substantially reduced the huge investment demand by mainland Chinese and foreign investors at that time. (*Note*: As the increase in demand by mainland Chinese investors was even bigger in Hong Kong and had created very serious problems there, the ABSD for foreign and mainland Chinese investors was soon adopted with higher rate (i.e., 15%) in the subsequent curbing measures in Hong Kong (see Chapter 4 for the detailed discussion).)

In addition to the 10% ABSD for foreigners and corporate entities, the Singapore government also introduced a 3% ABSD for (i) permanent residents purchasing their second property or beyond, and (ii) Singapore

---

[11] The 10–15 year cap for the second mortgage and beyond was meant to (i) help first-time buyers and (ii) reduce the risk or size of property bubble, as the shorter cap will curb investment demand and hence result in a lower long-run property price. The author believes that, in the long run, it will more fair to the citizens and less risky to the economy to move to the 10-year mortgage tenure cap for the second property and beyond. Nevertheless, for a smooth transition, it would be better to start with an 18-year mortgage cap and then gradually reduce the cap to 15, 12 and then 10 years over time.

[12] The demand from mainland Chinese investors was huge mainly because of the huge population and economic size of China. That is, even if a very small percentage (e.g., 0.1%) of the richer Chinese intended to buy properties in Singapore or Hong Kong, the demand would be huge from the viewpoint of these economies.

citizens purchasing their third property or beyond. Unlike the SSD introduced in the past, the ABSD did have an effect on both the long-term investors and the short-term speculators, as these buyers had to pay the ABSD at the moment they bought the property (i.e., no matter whether they hold or sell the property in the future). On the other hand, first-time buyers would not be affected as they did not need to pay the ABSD and their LTV cap was still 80%.

Such an experience would imply an important lesson for the future: *In case there is a need to pre-empt or curb a bubble in the future, the related government should consider going straight to the ABSD instead of the SSD*, as (i) the increase in long-term investment demand is usually much greater than the increase in speculative demand and (ii) the ABSD will affect both the long-term investors and short-term speculators, while the SSD will have little effect on long-term investors and, at most, moderate effect on speculators.

3.2.4 What was Wrong, the Fifth Round or the Sixth Round of Curbing?

The relatively large percentage of ABSD (on top of the close to 3% standard stamp duty) did have quite a dampening effect on the property market at that time. As we can see from Figure 3.1, it was the first time in that property boom that Singapore's private residential property price index was flat for 2–3 quarters. Unfortunately, as explained in Chapter 1, the developers could use their pricing power and hoarding power to keep the property price at the pre-curbing level, even if this would mean a significant drop in the number of new properties they could sell (and a significant drop in the number of resale property transactions). While such a consolidation would be relatively painful for the developers and property agents, the lower sales also meant an accumulation of pent-up demand during the consolidation period. That is, when potential home buyers took a wait-and-see stance after the curbing measures, there would be accumulation of pent-up demand over time. After a consolidation period of, say, 2–3 quarters, the cumulated pent-up demand would reach a decent level. By then, if there were any positive developments (such as a better external economic environment, higher prices and wages just because of normal inflation and economic growth, or just the fading out of the psychological impacts of the curbing measures), the developers would be able to use the cumulated pent-up demand and their pricing power to achieve another sharp surge in the prices of new properties, which would then pull up the price of resale properties through the indicator effect. Thus, even if the government introduced relatively severe curbing measures, property prices could still move toward a huge bubble in a pattern of *sharp surge — moderate consolidation — and another sharp surge.*

In fact, that was why the author proposed to use waves of severe curbing measures until the expectation of further rise in property prices change to one with "no clear confidence of a rise or fall in property prices". During the initial transitional period in which expectations change back to normal, there would be a significant drop in the number of property transactions from an exuberant level to a very low level, which would mean a lot of pain to the developers, property agents and some property investors. (*Note*: Such kind of pain would in turn induce them to lobby for a relaxation of curbing.) It should however be noted that these people had already made a lot of windfall from the property boom. Thus, it would be misleading to just focus on their temporary pain at that transitional period without counting their earlier windfall. Of course, from the economy point of view, it would be better to have less fluctuation of transactions instead of high volatility of transactions like that. However, given that the number of transactions was too high during the boom period, there was no better choice other than to accept a temporarily low number of transactions after the huge number of transactions. Besides, it would not be a wise choice to keep on satisfying these people, as this would mean an eventual bubble and then the bursting of such a bubble in the future. In fact, these are actually why the author has kept on emphasizing that the best time to pre-empt a bubble is at the seeding stage. Nevertheless, given that Singapore was already at the development stage of a bubble, we only had two choices at that time. The first one was to implement waves of severe curbing measures and hence take the implied moderate, but temporary, pain. The second choice was to let the bubble grow and then take the unbearable pain and the huge costs of a crisis in the future. For those who were aware of the high chance of the second outcome, the choice was obvious. (As explained, the chance of the second outcome was high because developers could offset the effect of curbing measures on property prices until the property prices became too high to be kept.) Unfortunately, many of the discussants at that time were not fully aware of the high chance of the second outcome. As a result, there were doubts and complaints on whether the fifth round of curbing was unnecessarily severe. Such doubts and complaints, or lobbying, had in turn delayed the next waves of severe curbing measures until January 2013, which was known as the seventh round of curbing measures.

Between the fifth and the seventh rounds, the government announced the sixth round of curbing in October 2012. Unfortunately, because of the above doubts and complaints on the fifth round of curbing measures, the Singapore government hesitated to implement any severe curbing measure. As a result, it turned out to be just a follow-up response to the curbing measures implemented in Hong Kong at that time and included the following: (i) a cap on the maximum length of mortgage tenure to 35 years, and (ii) a reduction of the LTV cap to 40% for those mortgages longer than 30 years (or those in which the mortgagee would be older than 65 before the end of the mortgage). In other words, there was no additional curbing other than discouraging middle-age and old-age investors from taking mortgages that span beyond their retirement age. Because of the relatively mild curbing measures and the cumulated pent-up demand discussed above, Singapore's private property price index made another rise in 2012Q4 (see Figure 3.1). This in turn forced the government to implement the seventh round of curbing measures in January 2013.[13]

3.2.5 The Seventh Round of Curbing

Among the various curbing measures implemented in the seventh round, the most powerful measures were the sharp increase in the ABSD and the further reduction of the LTV cap. For foreigners and corporate entities buying the first or second residential property, the ABSD was raised by another 5–15 percentage points.[14] Perhaps more striking was the sharp rise in the ABSD for permanent residents and Singapore citizens. For permanent residents, there would be (i) a 5% ABSD for the first property, and (ii) a further rise in the ABSD to 10% (from the previous 3%) for the

---

[13] There was also rumor that the by-election at that time was the reason for the seventh round of curbing measures. Whether true or not, the author believed the seventh round of curbing measures had to be implemented even if there was no by-election.

[14] Note that the ABSD for the third property and beyond was reduced from 10% to 5%.

second property and beyond. Even for the Singapore citizens, there would (i) a 7% ABSD for the second property, and (ii) a further rise in the ABSD to 10% (from the previous 3%) for the third property and beyond. Thus, only first-time Singaporean buyers were exempted from the ABSD. As the ABSD was on top of a close to 3% standard buyer stamp duty, the tax was quite heavy. Besides, this was the first time a heavy enough tax was imposed on all investment demand, including Singaporean's investment demand for the second property. The big jump in the ABSD also had a strong psychological impact to potential home buyers. Nevertheless, as explained in the footnote,[15] the developers were able to offset some of these impacts by offering a discount to "help absorb" the home buyers' ABSD.

In addition to the sharp increase in the ABSD, the Singapore government also tried to curb the investment demand by further reducing the LTV cap for those doing the second mortgage and beyond. For example, the LTV cap was further reduced to 50% for the second mortgage and to 40% for the third mortgage and beyond. In addition, the minimum cash downpayment was also raised to 25% for the second mortgage and beyond. The reduction in the LTV cap and the increase in cash payment could serve two purposes: (i) discourage "the hard-to-deal-with" investment demand, and (ii) increase the cushion to banks and investors in case there is a collapse of property price in the future.[16,17] Nevertheless, as will

---

[15] As the high ABSD could substantially dampen the investment demand, some property developers tried to offset the impact of such curbing measures by offering a discount to "help" property buyers absorb the ABSD. Such a strategy seemed to be effective as those offering the discount were able to sell quite a number of flats at that time. It should however be noted that it was debatable how much the true discount was, as developers could quote a higher price and then gave a discount based on the higher price.

[16] Parallel with the more powerful measures, the seventh round of curbing also included the following measures: (i) For HDB flat buyers, a new debt service ratio DSR (i.e., debt-service-to-income-ratio) cap of 30% was introduced if the mortgage was done with financial institutions. Meanwhile, the DSR cap for loans with the Housing Development Board were reduced from 40% to 35%; (ii) Permanent residents with a HDB flat are no longer allowed to rent the whole HDB flat out and (iii) Permanent residents buying private properties were required to sell their HDB flats within six months of the new purchase.

[17] In view that there was also growing speculative and investment demand for industrial properties, the government also introduced an additional seller stamp duty (ASSD) for industrial properties. The ASSD rates would be 15%, 10% and 5% if the buyer resold the

be explained in Section 3.2.6, with a lower LTV cap, property investors would switch to smaller size flats. In fact, there were signs that more and more investors were switching to one-room flats and two-room flats. This was very different from the past in which three-room flats were the most popular type. For example, in one of the new launch of private properties in March 2013, 60.1% were one-room flats, 30% were two-room flats, and only 2.2% were three-room flats, 4.4% were four-room flats, and 3.3% were penthouses.

3.2.6 The Effectiveness of the Seventh Round of Curbing

Despite the apparent severity of the seventh round of curbing, the author argued in April 2013 (see Yip, 2014) that the seventh round of curbing could at most cause a slowdown in the rise in property prices, but not any meaningful correction of property prices. Thus, it was important for Singapore to get itself ready for further rounds of curbing. The reasoning was as follows:

With the sharp surge of the ABSD to relatively high rates, the low LTV cap and the high property prices, most of the experienced investors (especially those who have experienced the pain of the Asian Financial Crisis in 1997) had already stopped investing in properties.[18] However, there were still quite a number of younger and perhaps less-experienced investors with only one property, and their desires to own another property were extremely strong after seeing the sharp surge in property prices over the past few years. Because of the high property prices, many of them could only go for smaller size flats (e.g., mostly shoe-box flats, with a smaller percentage

---

industrial properties within 1 year, 2 years and 3 years, respectively. The aim was to discourage short-term speculative demand while avoiding undesirable impacts on the long-term end-users.

[18] In fact, as explained in some of the author's articles in Hong Kong (see Yip, 2014 for the detailed discussion), the more profitable and less risky investment at that time should be shares, i.e., the property prices were already at the overvalued level, but many share prices were still at the undervalued levels, mainly because the global financial tsunami and then the European Debt Crisis had resulted in a *fear discount* in share prices (see Yip, 2011 for the discussion of fear discount in the global stock markets at that time).

opting for the two-room flats). As a result, there was still a decent investment demand for the smaller size flats. This was particularly the case if the developers offer them a discount to "help absorb" the ABSD.

In addition to the above investment demand for smaller size flats, there was still a decent demand for normal-size flats by HDB upgraders with only one property and one outstanding mortgage loan. [19] *In fact, in the new launches of private condominiums at that time, those in the outskirt areas with large number of HDB flats around and in proximity to the MRT stations could still sell very well. Meanwhile, with the relatively high population growth and normal pace of family formation, there was also a decent demand, and perhaps some panic demand, for normal-size flats by first-time homebuyers who would be exempted from the curbing measures.*

In short, despite the severity of the seventh round of curbing, the developers were able to offset part of the ABSD impacts through a temporary discount to "help" the buyers of new properties absorb the ABSD. Meanwhile, there was still a reasonably strong investment demand for smaller size flats (triggered by the sustained rise in property prices over the past few years), and a decent demand for outskirt normal-size flats by HDB up-graders and first-time homebuyers.

Due to the developers' pricing and hoarding power, they did not need a lot of demand to keep the price at the pre-curbing level. For example, only a moderate demand from just the upgraders or the first-time homebuyers would be enough for them to keep the price at the pre-curbing level. Thus, the developers would probably be able to hold the property prices with a temporary discount to help absorb the ABSD, and there would not be any meaningful correction of property prices after the seventh round of curbing. [20]

---

[19] That is, if a HDB upgrader bought a private property and then sold his HDB flat, he would be exempted from the ABSD and be eligible for the 80% LTV cap. As there was still quite a number of this type of HDB upgraders, there would still be a decent demand for normal size flats by these upgraders.

[20] Even in the case of a relatively severe medium-scale deterioration of the economic environment, they could offset the impact by extending the temporary discount for a longer period, increasing the discount by another few percentage points, or just accepting the pain of a lower transaction volume while waiting for the accumulation of pent-up demand during the consolidation period. After such an accumulation for a few months, if there was

The above deduction was soon confirmed by the subsequent statistics. As we can see from Figure 3.1, price indices for both private properties and resale HDB flats in 2013Q1 and 2013Q2 were slightly higher than those in 2012Q4.

3.2.7 The Eighth Round of Curbing: The TDSR

On 28 June 2013, the Monetary Authority of Singapore announced the TDSR framework, which required the financial institutes (FIs) to take into consideration borrowers' other outstanding debt obligation when granting property loans. When granting the new property loans, FIs were required to do the following:

(i)   Ensure the borrowers' monthly repayment for all debt (including personal loans, car loans, student loans, credit card debt and all mortgage loans) would not exceed 60% of borrowers' monthly gross income.
(ii) Apply a specific medium-term interest rate (i.e., 3.5%, which was about 2% higher than market mortgage rate) to the property loans that the borrower was applying for when calculating the TDSR.
(iii) Apply a new hair cut of at least 30% to the rental income and variable income (e.g., bonuses, commissions and business income).
(iv) Verify and obtain relevant documentation on a borrower's debt obligation.

As stated in the MAS press release, the aims of the TDSR were to (1) curb investment demand in the housing market, (2) prevent circumvention of the tighter LTV limits on second and subsequent housing loans, (3) encourage financial prudence among housing borrowers and (4) strengthen credit underwriting practices.

Interestingly, the TDSR did have quite a cooling effect on the property market. This was so because (a) it plugged some of the loopholes in the previous curbing measures; (b) the haircut on rental income and variable income substantially reduced the loan quantum that property buyers could apply for; (c) it was harder to stretch the loan tenure; (d) the need for

---

any improvement in the economic environment, the developers would be able to push for another sharp surge in property prices.

borrowers to provide the relevant documentation on their income and debt obligation did give them the necessary time to evaluate the costs and the risk of the purchase, thus making it more difficult for the developers or property agents to pressurize or mislead homebuyers to pay the deposit at the show flats. As a result, there was a significant reduction in the investment demand, panic demand and speculative demand, and hence a substantial reduction in the number of property transactions in the subsequent quarters. Thus, as shown in Figure 3.1, there were decent corrections of Singapore's property price indices, and hence a moderate squeezing of Singapore's property bubble since 2013Q3.

Despite the contribution of the TDSR in squeezing part of Singapore's property bubble, there were quite a few calls in 2015 by developers and even parliament members to relax the curbing measures on the property market. In response to that, the author published another policy article in the major Chinese newspaper in April 2015, explaining that any relaxation of the curbing measures would immediately cause a surge in Singapore's property prices (see Box 3.1 for a detailed discussion). Fortunately, the well-trained economic officials in the Singapore government were convinced by the argument, and had thereafter used politically[21] skillful ways to refuse the calls for the relaxation of the curbing measures at that time. This had in turn allowed the TDSR to achieve further squeezing of Singapore's property bubble. For example, as shown in Figure 3.1, there were 8.4% correction of the private property price index and 9.0% correction of resale HDB property price index between 2013Q2 and 2015Q4. As a result, the cumulated rise of the two property price indices between 2009Q1 and 2015Q4 were reduced to 41.6% and 34.8%, respectively. In other words, the moderate property bubble in Singapore was further reduced to a smaller one, thanks to the Singapore government's effort in introducing the TDSR as well as the fifth round and the seventh round of curbing measures.

---

[21] Note that the decision to keep or relax the curbing measures at that time was politically sensitive. Instead of a direct "no" to the calls for relaxation, the Singapore government was skillful enough to state that it was not yet the right time to relax the curbing measures. Such a statement without going into the details of the government's underlying professional analysis would avoid (i) unnecessary challenges on the analysis and (ii) the discussion on the potential bursting of Hong Kong property bubble from causing unnecessary panic in Singapore's property market.

Box 3.1: The author's press comment on 24 April 2015: Not the right time to relax Singapore's property curbing measures at that time

In response to the calls for the relaxation of the curbing measures (e.g., abolishing the ABSD and raising the LTV cap) at that time, the articles highlighted that the Singapore government should not adopt the suggestion. Otherwise, it would commit the same mistake as Hong Kong in 2013–2014: a moderate relaxation of the exemption of the curbing measures had resulted in another surge in Hong Kong's property prices, thus resulting in substantial profits for the developers while hurting the citizens' rating of the government (see Chapter 4 for the detailed discussion).

The article first reiterated the author's new theory on Asian property markets: Because of Asian developers' strong pricing and hoarding power as well as the indicator effect from new property prices to resale property prices, even if the government implements relatively severe curbing measures on the property market, developers would be able to hold the property prices slightly below the pre-curbing level. As a result, there would only be a substantial reduction in the transactions of properties and a moderate reduction in property prices. After a few months of such a consolidation period, there would be calls for relaxation of the curbing measures (see also the discussion in Section 3.2.4). Once the government mistakenly follows these suggestions, developers would be able to use their pricing power and the pent-up demand accumulated during the consolidation period to push the property prices up to a new high, thus pushing the property bubble to a bigger one through the pattern of "rapid surge — moderate consolidation — and another rapid surge".

A recent evidence of the above discussion was Hong Kong's experience in 2013–2014. In February 2013, the Hong Kong government followed Singapore's curbing measure in January 2013 (i.e., the heavy ABSD measure) by introducing a curbing measure called the "Double Buyer Stamp Duty" (DBSD) (see Section 4.1.6 for the detailed discussion). Such a curbing measure had temporarily stopped Hong Kong property prices from rising further. Unfortunately, the Hong Kong government had thereafter not only failed to adopt the TDSR curbing measure implemented in Singapore, but also in September–October 2013 accepted the developers' and parliament members' calls for an extension of the exemption period for the DBSD: According to the original announcement of the DBSD at that time, property buyers replacing their first and only property by another property within the exemption period would be exempted from the DBSD (i.e., if they sell their first property within

(*continued*)

Box 3.1: (*Continued*)

a few months of the *contract date* of the purchase). However, under the revised scheme, the exemption period was revised to 6 months after the *completion date* of the purchase. As the relaxation from the contract date to the completion date appeared to be moderate, the Hong Kong government thought that it would have little effect on Hong Kong's property prices. As such, it surrendered to the political pressure from the developers and parliament members by accepting the revised scheme without recognizing that the gap between the contract date and completion date could be 3–4 years for new properties. Meanwhile, the Hong Kong government also failed to use the political turmoil at that time (i.e., the "Occupy the Central" movement) to squeeze the property bubble to a smaller one. As a result, Hong Kong property price index was still around the pre-curbing level during the consolidation period between early 2013 and mid-2014. Because of the mistake on the relaxation of the exemption period and the failure to squeeze Hong Kong's property bubble amid the political turmoil, developers were able to push for another rapid surge in Hong Kong property prices since mid-2014: With the fading out of the political turmoil since June 2014, the loophole in the revised DBSD scheme for new properties and the accumulation of the pent-up demand during the consolidation period, developers were able use their pricing power to push Hong Kong's property prices further up. As a result, there was another 22.3% rise in Hong Kong's residential property price index between June 2014 and September 2015 so that the cumulated rise between March 2009 and September 2015 was 180%. As explained in Chapter 4, this mistake had resulted in a bigger property bubble. More importantly, it also meant that Hong Kong missed the only remaining good time to squeeze the property bubble, thus making the bursting of Hong Kong's property bubble unavoidable in the subsequent future.

Policy Implication for Singapore: Thus, according to the theory in Chapter 1 and Hong Kong's experience stated above, and bearing in mind the pent-up demand accumulated during the consolidation period (i.e., between 2013Q2 and 2015Q1), any relaxation of the curbing measures could trigger another surge in Singapore's property prices toward a bigger bubble, thus destroying the government's previous effort in squeezing the property bubble and making Singapore more vulnerable to a substantial plunge in property prices in the future. On top of the above risk of another surge in Singapore's property prices toward a bigger bubble, the article also reiterated the risk of a bursting of property in Hong Kong, India or another Asian city, which could trigger another Asian financial crisis through the contagion effect.

3.2.8 The Ninth Round of Curbing

Although the Singapore government managed to use the eighth round of curbing to squeeze the small bubble in Singapore's private property market to an even smaller one, its choice also implicitly implied a consolidation period with moderate decline in property prices and substantial reduction in property transactions. That is, given the developers' pricing power and hoarding power discussed in Chapter 1 and the previous sections, the inclination for (or, more correctly, the implicit choice of) a moderate consolidation would also mean smaller and smaller declines of property prices in the later phase of the consolidation period, and continued accumulation of pent-up demand throughout the consolidation period. By 2017Q2, the private property price index finally reached a local bottom, which was followed by a very moderate rise of 0.7% and 0.8% in the next two quarters. Nevertheless, as the pent-up demand accumulated during the consolidation period was substantial, private developers were able to use their pricing power to trigger a 3.8% rebound in 2018Q1 and another 4.3% rebound in 2018Q2, thus nullifying most of the −11.7% bubble-squeezing result achieved during the four years between mid-2013 and mid-2017.

Worse still, with a new fever of *en bloc* activities during the rebound, many of the owners of the *en bloc* flats used the compensated money to buy a new flat, thus creating a sudden rise in the demand for private properties (and a sudden reduction in the housing stock during the redevelopment stage of the *en bloc* housing estate). Meanwhile, within 6–9 months after the collective purchase of the *en bloc* housing estates, developers started the pre-selling of the new flats (i.e., before they started the construction and the completion of the new flats in the subsequent 3–5 years). As developers of these *en bloc* housing estates were able to use their pricing power to set a relatively high price for their redeveloped housing estates (i.e., with an initial premium of about 40–60% above the price of resale private flats nearby) and there was a strong indicator effect from the prices of new private flats to the prices of resale private flats, there was further upward pressure on Singapore's private property prices. If left unattended, Singapore's property market would be pushed to a new automatic bubble path.

In view of the potential danger, the well-trained Singapore monetary officials decided to announce Singapore's ninth round of curbing measures on 6 July 2018 (see the details in Table 3.1). After the announcement, the related officials were under heavy criticisms by developers and some owners of the potential *en bloc* flats. In response to the unfair criticisms, the author published another policy article in a major newspaper on 13 July 2018. In the article, the author first used the theoretical framework in Chapter 1 to explain that, without the curbing measures at that time, Singapore's property market would be pushed on to a new automatic bubble path (see the explanation in the previous two paragraphs). Thus, the curbing measures at that time were necessary. After explaining that the timing and the dosage of the curbing measures were more or less appropriate,[22] it also explained that the related economic officials' performance during the fifth, seventh and eighth rounds of curbing were good, while the performance in the ninth round of curbing represented a significant improvement when compared with the performance in 2009H2–2010H2:

(1) Although Singapore's economic officials missed the chance of pre-empting the bubble at the previous seeding stage of the current property bubble (i.e., between 2009H2 and 2010H2), it did manage to contain the growth of the bubble with the relatively severe measures in its fifth and seventh rounds of curbing. More importantly, the officials managed to squeeze the bubble to a smaller one with its eighth round of curbing, thus bringing Singapore's property market out from the automatic bubble path. According to the author's knowledge, Singapore was probably the only economy that managed to squeeze its property bubble to a much smaller one, and such an achievement should be recorded in the literature.

(2) The ninth round of curbing measures was meant to pre-empt the rebuilding of property bubble from the new seeding stage in 2018, thus suggesting that Singapore monetary officials in July 2018 had reached a much higher standard when compared with the monetary officials in 2009H–2010H2.

---

[22] It might be better for the government to announce the curbing measures in April–May 2018, as there were already signs in the market that the rebound was going to be substantial in the subsequent months.

Finally, the article highlighted that the above criticisms were very unfair to the monetary officials who were just doing their job to protect Singapore from the risk of another property bubble. It was necessary to point out the mistakes in these criticisms and encourage these well-trained and responsible monetary officials with positive rating. Otherwise, there would be no monetary officials willing to defend the nation against potential property bubbles in the future. In fact, these monetary officials should be promoted so that they could continue to contribute to the sound economic policies in Singapore.

3.2.9 Outlook and Policy Recommendations

While the effects of the ninth round of curbing are yet to be seen, some rough assessments on Singapore's property market could still be made, as follows:

(i) Without the ninth round of curbing, Singapore's property market would have already entered the development stage of a new bubble path.

(ii) Nevertheless, the 10% rebound of private property price index during the year between mid-2017 and mid-2018 had already nullified most of the −11.9% hard bubble-squeezing effort made in the four years between mid-2013 and mid-2017. As a result, cumulated (average) rise of private property price index between 2009Q1 and 2018Q2 was 50.3% (4.5% p.a.). Given that the prices of private properties in Singapore are still moderately high when compared with its median income, one can still argue that there is a small bubble in Singapore's private property market.

(iii) Fortunately, during the short period in 2018H1, the much higher offer prices of new private flats set by developers only had the time to pull up the offer prices of resale private flats through the indicator effect, and did not have enough time to pull up the offer prices of resale HDB flats. (With the implementation of the ninth round of curbing from 7 July 2018, it would be much more difficult for the prices of resale HDB flats to be pulled up (see further discussion below).) As a result, there was not yet any rebound of the price index of resale HDB flats in 2018H1. Given that (i) the cumulated (average) rise of the price index of resale HDB flats between 2009Q1 and 2018Q2 was only 31.7% (3.0% p.a.) and (ii) prices of resale HDB flats are much lower than the prices of private flats, it will be much harder to argue that there is a bubble in Singapore's resale HDB flats.

(iv) Developers will still be able to use their pricing power, hoarding power and temporary discount to offset the effect of the ninth round of curbing. So, there could at most be a small retreat in the initial price premiums between new and resale private flats from the very high 40–60% to about 20–40%. In fact, a checking of the offer prices in the market suggests that there is currently only a very mild retreat of the initial premiums to around 30–50%. With such a high initial premium, there is no sign of any visible reduction in the offer prices of resale private flats.

In short, the ninth round of curbing only managed to avoid a rapid surge in Singapore's property prices. With the developers' pricing power, hoarding power and excellent marketing techniques (such as a temporary discount), the end-result could at most be somewhere between the following "not-too-bad" and "not-so-good" scenarios:

(1) Even in the best scenario, the ninth round of curbing could at most extend the consolidation period with small changes in Singapore's property prices. Thereafter, the outcome will depend on what will happen in the internal and external economic environment (e.g., potential deterioration or ending of the Sino-US trade war, continuation or slowdown of interest rate hike in the US, possibility of widespread emergent market crises and possibility of bursting of property bubbles in Hong Kong, India or other Asian economies).

(2) In the not-so-good scenario, if the developers managed to sell well with the 30–50% initial price premium between new and resale private flats, prices of resale private flats will be pulled up (i.e., the currently high offer prices of resale private flats would become the transacted prices). Nevertheless, with the ninth round of curbing measures and the offer prices of resale HDB flats still at the level before the surge in 2018H1, it would be more difficult for developers to trigger a rampant rise in the prices of resale HDB flats. Even so,

the prices of new and resale private properties have become "not that affordable". Thus, the end result has to be either (i) a moderately painful correction, if there is a large enough negative event that could trigger a correction of private property prices in the future; or (ii) a heavy burden of "not that affordable" private housing for the current and future generation, if there is no large enough negative event to trigger the correction of private property prices.

Thus, in the forthcoming years, there is likely to be at most a moderate bubble in the private property market, and no-to-small bubble in the resale HDB market. Therefore, the no-to-moderate bubble in Singapore's property market would not be big enough to burst by itself. Nevertheless, Singapore's property market would still be vulnerable to the contagion effect of a bursting of property bubble in Hong Kong, India or another Asian city. In fact, even if Singapore property prices were at the fair value, such a contagion effect would be enough to push its property prices to levels well below that fair value, not to mention that its current private property prices are at a moderately overvalued level. As will be explained in Chapter 4, there is a high likelihood that Hong Kong's property bubble would burst between 2018H2 and 2021H1. In addition, as explained in Chapter 2, the cumulated (average) rises in property prices in India and other Asian cities over the past nine years are so huge that there is a high likelihood that some negative events (such as the deepening of the Sino–US trade war, the emergence of a widespread emergent market crisis, further rises in the US interest rate, geopolitical conflicts or global economic slowdown) would be able to trigger a collapse in their property prices.

By then, there would be a recession in Singapore even though there was basically no major policy mistake in Singapore. To prepare for this, the Singapore government should keep the curbing measures and be ready to introduce more severe curbing measures when deemed necessary. However, once the bursting of the property bubble in Hong Kong, India and another Asian city started to trigger a fall in Singapore's property prices through the contagion effect, the Singapore government should start to mitigate the fall through a few rounds of relaxation of the previously introduced curbing measures. Although a substantial portion of pent-up demand will disappear during the expected plunge, unwinding the cubing measures could still release a moderate amount of pent-up demand, which will help to contain the fall in property prices at that time. Even with such help, the less severe fall in property prices and the contagion effect of the expected Asian financial crisis will still trigger a mini-scale financial crisis and a recession in Singapore. Fortunately, during and after the 1997 financial crisis, the Singapore government has accumulated good policy experience to mitigate the recession and avoid massive layoffs by the following measures:

(i)   A substantial reduction in the employer CPF contribution rate to reduce employers' labor costs.
(ii) A substantial depreciation of Singapore's NEER.
(iii) Fiscal relief packages to reduce firms' labor costs, operating costs and rental costs.

As explained in Yip (2005), these curbing measures managed to keep firms' reputation cost of retrenchment high and therefore help avoid massive layoffs from happening in Singapore. That is, with these supporting measures of meaningful scale (e.g., almost 10% reduction in labor cost through the cyclical reduction of the employer CPF contribution rate, about 12% depreciation of the NEER and substantial fiscal relief package), employers in Singapore found it embarrassing (and damaging in reputation) to make massive layoffs unless their businesses were no longer viable. When the viable firms decided not to make massive layoffs (because of the damage to its reputation, and hence much higher recruitment cost in the future), firms' reputation cost of retrenchment was kept high, which in turn ensured most viable firms did not make massive layoffs in the subsequent stage of crisis and during the post-crisis recession. On the other hand, there was no such rescue packages in Hong Kong during the 1997 financial crisis. As a result, some viable firms in Hong Kong did not find it that embarrassing to make massive layoffs during the recession. The act of these firms, in turn, reduced the other viable firms' reputation cost of retrenchment, and hence induced some more viable firms to make massive layoffs. Thus, there was a vicious cycle between falling reputation cost of retrenchment and more viable firms making massive layoffs. In fact, during the 1997 financial crisis, some viable firms in

Hong Kong even laid off the more expensive senior workers and replaced them by the cheaper outsourcing or recruits of junior workers. As a result, the Hong Kong economy eventually reached the state where firms' reputation cost of retrenchment fell to zero and almost all the viable firms had made massive layoffs until their work force are trimmed to the new "optimal size" with respect to the severe recession at that time (i.e., these viable firms could recruit cheaper junior workers when the economy started to recover).

Thus, in case there is another Asian financial crisis triggered by a bursting of property bubble in Hong Kong, India and another Asian city, it will be important for Singapore to use the above policies to offset the crisis effect on its economy.

3.3 IMPORTANT LESSONS FROM SINGAPORE'S EXPERIENCE

With more severe curbing measures and other factors such as the existence of 80% of public housing in Singapore, the cumulative (average) rise in Singapore's property prices between 2009Q1 and 2018Q2 was much smaller than those in Hong Kong, India and many other Asian cities. In spite of that, Singapore still missed the best time to pre-empt the property bubble formation. One possible reason provided by a fellow economist of the author was that policymakers might prefer, or found it safer, to err on the side of insufficient curbing than on the side of excessive curbing, as the latter could destroy the economic recovery at that time. However, this would only be optimal if we were not aware of the risk of bubble formation. A check on previous asset bubbles, such as the current property bubble in Hong Kong and Singapore, China's stock market bubble in 2006–2007 and the asset bubble in Asia before the 1997–1998 financial crisis, suggests that policymakers in Asia *almost always* miss the best time to pre-empt the bubble. Given that we have continued to miss the best chance, economists should draw lessons from these mistakes so that policymakers could avoid making the same mistakes in the future. For example, as explained in Chapter 1, policymakers should be alert *if an asset price has a chance to have a sustained rebound from an undervalued trough for more than 3 or 6 months*, as such upward inertia of asset price could create an expectation of further rise in the asset price. Once there is such an expectation, it would be very hard to curb the rise in the asset price, and the chance of a bubble formation could be much greater as compared to normal times. Worse still, more and more market participants would sooner or later lose their trust in the government's ability to contain the rise.

Thus, one important lesson could be drawn from here — if we see an asset price having a sustained rebound from an undervalued level for more than a few months, it would in fact be safer to implement curbing measures for at least a partial correction of the cumulated rebound (say, until the cumulated rebound of asset price is reduced by at least 30–50%). Once there is such a correction of asset price, it will take a longer time of sustained rise in asset price to cause an expectation of further rise in asset price. Before that, the government could introduce another round of curbing measures to pre-empt an expectation of further rise in asset price.

Having said that, Singapore's persistent and determined effort in (i) curbing the bubble during the development stage of bubble and then (ii) gradually squeezing the bubble between mid-2013 and mid-2017 deserve special respect. According to the author's knowledge, Singapore was probably the only economy that managed to squeeze its property bubble to a much smaller one. In addition, Singapore's ninth round of curbing managed to pre-empt the rebuilding of property bubble from the new seeding stage in 2018, thus suggesting Singapore's monetary officials in July 2018 have learned from the mistake of, and therefore have reached a higher standard than, their predecessors in 2009H2–2010H2.

CHAPTER 4

LESSONS FROM THE FORMATION OF PROPERTY BUBBLE AND THE CURBING MEASURES IN HONG KONG

In Section 4.1, the author will first provide a detailed discussion on the lessons from (i) the rapid formation of a property bubble in Hong Kong between March 2009 and February 2013 and (ii) the insufficient curbing measures during this period. In Section 4.2, he will explain that it was necessary at that time for Hong Kong to adopt a bubble-squeezing strategy to pre-empt an eventual bursting of the bubble. Otherwise, the bursting could cause enormous damages to the Hong Kong economy and could trigger another Asian financial crisis through the contagion effect. In Section 4.3, he will then report the detailed design of his proposed bubble-squeezing strategy at that time. Unfortunately, as Hong Kong policymakers failed to appreciate the importance of implementing the bubble-squeezing strategy, he will explain in Section 4.4 that an eventual bursting of Hong Kong's property bubble seems unavoidable. In Section 4.5, he will propose some policy measures that could mitigate the economic damages during the expected crisis and post-crisis recession.

As Hong Kong policymakers had performed badly in (a) pre-empting the emergence of the property bubble at the seeding stage, (b) stopping the property bubble from growing at the development stage and (c) realizing the need to implement the proposed bubble-squeezing strategy before it was too late, the author has written down the related lessons in this chapter with the hope that

(i) policymakers could, in the future, avoid similar mistakes; and
(ii) citizens in Hong Kong and other developing economies would be more aware of the importance of having qualified economists (with solid foundation in economic theories and policy insight) to monitor and manage their economies.

4.1 LESSONS FROM THE INACTION AND THEN INSUFFICIENT CURBING IN HONG KONG

4.1.1 Lessons from the Inaction between April 2009 and August 2010

Before discussing the property bubble in Hong Kong, it should be noted that there was a shift of power from one Chief Executive (Mr. Donald Tsang) to another (Mr. C.Y. Leung) on 1 July 2012. The first Chief Executive was a believer, or more correctly, a dogmatic believer of free market force.[1] Despite the widespread public calls at that time for restarting the construction and sale of public flats to the middle-low income group (i.e., the Home Ownership Scheme) and the sale of sandwich-class flats to the middle-income group, Mr. Tsang kept on refusing to do so until he was "urged" by the Chinese government to restart the public housing schemes and consider curbing measures on the property market.[2] Even so, he did these with a time delay (up to August 2010 for the first curbing and up to October 2010 for the announcement of a public housing scheme), and only announced a small-scale and highly distorted form of a public housing scheme. For example, there was only a plan of 5,000 units in the new scheme called "My Home Purchase Scheme", and

---

[1]There are people (including the author) that would classify him as a dogmatic market believer instead of a believer of free market force, mainly because there was evidence that he did not really know how the market force works in the Hong Kong property market and other areas. An important difference between the two is that a proper believer of free market force knows how the market force works, while a dogmatic believer does not. There was also debate on whether he intentionally or unintentionally left the property bubble to the next Chief Executive. Thus, the wording of "a believer or a dogmatic believer of free market force" could be a big bias to the good side.

[2]The Chinese government usually has channels to receive public views and feedbacks on Hong Kong economic and political issues. As many Hong Kong people including the author were making complaints that Mr. Tsang was trying to leave a property bubble to the next Chief Executive, the Chinese government was convinced and therefore urged him to settle the issue.

successful applicants of the new scheme could rent the flat for a few years before deciding to buy the flat or a private flat in the market.[3] As a result, there was no curbing measure and basically no provision of affordable public housing for sale between April 2009 and August 2010 (i.e., the seeding stage and the early phase of the development stage of Hong Kong's property bubble). As predicted by the theoretical discussion in Chapter 1, the sustained rebound of property prices in that period triggered an expectation of further rise in property prices and hence enormous investment demand, speculative demand and panic demand for housing.

Worse still, because of his other mistake in the land supply for private housing, the annual quantity of supplied private flats at that time was well below the historical norm as well as the normal annual absorption. While a moderately larger quantity supplied may not be able to stop the developers from using their pricing power and hoarding power to push for higher property prices (see the discussion in Chapter 1), an insufficient quantity of supplied private flats will definitely allow them to push for a sharp rise in property prices. Even more disappointing was that Mr. Tsang did not make any effort to contain the huge demand by investors from mainland China. As a result, there was an almost uninterrupted 42% surge in Hong Kong's residential property price index during the 18 months between March 2009 and August 2010 (see Figure 4.1).[4]

4.1.2 Lessons from the First and Second Rounds of Curbing

In August 2010 and November 2010, the Hong Kong Monetary Authority (HKMA) finally announced its first and second rounds of curbing measures.[5] The first round of curbing included the following:

---

[3] In case a successful applicant decided to buy the flat or a private flat, he/she could get a subsidy equivalent to half of the accumulated rentals that the applicant has paid in the past. Many people including the next Chief Executive believed the scheme did not make much sense. In 2013, the scheme was scrapped, and the planned units in the scheme were reclassified into the standard Home Ownership Scheme.

[4] Even during the outbreak of the Greek sovereign debt crisis in May 2010, Hong Kong's property prices only stayed flat for 2 months before making another sharp surge from July 2010.

[5] One reason for the two rounds of curbing could be Bernanke's indication of the inclination of another round of QE (i.e., QE2) in August 2010 and the formal implementation of QE2 in November 2010.

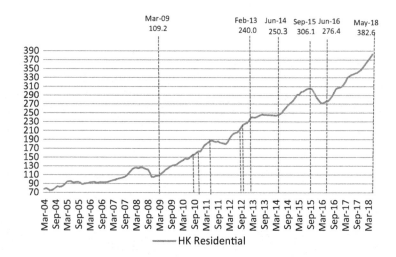

Figure 4.1:   HK Residential Property Price Index

Source: CEIC.

(i)   a reduction in the loan-to-value-ratio (LTV) cap to 60% for non-owner-occupied properties and for luxurious properties with a price at or above HK$12 million;

(ii) a reduction in the cap on the mortgage service ratio (i.e., the ratio of mortgage installment to income) to 50%; and

(iii) a new requirement for banks to conduct a stress test to ensure the mortgagee's mortgage service ratio would stay below 60% should mortgage interest rates rise by at least 2 percentage points.

Nevertheless, as the substantial rebound of property prices between March 2009 and August 2010 had already triggered a substantial increase in the investment demand, speculative demand and panic demand for properties, the relatively mild curbing measures only resulted in a less sharp rise in property prices in the next month. Thereafter, the property price index made another sharp surge. Such an experience further confirms the following lesson drawn from previous asset bubbles: *once there is an expectation of further rises in the asset price, and hence the implied increase in the asset demand, moderate curbing measures could not stop the asset price from rising and the asset bubble from growing.*

The second round of curbing announced in November 2010 included the following measures:

(i) a seller stamp duty (SSD) for residential properties resold within 2 years (i.e., 15% for properties resold within 6 months, 10% for properties resold within 6–12 months and 5% for properties resold within 12–24 months);

(ii) an LTV cap of 50% for non-owner-occupied residential properties, luxurious residential properties with a price at or above HK$12 million, commercial and industrial properties, properties held by companies and properties with mortgage loans based on customers' net worth;

(iii) an LTV cap of 60% for residential flats with a price above HK$8 million and below HK$12 million.

As explained in Chapter 3, the SSD would not affect long-term investors (i.e., they do not need to pay the tax as long as they hold the property for more than 2 years). The effect on speculative demand would also be limited as speculators could extend their speculative horizon to 1–2 years (i.e., changing from short-term speculators to medium-term speculators: no need to pay anything if they hold the properties for 2 years, or only need to pay 5% if they hold it for 1 year).[6]

In fact, as shown in Figure 4.1, the second round of curbing only caused an extremely mild and short-lived knee-jerk in the property price index (i.e., only 0.4% for just 1 month), before it made another sharp surge from January 2011. The above experience reconfirmed Chapter 1's conclusion that mild curbing measures during the development stage of an asset bubble would not be able to stop the bubble from growing (i.e., it could at most caused a very short-lived correction which would soon be made up by a sharper rise in asset price in the subsequent months). It also

---

[6] Some discussants at that time even argued that when the short-term speculators (with properties in hand) switched to medium-term speculators because of the SSD, their hoarding of properties at that time would imply a temporary decline in the speculators' supply, which could contribute to a further rise in property prices at that time. Nevertheless, as the SSD still implied a psychological impact at least on short-term speculation, there was still a very short-lived knee-jerk in the property price index.

reconfirmed that the SSD would have little effect on long-term investment demand and at most moderate effect on speculative demand. From the lessons drawn from past experience, the author also believes that *if the curbing measures were implemented at the seeding stage (say, in 2009Q4–2010Q1, or preferably 2009Q3) and if the authority went straight to the additional buyer stamp duty (ABSD) instead of the SSD, Hong Kong might have been able to pre-empt the property bubble.*

4.1.3 Lessons from the Third Round of Curbing

With further rises in property prices, the author presented a seminar at the HKMA and did an interview with a major Hong Kong finance newspaper in June 2011, warning that Hong Kong's property bubble had already entered the development stage, highlighting the need for more severe curbing measures to stop the bubble from growing. Later that same month, the HKMA announced the third round of curbing measures, which included the following:

(i) a further reduction of the LTV cap to 50% for residential properties with a price at or above HK$10 million, and to 60% for residential properties with a price at or above HK$7 million but below HK$10 million; and

(ii) a further reduction of the LTV cap to 40% for buyers whose main incomes came from outside Hong Kong SAR, and for net-worth-based mortgages regardless of property values.

As we can see from Figure 4.1, there was a moderate decline of property price of about 4–5% for a more sustained period of 7 months between June 2011 and January 2012. Nevertheless, one should be cautious about whether it was the relatively mild curbing measures or other factors that had caused the moderate decline. As there was a risk that the European Debt Crisis at that time could develop into a full-blown crisis, it would be debatable whether it was the moderate curbing measures or the deterioration of the European Debt Crisis that played the major role[7] in the moderate

---

[7] Judging from the strength of the measures in the third round of curbing and the potential damage of a full-blown European Debt Crisis, the author was inclined to believe that it was

correction of Hong Kong's property prices at that time. Either way, with better news about the European Debt Crisis and the accumulation of pent-up demand in the subsequent months, Hong Kong developers were able to engineer a sharp surge of property prices between January 2012 and May 2012. As shown in Figure 4.1, the moderate decline between June 2011 and January 2012 was easily offset by the subsequent surge, leaving the tendency of a growing bubble relatively intact. That is, the moderate decline had at most caused a delay, but not a change, in the tendency of, the growth of the bubble.

4.1.4 The Inauguration of the New Chief Executive

In March–April 2012, a new Chief Executive (Mr. C.Y. Leung) was elected in the Hong Kong SAR. As the newly elected Chief Executive was more inclined to provide sufficient public housing to eligible Hong Kong citizens and was concerned about the high property prices in Hong Kong, market participants were worried about a substantial supply of public flats similar to that announced in 1997–1998 and more severe curbing measures on the property market. As such, there was a moderation in the rise of property prices between May 2012 and July 2012. After recommending Mr. C.Y. Leung (the eventually elected candidate)[8] to the Chinese leaders in the form of internal reports through the Xinhua News Agency (the article was also published in a major newspaper in Hong Kong), the author started to write a series of policy articles on the Hong Kong economy. In those articles on the property bubble in Hong Kong, the author warned that Hong Kong's property market was already in the development stage

---

the latter that played the major role in the moderate decline of Hong Kong's property prices at that time.

[8] There were actually three candidates for the election and two of them were "acceptable" to the Chinese central government. Among the two, Mr. Tang was actually the favorite at the beginning. However, because of his weak administrative ability and his lack of devotion to work for Hong Kong people, some people including the author tried to convince the Chinese leaders by writing internal reports through China's various official channels that it would be better to have the other candidate as the Chief Executive. With subsequent scandals that illustrate Mr. Tang's inability to tackle complicated issues and crisis, the Chinese leaders eventually decided to support the other candidate as the Chief Executive of the Hong Kong SAR.

of a bubble. After spelling out the characteristics of the development stage, these articles explained why some discussants' views that there would be no further rise in Hong Kong's property prices could be wrong.[9] The article then highlighted that the risk at that time was not a correction in property prices, but further rise of property prices toward a huge bubble. Thus, it was important for the newly elected government to select well-trained economics experts to stop the growth of the property bubble and sort out the future economic development strategies for Hong Kong.

Unfortunately, there were people (including the developers and property agents) expressing their concern of a repetition of the collapse of property prices between 1997 and 2003; the new Chief Executive as well as his team of improperly trained think-tank (mainly practitioners in the property market) did not seem to have enough theoretical foundation in economics to appreciate the importance and likelihood of the above warnings made by the author. As a result, the new Chief Executive made the very wrong decision of taking a relatively mild tone on the rise of property prices at that time. Meanwhile, the European Central Bank's (ECB) announcement of the Outright Monetary Transactions (OMTs) at that time had basically removed the possibility of a full-blown European Debt Crisis.[10] These two developments in turn allowed the developers to use

---

[9] These discussants argued that Hong Kong property price was already at the "crazy" (or overvalued) level, and therefore could not go up further. However, based on the theoretical framework outlined in Chapter 1, the author highlighted in the article that it was highly possible that the overvalued property prices could rise to even more overvalued levels.

[10] As explained in the author's policy articles published in the *Hong Kong Economic Journal* in August–September 2012, the worst case was for Spain to apply for a bailout while agreeing to follow the austerity conditions specified by the European Union. Such a worst-case scenario would at most mean a severe recession in Spain, but not a full-blown European Debt Crisis. That is, as long as Spain was willing to keep the tight fiscal budget, the ECB and the European Stabilization Mechanism (ESM) would support and buy the Spanish government bonds. Because of the ECB's unlimited capacity in printing Euro, there would no longer be any default risk of the Spanish government bonds. More importantly, when the market sooner or later recognized that this would be the worst-case scenario, more and more investors would find it highly profitable to buy the Spanish government bonds, which would in turn push down the Spanish bond yields. The actions could in turn imply the Spanish government might not need to apply for a bailout, i.e., the worst-case scenario would never happen.

their pricing power (and the cumulated pent-up demand during the consolidation period) to push for another surge in property prices between July 2012 and October 2012.

4.1.5 The Fourth and the Fifth Rounds of Curbing

With the sharp rise in property prices and US's announcement of quantitative easing three (QE3), the HKMA announced its fourth round of curbing in September 2012. The curbing measures in the fourth round included

(i) the introduction of a mortgage tenure cap of 30 years; and
(ii) for mortgage loan applicants with outstanding loans, (a) the cap on mortgage service ratio being reduced to 40% (from 50%) and (b) the LTV cap being reduced to 30% for net-worth-based mortgage and for buyers whose main income comes from outside Hong Kong SAR.

As we can see from Figure 4.1, Hong Kong's property price index continued to rise after the fourth round of curbing mainly because of the following reasons:

(a) the upward pressure due to the expectation of property inflation and changes in economic behaviors was far greater than the effect of the curbing measures; and
(b) on top of the higher investment demand, speculative demand and panic demand by Hong Kong citizens, there was also a huge investment demand by the rich mainland Chinese.

With these mainland Chinese investors buying new Hong Kong properties at prices well beyond the acceptable norm in Hong Kong, there was a surge in the price premiums between new flats and resale flats. Such a surge in the price premiums also resulted in a psychological effect for further rise in property prices.

With the seemingly uncontrollable rise in property prices and Hong Kong citizens' complaints on the above impacts of mainland Chinese investors, the Hong Kong government soon announced its fifth round of curbing in October 2012, which included

(i) a higher SSD rate for a more extended period (i.e., 20% for residential properties resold within 6 months, 15% for residential properties resold between 6 months and 12 months and 10% for residential properties resold between 12 months and 24 months); and

(ii) an ABSD of 15% for residential property buyers from mainland China and foreign countries.[11]

Of these, the more powerful curbing measure was the 15% ABSD, which had at least discouraged most mainland Chinese investors from buying Hong Kong properties in the subsequent months. The disappearance of most mainland Chinese investors during that period also had a psychological effect on domestic investors and speculators. Meanwhile, property market participants were concerned with the risk of strong curbing measures and substantial increase in public housing in the Chief Executive's policy report to be announced in January 2013. As a result, there was a less rapid rise in property prices and a decline in transaction volumes in October–December 2012.

Unfortunately, because of the misleading recommendations of his improperly trained think-tank, the Chief Executive's policy report only announced an increase in the supply of land for housing as a solution for the rise in property prices. That is, without the theoretical framework outlined in Chapter 1, the think-tank, and hence the Chief Executive's policy report, did not recognize the importance of curbing the enormous investment demand, speculative demand and panic demand triggered by the rise of property prices over the past few years. Worse still, because of the lag effect of the previous Chief Executive's mistake on Hong Kong's land supply for housing, the short-term and medium-term increase of land supply for housing announced in the 2013 policy report were rather limited. With the uncertainty on "heavy curbing measures" and "substantial housing supply" removed, Hong Kong property prices made another sharp surge immediately after the 2013 policy report. The above experience also reconfirmed the following lesson: *during the development stage of a*

---

[11] The measure was first implemented in Singapore's fifth round of curbing in December 2011, and then adopted in Hong Kong with appropriate modification (i.e., an ABSD of 15% instead of the 10% in Singapore's fifth round of curbing).

property bubble, a normal increase in the land supply would not be sufficient to stop the bubble from growing, as the expectation of further rise in property prices has already triggered an enormous increase in demand for flats. To stop the bubble from growing, there has to be strong enough curbing on demand.

4.1.6 The Sixth Round of Curbing

In view of the inability of the senior Hong Kong monetary officials in dealing with the property bubble, the author published two very critical policy articles and a follow-up press interview in January–February 2013 highlighting that waves of severe curbing measures were required to stop the property bubble from growing. In particular, the government should at least consider adopting Singapore's latest policy of extending the ABSD to non-first-time domestic homebuyers. Otherwise, Hong Kong's property bubble would continue to grow and then burst. By then, the Chief Executive and his cabinet would lose people's respect and their moral authority, not to mention the chance of winning the election for the second term. Moreover, the expected collapse in Hong Kong's property prices at that time would, through the contagion effect, trigger severe correction of property prices in China, Singapore and other Asian economies. Worse still, if the property bubble in Hong Kong and the above economies continued to grow from the current level, the disaster during the subsequent bursting would be more severe than that during the Asian financial crisis in 1997–1998.

With the author's critical comments and the pressure from other government officials, the then Financial Secretary finally announced the sixth round of curbing on 23 February 2013, which included

(a) a doubling of the standard buyer stamp duty for those buying the second and subsequent properties[12];

---

[12] Note that Hong Kong's buyer stamp duty is charged in the form of progressive rates. The new (and old) rates are as follows: 1.5% (HK$100) for properties at or below HK$2 million, 3.0% (1.5%) for the next trench until HK$3 million, 4.5% (2.25%) for the next trench until HK$4 million, 6.0% (3.0%) for the next trench until HK$6 million,

(b)   a more stringent stress test requiring the mortgage installment to stay below 60% of family income should the mortgage interest rate rise by at least 3 percentage points[13];

(c)   a further reduction of the LTV cap to 40% for commercial properties (to 30% for investors whose main income came from outside the Hong Kong SAR);

(d)   an LTV cap of 40% and a maximum mortgage tenure of 15 years for mortgages on car parks;

(e)   a measure raising the speculators' transaction cost by requiring the payment of stamp duty at an earlier period (i.e., at the contract date instead of the completion date).

It should be noted that the doubling of the standard buyer stamp duty was basically the same as the ABSD adopted in Singapore. That is, it was just the choice of a different name to avoid any unnecessary query of a copying of policy in Singapore.[14] With the curbing, there was drastic reduction in the number of property transactions in the subsequent months. Nevertheless, similar to the case of Singapore, the Hong Kong developers were able to keep the price with a discount to "help" buyers absorb the higher stamp duty. Meanwhile, sellers of resale flats in Hong Kong also adopted the developer's strategy of giving a temporary (and perhaps partial) discount. As a result, Hong Kong property price managed to stay around the pre-curbing level with at most a temporary and occasional discount of a few percentage points (see Figure 4.1).

7.5% (3.75%) for the next trench until HK$20 million and 8.5% (4.25%) for properties above HK$20 million.

[13] About 1–2 weeks after this announcement, there was a moderate rise in Hong Kong's mortgage rate, and there was news of occasional moderate reductions in resale property prices. Nevertheless, as the rise in mortgage rate was rather moderate, the reduction in property prices was mild and at most in the form of occasional discounts. However, such an incident did suggest that a substantial rise in the mortgage rate (say, during the US interest rate hike amid the later phase of the US economic recovery from the global financial tsunami) would have substantial impacts on Hong Kong's property price (see the detailed discussion in Section 4.3).

[14] Actually, there were plenty of cases that the two governments learned from each other in the policy front, which should be a good practice. Queries on that are in fact counter-productive.

4.2 THE NEED FOR A BUBBLE-SQUEEZING STRATEGY FOR HONG KONG

With the significant fall in the number of property transactions, many market analysts, and even some government think-tanks, were predicting a medium size (say, 5–15%) correction in Hong Kong property prices. Nevertheless, in the follow-up policy articles published in major Hong Kong newspapers between June 2013 and February 2014, the author explained that the above prediction would likely be wrong.

In these articles, the author first welcome the Hong Kong government's adoption of the proposed curbing measures in February 2013, which had at least temporarily avoided further rises in Hong Kong's property prices. Without these curbing measures, Hong Kong's property bubble would grow bigger, and the potential damage of the subsequent bursting would be far greater than that in the financial crisis in 1997–1998. Thereafter, the articles explained that, unless the Hong Kong government could squeeze part of the property bubble in the subsequent 6–8 quarters, the bubble would eventually burst in the distant future (see Section 4.2.1 for the detailed discussion). However, the external economic environment was not yet ripe for an immediate bursting, and there remained a high risk that the bubble would grow further before the eventual bursting (see Sections 4.2.2 and 4.2.3 for a detailed discussion). Nevertheless, seeing this from a different point of view, this would also mean the subsequent 6–8 quarters (i.e., between 2013Q2 and 2015Q2) would be a reasonably good period for Hong Kong to adopt a bubble-squeezing strategy. The remaining part of this section will explain the rationales for the above view. Section 4.3 will then discuss the proposed bubble-squeezing strategy.

4.2.1 High Likelihood of an Eventual Bursting of Hong Kong's Property Bubble

To highlight the importance of the bubble-squeezing strategy, the articles first noted that Hong Kong's residential property prices had already surged by 120% between March 2009 and February 2013. According to the affordability measures computed by the HKMA, residential property prices were already at an extremely overvalued level.[15] Perhaps more worrisome was that many Hong Kong property investors were not fully aware of the potential damages of a substantial rise in Hong Kong's mortgage rate and a substantial appreciation of the Hong Kong dollar during the later phase of the US economic recovery. (Note: Given the substantial size of Hong Kong's property bubble, some other negative events (such as a widespread emergent market crisis, a global economic slowdown or financial turmoil, the Sino–US trade war or military conflict) could also trigger a bursting of the bubble. That is, the rise in the mortgage rate is only one of the potential triggering causes for the eventual bursting of the bubble. Even in the absence of these events and government curbing measures, the theory in Chapter 1 would suggest that the Hong Kong property bubble would continue to grow to such a gigantic size that even a mild or moderate negative economic event is sufficient to trigger the bursting of the bubble).

4.2.1.1 *The effect of a rise in Hong Kong's mortgage rate*

The articles then explained that it would be just natural for Hong Kong's mortgage rate to rise from the extremely low level of around 1% in 2009 back to the normal level of 6–7%. Even if it just rises back to 3–5%, this would mean the mortgage rate would rise by at least 2–4 percentage points between the trough and the peak of the current economic cycle. (Note: In case there is a speculative attack on the Hong Kong dollar similar to that during the financial crisis in 1997–1998, the mortgage rate could rise to more than 9–10%.[16]) Unfortunately, many of the property buyers were not fully aware of the huge surge in monthly mortgage installment burden with the above expected rise in mortgage rate. As such, the author presented Table 4.1 in the press article to demonstrate these property owners' potential risk to the rise in the mortgage rate[17]:

---

[15] As reported in the HKMA Quarterly Bulletin in 2013Q2, *"Housing affordability has deteriorated further, with the price-to-income ratio just slightly below its 1997 peak of 14.6 and the income-gearing ratio rising to a 13-year high of around 63%. The currently low rental yield also signals risk of housing prices running ahead of fundamentals, whether from a user-cost or asset-pricing perspectives."*
[16] During the 1997–1998 financial crisis, Hong Kong's mortgage rate did rise to the 9–10% range.
[17] The author would like to express his thanks to Professor Y. K. Tse of the Singapore Management University for suggesting him to prepare the table in the press article.

Table 4.1: Monthly Mortgage Installment (for Every HK$1 Million Mortgage Loan)

Mortgage rate	Tenure of mortgage				
	10 years	15 years	20 years	25 years	30 years
1%	8,760	5,985	4,599	3,769	3,216
2%	9,201	6,435	5,059	4,239	3,696
3%	9,656	6,906	5,546	4,742	4,216
4%	10,125	7,397	6,060	5,278	4,774
5%	10,607	7,908	6,600	5,846	5,368
6%	11,102	8,439	7,164	6,443	5,996
7%	11,611	8,988	7,753	7,068	6,653
8%	12,132	9,557	8,364	7,718	7,338
9%	12,668	10,143	8,997	8,392	8,046
10%	13,215	10,746	9,650	9,087	8,776

As shown in the table, for a mortgagee with a 20-year mortgage loan, a rise in the mortgage rate from 1% to 3–5% (6–7%) would mean a 21–44% (56–69%) rise in the monthly mortgage installment. If there is a speculative attack on the Hong Kong dollar so that the mortgage rate rises to 9–10%, the monthly mortgage installment would rise by 96–110%. Thus, even for relatively prudent mortgagees whose monthly mortgage installment is only 50% of their before-tax income, their after-tax income would not be sufficient to cover the new monthly mortgage installments and usual living expenses. Worse still, for those mortgagees with a 30-year mortgage loan, the corresponding rises in monthly mortgage installments would be sharper at 48–53% (86–107%) and 150–173%, respectively!

Thus, when Hong Kong's mortgage rate started to rise to 3%, 4% and then above 5%, it could be easily envisioned that at least a certain number of financially overstretched property owners would be forced to sell their properties. Even for those property owners with substantial amount of liquidity, anticipation (or observation of early signs) of the above rise in mortgage rate and forced selling would induce some of them to sell their properties at the early stage. For the developers who are usually smarter than these property owners, some may start massive offload of their flats with a medium price cut (of, say 5–10%).[18] These would in turn induce more property owners and more developers to sell their flats at even lower prices. The fall in property prices would then deter potential new buyers from buying flats. All these would then trigger further fall in property prices. Sooner or later, there would be vicious cycles among plunge in property prices, collapse in share prices, severe recession, massive layoffs and huge surge in banks' non-performing loans. Thereafter, banks would have to cut their loans and make fire sales to keep their capital adequacy ratio from falling too much. Enterprises and individuals would also be forced to deleverage. These would in turn trigger more downward spirals, thus resulting in vicious cycles among financial crisis, severe recession and widespread unemployment.

4.2.1.2 The effect of a rebound in the US dollar and Hong Kong dollar

Another reason for many property owners not being fully aware of their potential risk was as follows: as noted in Yip (2011), the US dollar, and hence the Hong Kong dollar, had depreciated substantially during the US QE. That is, the surge and hence the overvaluation of Hong Kong property prices were partially offset by the decline of the US dollar and Hong Kong dollar over the past few years. Nevertheless, when the Federal Reserve unwinds its QE and then starts its interest rate hike during the later phase of the US economic recovery, the US dollar and Hong Kong dollar could rebound by at least 30% between the trough and the peak of the exchange rate cycle at that time. By then, Hong Kong property prices in terms of foreign currency (i.e., nominal effective exchange rate) could surge by at least 30%, which would then make Hong Kong property investors suddenly aware of the "hidden" overvaluation of Hong Kong property prices.

4.2.1.3 Cumulated rise in other asset prices was also gigantic

Similarly, as shown in Figure 4.2, the cumulated rise of non-residential property prices during the same period was also gigantic. Worse

---

[18] In fact, the collapse of Hong Kong's property price in 1997–1998 began with a major developer's massive offloading of flats with a medium price cut.

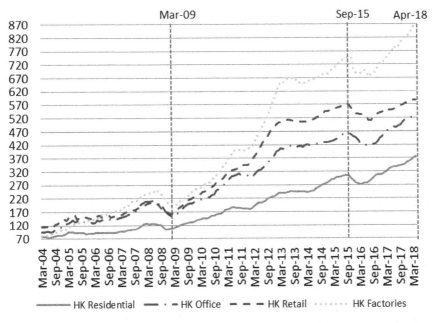

Figure 4.2:   Hong Kong's Property Price Indices

still, other asset prices, such as the prices of car park and taxi licenses, had also surged substantially and were generally believed to be substantially overvalued. When all these asset prices plunged with the collapse of residential property prices, the damage would be enormous.

4.2.2   Risk of Further Rise in Hong Kong's Property Prices before the Eventual Bursting

Nevertheless, the articles noted that the most worrisome case was not the above scenario, but further rise in Hong Kong's property prices before the eventual collapse. As explained in the previous sections, Hong Kong's developers had successfully offset the effects of the sixth round of curbing. Although there was significant reduction in the number of property transactions, the level of property prices was basically similar to the pre-curbing level. Meanwhile, there was continuous accumulation of pent-up demand during that consolidation period. With the expected recovery of the US economy, the expected rise in share prices at that time[19], upward revisions of wages with inflation and economic growth and the fading out of the psychological effect of the curbing measures over time, Hong Kong developers might be able to use their price setting power (and the powerful indicator effect from new flats to resale flats) to engineer another surge in property prices. Thereafter, there could be a few vicious cycles, upward spirals and then herding behaviors that push the domestic property prices further up (see the detailed discussion in Chapter 1). Thus, there was a risk that Hong Kong's property prices would increase further before the eventual collapse. If this happens, the damage of such a collapse could be more severe than that in the 1997–1998 financial crisis. Thus, the Hong Kong government should at least prepare itself for more curbing measures so as to ensure Hong Kong property prices would not increase further. The articles then explained that standard curbing measures would not be powerful enough to help squeeze part of the property bubble, and therefore would not be able to help Hong Kong avoid the eventual bubble bursting (see Section 4.3.2 for the detailed explanation). Thus, it would be safer for the Hong Kong government to consider the truly powerful proposed bubble-squeezing strategy (see Section 4.3 for the full proposal).

4.2.3 The External Economic Environment was Not Yet Ripe for a Major Correction

The articles also highlighted that the external economic environment was not yet ripe for a bursting of Hong Kong's property bubble, and a major

---

[19]As explained in Yip (2011) and the author's follow-up policy articles in 2012, the risk of a full-blown crisis in the US in 2008–2009 (and the risk of a full-blown European Debt Crisis in 2011–2012) had resulted in a sharp plunge and hence a substantial *fear discount* in the global stock price. The subsequent rebound of the global stock market was actually a gradual recovery from an extremely undervalued level toward a more normal level. From a lot of objective measures such as the price-to-earnings ratios, the dividend yields and the price-to-book ratios, the global stock market at that time was still moderately undervalued, not to mention that the expected recovery of the US economy would justify further upside beyond the above static gap of undervaluation. More importantly, as explained in Yip (2011, 2014), if the share price falls to a substantially undervalued level during the trough of the economic cycle and starts to rebound from there, it is likely that the share price will rise beyond the normal level and reach an overvalued level during the overheated phase of the economic cycle. Thus, there was still plenty of upsides for the US and domestic stock markets at that time.

correction of property prices in Hong Kong in the subsequent 6–8 quarters was rather low, if not out of question. This was so because (i) the US economy was still recovering, (ii) the global stock market was still rebounding and (iii) it would take at least a few years before the cumulated rise in the US (and Hong Kong) interest rate and the cumulated appreciation of the US dollar (and Hong Kong dollar) reach a high enough level to trigger the collapse of Hong Kong's property prices. Thus, the subsequent 6–8 quarters could be a good period to adopt the proposed bubble-squeezing strategy. If the Hong Kong government missed this chance, as it usually did, the only thing Hong Kong could do was to wait for the eventual bursting of the bubble.

4.3 POLICY RECOMMENDATION: THE BUBBLE-SQUEEZING STRATEGY

After explaining the high likelihood of a further surge and then an eventual bursting of Hong Kong's property bubble, the articles proposed a bubble-squeezing strategy that could help to avoid the potential disaster. Below, the author will outline the proposed strategy in Section 4.3.1 and then discuss the proposed implementation details in Section 4.3.2.

4.3.1 An Outline of the Strategy

Applying the bubble-squeezing strategy first proposed in Yip (2011), the Hong Kong government could use *waves of severe enough curbing measures* to reduce the size of the asset bubble *step by step to less overvalued levels* so as to reduce the damages, or even the probability, of the subsequent collapse. That is, the Hong Kong government could first use sufficient curbing measures to achieve a moderate correction of the asset price to a less overvalued level, and then gave the asset market some time (say, a few months) to consolidate around that less overvalued level. Thereafter, if the condition allowed,[20] the government could consider another round of curbing measures to achieve another moderate correction of the asset price to an even less overvalued level. After two, three or more rounds of

---

[20] Even if condition did not allow, the first-round curbing would still help reduce the subsequent plunge.

moderate correction of the asset price to much less overvalued levels, there could be a chance for the related economy to avoid a disastrous bursting of bubble in the subsequent future. Even if a disastrous bursting could not be avoided, the few rounds of moderate corrections to less over-valued levels could still mitigate the subsequent overcorrection of the asset price and hence the implied damages.[21] On top of that, the curbing measures used during the bubble squeezing would allow the related government to reduce the subsequent plunge, and hence the implied damages, by a speedy unwinding of the curbing measures during the collapse.[22,23]

4.3.2 Implementation Details

Crucial to the above bubble-squeezing strategy was whether the adopted curbing measures would be powerful enough to achieve a moderate correction of property prices. In Section 4.3.2.1, the author will explain that the "severe" measures so far adopted by the Hong Kong government were in fact not that severe. A more powerful measure is then proposed in Section 4.3.2.3.

---

[21] As a plunge of asset price from a more overvalued level would usually cause a bigger overcorrection, bringing an asset price to a less overvalued level would also reduce the subsequent overcorrection.

[22] Even so, the downward pressure on property prices at that time would still be enormous (i.e., see Chapter 1 on the enormous impacts of herding behaviors, downward spirals and vicious cycles, as well as changes in expectation and economic behaviors in the reverse direction).

[23] The Hong Kong government could also consider the following modification: use sufficient curbing measures to stop the property bubble from growing, while waiting for large enough negative economic or political events to trigger a moderate correction of property prices to less overvalued levels. The advantage of the modified choice was political: the Hong Kong government could avoid unnecessary blames, as it would be the negative economic and political events instead of the government curbing measures that trigger the correction. The disadvantage of the modified choice was that there might not be any large enough negative event to trigger a correction of property price in the near future. Even if there was a large enough negative event in the near future, its size and arrival time were unlikely to be optimal for the bubble-squeezing strategy. As an economist who strongly prefers a good control of the situation instead of hoping for uncertain events with unknown size and unknown arrival time, the author is in favor of the first choice.

4.3.2.1 *Existing curbing measures not powerful enough to squeeze the bubble*

It should be noted that most of the adopted curbing measures, such as the ABSD, lower LTV cap, lower mortgage tenure cap and lower DSR (Debt Service Ratio) cap,[24] were curbing measures on *new buyers* of properties, and would not apply to *existing property owners* who bought their properties and fixed their mortgage terms before the new measures. Thus, even though these curbing measures were said to be severe measures, they were actually not that severe as the *net* number of properties bought by the *new buyers* would be just a very small percentage (e.g., 1–3%) of the number held by the *existing owners*. Furthermore, even among the much smaller *net* number of new purchases, there would be exemptions for first-time homebuyers and related loopholes (e.g., using son's, daughter's or parent's first-time home-buyer qualification to circumvent the curbing measures). As a result, only the non-first-time new buyers would be affected by these curbing measures.

Thus, as long as existing property owners believed that these curbing measures would not cause an immediate collapse of property prices and chose not to sell their flats, these curbing measures would only have very limited effect.[25] (In fact, with an expectation of further rise in property prices, many market participants had in the past rushed to buy another property if they anticipated such kind of announcements in the near future. This also explained why, immediately after the announcements in the previous rounds of curbing in Hong Kong and Singapore, some investors had rushed to buy a property that same night, i.e., before the announced measures became effective the next day.[26])

---

[24] As explained in Chapter 3, the SSD would be even weaker than the ABSD and the other curbing measures.

[25] With previous curbing measures failing to cause any major correction of property prices, most property owners would usually take a wait-and-see attitude with respect to the curbing measures. If most of them take a wait-and-see attitude, then the realized outcome would be no major correction of property price. When the realized outcome confirms the property owners' initial expectation of no major correction of property prices, the property owners would continue to hold their properties.

[26] The above experience (and similar experience in China) suggests the following lesson: if the government adopts insufficient curbing measures (say, because of the overestimation of the power of the curbing measures or the overworry of a moderate correction of

4.3.2.2 *Subsequent interest rate hike would be sufficient to trigger a disastrous correction*

Unlike the above curbing measures, a rise in the US interest rate and hence the domestic mortgage rate will affect *all existing owners and new buyers with a mortgage loan.* When the cumulated increase in interest rate reaches a certain level, there will be a certain number of existing owners who start selling their properties, which will in turn trigger a collapse in property prices by inducing more existing owners and developers to sell their flats, and deterring new buyers from buying flats (see the discussion in Section 4.2.1). That is, there will be *herding behaviors in the downward direction,* which would mark the first phase of the deep plunge in property prices.

With further fall in property prices, there would be *a few vicious cycles in the downward direction* (e.g., vicious cycles among the fall in property prices and share prices, severe recession, massive retrenchments, widespread bankruptcy, banking and financial crisis, liquidity crunch, attacks on the currency board system and further surge in Hong Kong interest rate beyond the rising US interest rate). The fall in asset prices and hence the expectation of further fall in asset prices would also trigger *a few changes in economic behaviors in the downward direction.* For example, there would be *panic selling* (or massive fire sales) of all type of assets which would include at least the residential properties, shares, retail premises, offices, flatted factories, car parts and the very expensive taxi licenses. There would also be widespread *financial deleveraging* by individuals, firms and financial institutions, and a substantial degree of *financial disintermediation* (e.g., substantial reduction of bank loans, partly because the banks' lending capacities are substantially hurt by the provisions for non-performing loans, and partly because of the surge in the adverse selection problems and moral hazard problems during the crisis).

As we have seen in the US during the global financial tsunami, the financial disintermediation and hence the substantial reduction in bank loans would force many firms not only to shelve their investment plans but

property price) so that it keeps failing to stop the property price from rising further, more and more market participants will lose confidence in the government's ability to contain the rise in property prices. This would in turn weaken the effectiveness of the government's curbing measures in the subsequent rounds. To reverse the difficult and embarrassing situation, heavier curbing measures are needed.

also to cut their non-core operations, both of which would contribute to more severe recession and further rise in the unemployment rate. Meanwhile, the financial deleveraging could cause further plunge in asset prices, which would further worsen the balance sheets of financial institutions, thus forcing them to make more *fire sales* and hence deeper overcorrection of asset prices (Shleifer and Vishny, 2011). Furthermore, as we have seen in the 1997 Asian Financial Crisis, a crisis could trigger massive retrenchment through a temporary reduction of all firms' *reputation cost of retrenchment* toward zero (see Section 3.2.9 and Yip, 2005). That is, a crisis would first force some firms to make lumpy retrenchments. Even if some of the other healthy and profitable firms decide to make similar retrenchments at that time, the decision would have much less harm to their reputation as employers, simply because many firms are making retrenchment at that time. When more and more firms make lumpy retrenchments, there will be further reduction in the reputation cost of retrenchment. Such process could go on until most firms made massive retrenchments and the reputation cost of retrenchment fell to negligible levels. (In fact, that was what had happened in Hong Kong during the Asian Financial Crisis: many of the still healthy and profitable firms found it beneficial to retrench the higher-paid senior employees during the crisis and then hired lower-paid junior employees during the recovery stage. Such type of retrenchment had substantially raised Hong Kong's long-term unemployment rate, and it had taken Hong Kong many years to clear this long-term unemployment problem.) By then, the Chief Executive of Hong Kong and his cabinet would lose the credibility and moral authority of ruling. Thus, it would be important for them to consider the proposal outlined in Section 4.3.2.3.

4.3.2.3 *Additional safeguards and designs to ensure a gradual and safe squeezing of bubble*

In Section 4.3.2.1, the author has explained that the existing curbing measures in Hong Kong would not be powerful enough to help squeeze the bubble and hence avoid the expected crisis. Nevertheless, the discussion also suggests that those curbing measures that affect the *existing owners* with a mortgage loan could be powerful enough for the bubble-squeezing strategy. One such measure is the mortgage tax first proposed by the author.

Nevertheless, after finding out that the proposed tax bill will have little chance of being passed by Hong Kong's Legislative Council, the author thereafter modified it to the proposal of a *pre-paid mortgage rate.*[27] In this modified proposal, the HKMA will announce that banks have to collect and keep a progressive pre-paid mortgage rate for their mortgagees. It should be noted that the mortgage pre-payments should be recorded under the names of the mortgagees, and are not assets of the banks. That is, when the property bubble collapses in the future, the HKMA would announce that these mortgage pre-payments could be used to help pay part of their owners' (i.e., the mortgagees') monthly mortgage installments. As all existing owners and new buyers with a mortgage (i.e., all mortgagees) are required to pay the pre-paid mortgage rate (or the mortgage tax), the effect of these measures would be far greater than the existing curbing measures which affect only the *new buyers.* That is, there will be a high enough pre-paid mortgage rate (or mortgage tax rate) that could cause a meaningful correction of property prices. In fact, the problem of these strong enough measures is that they could have too strong an effect at the early stage of the curbing. As such, it has to be supplemented by the following policy designs to ensure a safe squeezing, and yet no early bursting, of the bubble.

In view that the economic environment in the subsequent year was not yet ripe for a bursting of Hong Kong's property bubble and there was a risk of further rise in Hong Kong's property prices, the author recommended the Hong Kong government to consider

(i)   further increases in the severity of the adopted curbing measures; and
(ii) initiating a public discussion on whether there would be a need to start imposing a relatively low pre-paid mortgage rate.

Increasing the adopted curbing measures could include further reduction of the debt service ratio cap, the LTV ratio cap and the mortgage tenure cap, increase in the buyer stamp duty and plugging the loopholes

---

[27] Another effective measure would be the TDSR adopted in Singapoer in June 2013, which focused on plugging the loopholes in the existing curbing measures. Unfortunately, Hong Kong's senior monetary officials again did not adopt the measure. As a result, Hong Kong property bubble had the chance to grow to a more gigantic one.

in existing curbing measures. These actions could on one hand help slow down the rise of property prices, and on the other hand help mitigate the potential damage of a bursting of the property bubble by a speedy unwinding of these measures during the crisis and post-crisis periods.

Nevertheless, as explained in Section 4.3.2.1, these curbing measures could only directly affect the relatively small number of *non-first-time new buyers*. Thus, the major responsibility of the bubble-squeezing strategy has to fall on the pre-paid mortgage rate. However, imposing the required pre-paid mortgage rate in one goal would imply too much impact at the beginning. Therefore, it is necessary to first start (a) a discussion on whether it should be implemented and (b) a discussion of a relatively low pre-paid mortgage rate. The use of the former is that it could partition the total effect of the pre-paid mortgage rate into two parts: the first part is the effect through changes in expectation during the discussion stage, and the second part is the remaining effect during the implementation stage (say, after a few months of discussion). Even so, as the discussion of the pre-paid mortgage rate would change the market's expectation of the mortgage burden for *all the periods in the subsequent years*, and some market participants would expect the possibility of upward revision of the pre-paid mortgage rate in the future, one should not underestimate the potential size of the initial impacts. Therefore, it would also be important to start the discussion with a relatively low pre-paid mortgage rate. For example, the HKMA can start talking about (i) a 0.50% pre-paid mortgage rate if the mortgagees' LTV ratios are higher than 60%, (ii) a 0.25% pre-paid mortgage rate if their LTV ratios are within the range of (50%, 60%] and (iii) no additional pre-paid mortgage rate for the time being if their LTV ratios are at or below 50%. In addition, as the property's market will price in future increase in the pre-paid mortgage rate, the HKMA should also indicate that the tentative (but revisable) target of the total increase in the pre-paid mortgage rate will be 2%.

With the two additional safeguards, we can substantially reduce the initial impacts of the pre-paid mortgage rate, and therefore (i) avoid the possibility of too much correction at the early stage and (ii) give the related government authority the necessary *opportunity* and *time* to observe the market response and make appropriate adjustment in the severity of the squeezing plan. For example,

(1) If Hong Kong's property prices make a 5–8% correction during the discussion stage, the related authority could stick with the initial plan of imposing the pre-paid mortgage rate, say, 3 months after the public discussion. This will give the market a 3-month resting and adjustment time before the second round of smaller correction in the implementation stage.[28] After observing the total amount of correction during the discussion stage and the implementation stage, the related authority could then decide whether it should continue the squeezing of the bubble with another round of discussion and implementation of a higher pre-paid mortgage rate, or give the market more resting time before the second round of squeezing.

(2) If there is only a negligible correction (of, say, 1–3%) in property prices, the related authority could start discussing a higher pre-paid mortgage rate (and push for a faster implementation), with the aim to achieve a 5–8% correction at the discussion stage before the second correction in the implementation stage.

(3) In the unlikely case that that there is 10–15% correction in property prices, the HKMA could slow down the squeezing plan a bit. In the extremely unlikely case of over 15% correction in property prices, the related authority could state that there are still a few months of discussion and consultation, and the authority's final decision will depend very much on whether the total correction of property prices during the discussion stage has reached its initial target. (*Note*: Unless in the extremely unlikely case of a collapse of property price, the related authority should avoid announcing the withdrawal of the measure, as such kind of announcement would cause an immediate jump in property prices back to the highly overvalued levels. Worse still, the rebound could trigger another round of surge in property prices. Instead, the related authority could indicate that it is open to the idea of starting the pre-paid mortgage rate (i) at a lower rate and/or (ii) for only mortgage loans for non-owner-occupied-properties.)

---

[28] As the market would gradually raise the expected probability of the measure during the discussion stage (e.g., from 0% to 50–60% and then 70–80% chance), the effect of the actual implementation of the measure would be much smaller than the cumulated effects during the discussion stage.

4.4 PROPERTY PRICE MOVEMENTS BETWEEN JUNE 2014 AND MAY 2018

Unfortunately, despite the author's well-planned bubble-squeezing proposal and follow-up visits to the related government authorities in Hong Kong, the top economic and monetary officials lacked the knowledge, vision and devotion to undertake the bubble-squeezing strategy before it was too late. Worse still, because of another policy mistake committed by the Hong Kong government (see the detailed discussion in Section 4.4.2), there were signs in June–July 2014 supporting the author's worry highlighted in Section 4.2.2, i.e., the Hong Kong property bubble could grow bigger before the eventual collapse. As such, the author published another policy article in July 2014, pointing out that there was too little time left to squeeze the huge property bubble to a safe enough level, and an eventual disastrous bursting of Hong Kong's property bubble could be an unavoidable reality. In this section, the author will discuss the property price movements in Hong Kong between June 2014 and May 2018.

4.4.1 Insufficient Time to Squeeze the Property Bubble to a Safe Enough Level

After pointing out that there was too little time left to squeeze the huge property bubble to a safe enough level before the eventual bursting, the July 2014 article also warned Mr. John Tsang (the then Hong Kong Financial Secretary) and Mr. Norman Chan (the then Chief Executive of the HKMA) that, once the expected bursting of Hong Kong's property bubble was realized, they would be heavily criticized and things would turn very ugly for them. As there was still a safe period of at least 6–9 months to perform a decent curbing on the property market, and there was a growing risk that Hong Kong's property prices would surge further before the eventual bursting, they better implemented more curbing measures to squeeze part of the bubble, or at least stop the bubble from growing. Although there might not be enough time for Hong Kong to squeeze the property bubble to a safe enough level before the eventual bursting, the curbing could still mitigate the subsequent damages. Such an effort would also help mitigate the criticism they would face in the future. In addition, to mitigate the damages of the expected bursting, the HKMA should (i) start studying the various vicious cycles (including financial deleveraging, financial disintermediation, fire sales and speculative attack on Hong Kong's currency board system) highlighted in the author's previous publications and (ii) plan for mitigating measures during the crisis triggered by the bursting of the bubble. The article also warned the Chief Executive of Hong Kong that during the crisis he would be the one most seriously blamed, even though the mistakes committed by Hong Kong's top economic and monetary officials as well as his predecessor were more serious than the mistakes committed by him. Nevertheless, it would still help a bit if he could pressurize his top economic and monetary officials to implement more curbing measures as soon as possible and start planning measures to mitigate the expected crisis.

The article also recommended the banks in Hong Kong to further reduce their exposure to the property-related loans and make all necessary pre-arrangements for the expected crisis. For those banks that failed to do the necessary preparation, the subsequent crisis would cause a substantial surge in the banks' loss provisions and hence a plunge in the banks' capital adequacy ratios below the acceptable norm, as well as potential bank runs due to numerous negative news and whispers on the healthiness of these banks. These could in turn force the government to take over these troubled banks and then sell them to potential buyers at distressed prices. On the other hand, for those banks which made sufficient preparation against the expected crisis, the preparation would not only help them to survive through the crisis, but would also allow them to grow their market share by buying the troubled banks at extremely low prices.

The article also warned Hong Kong's potential homebuyers to avoid buying properties at those highly overvalued levels, as the risk of an eventual bubble bursting and hence the potential losses to them were just too high. In addition, the article warned that there would be a substantial rise in the unemployment rate during the crisis. On the other hand, for those potential homebuyers who were willing to wait, the bursting of the property bubble would one day enable them to purchase their properties at extremely attractive prices[29] and yet help providing a support on the property prices during

---

[29] The article also warned that a significant portion of these potential homebuyers might lose their jobs during the crisis, and would therefore be unable (or unwilling) to buy properties at the distressed prices. Nevertheless, their choice of not buying overvalued

the crisis triggered by the bursting. Finally, the article noted that, as an economist, the author preferred to hope that the bursting would never happen. Unfortunately, it seemed that the chance of such a hope was rather slim.

4.4.2 The Surge between June 2014 and September 2015: Another Mistake by the Hong Kong Government

Unfortunately, again, the Hong Kong government failed to recognize the need to implement more curbing measures. Worse still, because of the lobbying of some politicians closely linked with the developers, the Hong Kong government made another mistake by accepting the developer-related politicians' request to extend the grace period for the exemption of the Double Buyer Stamp Duty (DBSD)[30] (see Box 4.1 for the detailed discussion). As such, the developers were able to use their pricing power, the pent-up demand accumulated during the consolidation period and the subsequent improvement in the political environment[31] to engineer another jump in property transactions and then another surge in property prices. As we can see from Figure 4.1, property prices in Hong Kong made another 22.3% surge between June 2014 and September 2015.

---

properties before the bursting would at least help them avoid an additional pain (i.e., the stress to service the mortgage installment of a property of negative asset value), while being unemployed during the crisis.

[30] Obviously, the related government officials believed that the apparently mild extension would have little effect on Hong Kong's property prices. However, as already clearly explained in the author's posted articles and journal paper to these senior officials, the DBSD could at most temporarily suppress the rise of the property prices and there would be continued accumulation of pent-up demand during the consolidation period. Once there was any meaningful change in the economic and political environment, the developers would use their pricing power and the cumulated pent-up demand to engineer another rapid surge in property prices, therefore pushing the property bubble towards a bigger one. Thus, it was extremely important for the Hong Kong government to start squeezing the bubble before these meaningful changes in the economic environment.

[31] Because of the DBSD and the political uncertainty due to the "Occupy the Central" movement at that time, property prices in HK stayed relatively flat between February 2013 and June 2014. However, with the extension of the grace period for the exemption of the DBSD and the improvement in the subsequent political environment, property prices in Hong Kong started to surge again.

Box 4.1: The mistake of agreeing to extend the grace period for the exemption of the DBSD

In the initial announcement of the DBSD, property buyers would be exempted from the additional stamp duty if they sell their original owner-occupied property within 6 months after the purchase contract date so that the newly purchased property would become their one and only one owner-occupied property in Hong Kong.[32] Thereafter, because of the influence of the powerful developers in Hong Kong and other political complications, there was a delay in the formal approval by the Hong Kong Legislative Council for the new tax. During this process, the Hong Kong government mistakenly compromised to the developer-related legislative members' request to extend the starting point of the above 6-month grace period from the purchase *contract date* to the transaction *completion date*.

While this would mean an extension of the grace period by about 3 months for an upgrading or switching to another resale flat, it could mean up to 3 years extension for an upgrading or switching to new properties, as property developers in Hong Kong usually sell their properties 3 years before the completion of their new housing estates. Such a long enough extension had made many property owners reconsider upgrading or switching their properties to new properties (i.e., buy a new flat and then sell the original flat near the end of the 3-year grace period), as (i) the switching will be exempted from the additional stamp duty and (ii) the up to 3-year grace period would allow them to profit from the rises in property prices during such a long grace period. In other words, the extension of the grace period had unlocked a huge "suppressed" or "hidden" pent-up demand for new properties. (Note that these switchers or upgraders were at least rational in the following sense: they believed their switching would enable them to gain during the extended grace period, and the subsequent property prices did rise during the extended grace period. Of course, when they sell their original properties, there would be a much greater amount of properties for sale in the resale market. However, given that there is a strong indicator effect from new property prices to resale property prices, the expected surge in new property prices during the grace period extension would be able to pull up the resale property prices so that these switchers would in fact be buying the new properties at an early period and selling their original properties at a later period (with a higher price). Of course, subsequent buyers of the upgraders' original properties would be at

(Continued)

---

[32] Such an exemption was meant to avoid the DBSD from affecting homeowners' need to change their flats to another flat of a different location, size or class.

Box 4.1: (*Continued*)

a much higher risk as the bubble did grow bigger because of the above over-whelming upgrading activities. Nevertheless, most of these subsequent buyers did not seem to be aware of the high risk of their purchase.)

4.4.3 The Correction between September 2015 and March 2016

In August–September 2015, the anticipated rise in the US interest rate caused a substantial rise in the US dollar. The strong US dollar in turn contributed to a substantial plunge in oil prices and other commodity prices as well as a mini devaluation of renminbi. The latter in turn triggered a vicious cycle of "substantial capital flight from China and plunge in China's stock market index — further depreciation of renminbi — further capital flight and further plunge in China's stock market index." Worse still, with the fall in the renminbi and the China stock market index, some huge speculative funds were able to trigger substantial plunges in the global stock markets as well as excessive fall in the oil prices (e.g., well below the non-sustainable level of 25 US dollar per barrel) and other commodity prices.

With (i) the above turmoil in the global financial markets, (ii) the growing awareness of the potential impacts of the expected US interest rate hike and (iii) the poor retail sales in the Hong Kong economy at that time, Hong Kong property prices started to fall from the peak in September 2015. The fall in property prices in turn triggered a more pessimistic view on the outlook of property prices (and hence more selling of properties). As a result, there was 11.3% correction of the residential property price index between September 2015 and March 2016.

Unfortunately, as shown in Figure 4.1, the 11.3% correction was still much smaller than the 22.3% rise between June 2014 and September 2015. That is, if the Hong Kong government had

(i)   introduced more curbing measures as suggested in Section 4.4.1; and
(ii) avoided the policy mistakes highlighted in Section 4.4.2,

the 11.3% correction between September 2015 and March 2016 would have helped squeezing part of the property bubble. Unfortunately, because of the above two mistakes by the Hong Kong government, the size of the bubble in June 2016 was still 10.4% bigger than that in June 2014.

On the other hand, as explained in Chapter 3, the Singapore government's TDSR measure introduced on 29 June 2013 was able to achieve a gradual squeezing of its moderate property bubble to a smaller one. Such a comparison further illustrates the poor standard of Hong Kong's top economic and monetary officials in managing its macroeconomic risk. Worse still, as will be discussed in Section 4.4.4, the delay in the US interest rate hike due to the Brexit referendum and the subsequent inaction of the Hong Kong government contributed to another sharp surge in Hong Kong property prices from July 2016.

4.4.4 The Brexit Referendum and the Surge between June 2016 and May 2108

In view that the delay in the US interest rate hike would cause a rebound of Hong Kong's property bubble back to more dangerous levels, the author published another policy article on 30 July 2016, highlighting the need of another round of curbing measures. The article first noted that, based on the Federal Reserve's actions over the first seven months in 2016, it appeared that the Federal Reserve was quick to notice that

(i) the strong US dollar could cause sharp plunges in the commodity markets, the emerging markets and even some mature markets, which could in turn cause substantial negative repercussion and hence affect the US economic recovery; and
(ii) the US and global economic growth in 2016H1 was lower than expected, although the US job market was recovering well.

As a result, the Federal Reserve would opt for a more gradual pace of interest rate hike. In particular, it had given up its original plan of four interest rate hikes in 2016, and would probably only make one rate hike in 2016 (although one could not rule out the possibility of two or zero rate hike).[33] More importantly, on top of a slower pace of rate hike, the cumu-

---

[33] Because of (i) another turmoil in the global financial markets in January–February 2016; (ii) the potential risk of the Brexit Referendum on 23 June 2016; (iii) the surprisingly weak

lated amount of rate hike in 2017 and the subsequent years would be smaller than what was previously indicated by the Federal Reserve. For example, the cumulated amount of rate hike in 2017 would probably be only around 1% (e.g., four rate hikes, each with a 0.25% hike). This would imply, on top of the previous analysis of no bursting of Hong Kong's property bubble in 2016, the cumulated rate hike in 2017 would not be large enough to trigger a bursting of Hong Kong's property bubble.

If appropriately used, such a change would actually mean that Hong Kong has a decent extra time to squeeze the property bubble to a safer level (i.e., still a bubble but not big enough for a bursting). However, in view of

(i)   the weak ability of Hong Kong's top economic and monetary officials at that time;
(ii) the speculative culture in Hong Kong; and
(iii) the developers' powerful influence on Hong Kong's property market as well as the political circle,

the article admitted that the author was not optimistic with the outcome.

Firstly, with the delay in the US interest rate hike, a large number of property market participants mistakenly interpreted it as no rate hike in the future while another large portion of participants only consider the amount of rate hike until 2017. Even for the remaining portion of property market participants who might be roughly aware of further rate hikes after 2017, a significant portion of them would think that it would be too long to consider the rate hikes after 2017, and preferred to engage in another round of speculation at that time (i.e., they believed there would be enough time to make another round of speculation). As a result, the delay in the US interest rate hike could result in a large number of property market participants rushing into Hong Kong' property market. In fact, that was also why Hong Kong property prices thereafter made a substantial surge at that time.

Unfortunately, the "not-that-well-trained" monetary and economic officials in Hong Kong once again failed to recognize the need (or lacked

---

job figure in May 2016 and (iv) weak GDP growth in 2016H1, the Federal Reserve had rationally decided not to raise interest rate in March 2016 and June 2016, thus changing its original plan of four interest rate hikes to only one hike in 2016.

the ability to design good enough curbing measures) to stop the bubble from growing again, not to mention the need to squeeze the huge property bubble to a smaller and less dangerous one. Therefore, Hong Kong's residential property price index had the chance to surge by another 38.4% between June 2016 and May 2018. As a result, the cumulated (average) rise in Hong Kong's residential property price index during the 9 years 2 months between March 2009 and May 2018 was 250% (14.7% p.a.). In addition, the housing price-to-income ratio in 2017Q4 surged to the record high of 16.4 years, which was much bigger than the 14.6 years recorded during the peak of the 1997 property bubble.

With such a gigantic property bubble, it will be a just a matter of time the bubble will burst. By then, the bursting will trigger a financial crisis and severe recession in Hong Kong. Worse still, the bursting of Hong Kong's property bubble and the collapse in Hong Kong's stock market will, through the contagion effect, trigger plunges in the property markets and stock markets in other Asian economies. Given that there are reasonably big property bubbles in many other Asian economies, the chance of another Asian financial crisis is high. Even for well-managed economies such as Singapore, the expected crisis would still trigger a mini financial crisis and a moderately severe recession.

4.5 PROPOSED POLICY MEASURES AFTER THE BURSTING OF THE PROPERTY BUBBLE

In view of the expected bursting of Hong Kong's gigantic property bubble, the author will in this section propose policy measures that would mitigate the damages during the crisis period and post-crisis recession.[34]

4.5.1 Lessons from the US Experience During the Global Financial Tsunami

The first set of proposed measures are drawn from the following US measures adopted during the global financial tsunami: the Trouble Asset Relief

---

[34]The proposals in Sections 4.5.1.1–4.5.1.3 were already publised in the Hong Kong Economic Journal in 2018. Yip (2018) also provided a discussion on the important characteristics of financial crises and the policy measures adopted in the US during the Global Financial Tsunami.

Program (TARP), the temporary change in the mark-to-market rule, the stress test on banks and the associate encouragement of capital injection, and the QE programs.

4.5.1.1 *The effect of TARP and its potential application in Hong Kong*

The TARP was the US Treasury's direct capital or loan injection into most US banks (e.g., Citigroup), foreign banks' subsidiaries in the US, non-bank financial institutions (e.g., AIG) and some non-financial corporations (e.g., General Motors). The first effect of the TARP was to stop these too-big-to-fail corporations from shutting down, which could trigger further rounds of contractions through the multiplier effect (i.e., the vicious cycles between shutting down of firms, massive layoffs, plunge in consumption, plunge in aggregate demand, and more shutting down of firms) and the accelerator effect (i.e., the vicious cycle between fall in output, plunge in investment and further fall in output).

The second effect was to stop the potential failure of these too-big-to-fail corporations from triggering failures of other firms through the **counterparty risk**. For example, if the US government let Citigroup and AIG fail at that time, the implied counterparty risk would pull many other financial and non-financial corporations into the spiral of troubles. Once so, the whole US financial system will experience serious malfunctioning or could even be unable to functioning properly. In fact, when the US Congress decided not to support the rescue of the Lehman Brother in late 2008, the implied surge in the counterparty risk and fear had caused a partial malfunctioning of the US financial system, and pulled more financial institutions into the spiral of troubles. Fortunately, the shock had subsequently forced the US Congress to support the US Treasury's use of the TARP funds for capital injection into financial institutions (such as AIG, Citigroup, Fannie Mae and Freddie Mac) that were on the verge of shutting down in the subsequent quarters. As a result, the problem was localized and was stopped from spreading to other corporations. In addition, the TARP loans to the top three US car manufacturers (i.e., General Motors, Ford and Chrysler) helped avoid the shutting down of these major firms, whose failure would have severe spillover effects on the steel and other related industries. (Of course, during the subsequent safety violation of Toyota, the US Government's additional and possibly excessive effort against Toyota also played an important role in helping the three major US car manufacturers regain demand and return to long-term profitability.)

The third effect of the TARP was to cut off the vicious cycle between loss provisions and fire sales of assets by banks: to understand this, first note that banks need to keep the legally required 8% capital–asset (K/A) ratio and follow the mark-to-market rule to make loss provisions due to any fall in the prices of their asset holdings (or any increase in doubtful loans). As almost all the securities (such as shares, bonds, mortgage backed securities and collateral debt obligations) experienced drastic decline during the crisis, the banks had to make substantial loss provisions even though they were still holding the securities with paper losses instead of realized losses. Such loss provisions had to be deducted from banks' capital (K), which would cause a fall in the K/A ratio below the legally required 8%. As it would be extremely difficult to raise capital (i.e., increase K) during the crisis period, banks could only restore their K/A ratio by fire sales of assets (i.e., reducing A). Unfortunately, the 8% capital–asset ratio would mean a leverage of 12.5 times. That is, every 1 dollar of loss provision would require the banks to sell 12.5 dollars of assets! Naturally, such huge amount of fire sales of assets would cause further plunges in the prices of these assets. Worse still, with further plunges in these asset prices, banks will need to make another round of fire sales to restore the 8% capital–asset ratio. As a result, there was a vicious cycle of loss provisions — fire sales — more rounds of loss provisions and fire sales.

The aim of TARP was to use the direct injection of capital into the banks (and non-bank financial institutions) to restore the K/A ratio so that they did not have to make the fire sales, which would cause further plunges in asset prices and further rounds of loss provisions. This would in turn reduce the fall in securities prices and the related vicious cycles (such as further deleveraging by individual investors and other corporations, and the vicious cycle between plunge in asset prices, negative wealth effect and deeper recession). In fact, because of the above-mentioned leverage of 12.5 times for banks, the effect of each dollar spent on the TARP would be much greater than the effect of each dollar spent on the QE (although the gigantic size of the QE still made it the most important measure to stop the US economy from dipping into a great depression).

In short, the effect of the TARP was to use direct capital or loan injection to localize the problem to only those distressed financial institutions, thus cutting off the potential vicious cycles and containing the counterparty risk so that the US financial system could continue to function, albeit with moderate malfunctioning. When undertaking the capital injection, the US government also heavily penalized these distressed financial institutions and their shareholders. For example, when rescuing Citigroup and the AIG, the US government only used a relatively moderate (but very much needed) capital injection to purchase 80% of the shares of these financial institutions, thus resulting in a significant dilution of the percentage holding of the original shareholders and enabling the US government to earn a decent profit during its subsequent exit from these financial institutions. Thus, the heavy penalty to the original shareholders was enough, and the moral hazard argument against the rescue package was simply invalid. Nevertheless, while the greedy CEOs of these financial institutions had eventually lost their jobs during the crisis, they had already received huge amounts of bonus before the crisis. Thus, while many economists believed these CEOs should be penalized, the existing legal system had ironically helped them avoid the punishment.

Potential Application in Hong Kong: In order to apply similar rescue package in Hong Kong during the expected crisis, the Hong Kong government should first put a significant amount of budget surpluses cumulated during the bubble period into a rescue fund. When a bank or non-bank financial institution falls into trouble after the bursting of the bubble, the Hong Kong government can perform a capital injection by using the funds to buy up a significant portion of the shares of the distressed financial institution, thus localizing the problem to the distressed financial institution and cutting off the potential vicious cycles. In view that the Hong Kong government might not have enough funds to deal with the expected disaster, the Hong Kong government should also make early contacts or establish pre-crisis connections with major sovereign funds as well as large local and foreign corporations so that it can quickly find a potential buyer for the distressed financial institution when deemed necessary. For the CEOs and major shareholders of the banks in Hong Kong, it would be a good idea to raise their capital–asset ratios to levels that would enable them to go through the crisis without severe fire sales. Otherwise, the major shareholders would have to take the risk of selling their banks at extremely low prices (and the CEOs would probably lose their jobs during the crisis). On the other hand, if they could keep a high enough capital–asset ratio, they would be able to buy up other banks at extremely low prices, which would significantly raise their market shares and influences after the crisis.

4.5.1.2 *The temporary change in the use of mark-to-market rule and its potential application in Hong Kong*

As noted above, banks (and other listed companies) are required to use the market price to compute and report their total asset values. During normal time, such a mark-to-market rule would ensure all firms report their profits and asset values according to a uniform, standard and representative format. Nevertheless, with the plunges in the prices of all the toxic and non-toxic securities during the crisis to levels that were well below the long-term values, the mark-to-market rule would require banks and other listed companies to make loss provisions that were well beyond what was required for the long term. As the loss provisions had to be deducted from the equity capital (K) in the balance sheet and included as a loss item in the profit and loss account, the latter would imply that banks and many listed firms would change from profit-making status before the crisis to huge-loss status during the crisis. These big losses in the quarterly earnings results would then cause severe plunges in the shares prices, which would in turn trigger widespread panic in the financial system and more adverse vicious cycles in the economy. To stop the financial system and the economy from deteriorating further, the US government announced an alternative computation rule that is based on the long-term asset values, and temporarily allowed the listed firms to use this long-term valuation rule or the mark-to-market rule to value their assets. With such an option on the asset valuation rule, the listed companies no longer needed to make substantial loss provisions, which had initially helped stabilizing the earnings results and then supporting the subsequent rebound in the shares prices. Thus, the related department of the Hong Kong government should carefully study the long-term valuation rule announced in the US so that it could be used during the expected crisis. Such an announcement would mitigate the decline in the listed firms' earnings results and shares prices, reducing banks' fire sales pressure for the restoration of the capital–asset ratio, and hence avoid the more serious vicious cycles triggered by these changes.

During the expected crisis, banks and the Hong Kong Government should also flexibly give the distressed mortgagees the option of temporarily paying the mortgage interest portion but not the principal repayment portion. This will not only substantially reduce the number of forced sale properties and the implied vicious cycles, but will also substantially reduce the amount of banks' loss provisions. The latter will in turn substantially reduce the downward pressures on banks' reported earnings and share prices as well as the pressure on banks' capital–asset ratio and fire sales, thus stopping them from triggering more serious vicious cycles. Of course, when the crisis is over, Hong Kong should go back to the usual mark-to-market rule and the original practice of including both the interest payment portion and principal repayment portion in the mortgage installment.

4.5.1.3 *The stress test on banks and the associate encouragement of capital injection*

During the global financial tsunami, there was a significant fall in the market's confidence on the US banks and non-bank financial institutions. This had in turn caused a certain degree of financial disintermediation, i.e., difficult for these financial institutions to function normally, and therefore affect the normal running of the real economy.

To restore the market confidence on these financial institutions, the US government had developed the following strategy: on one hand, announced the plan of conducting a fair stress test on these financial institutions a few months after the announcement, and on the other hand allowed these financial institutions to take the pain to raise capital through the issuance of new shares at very low prices. As the consequence of not passing the stress test would be too serious for these financial institutions, almost all the financial institutions had made an effort to raise capital before the test. As a result, most of these financial institutions were able to pass the stress test in the first round, thus enabling the US government to achieve the dual purposes of improving the capital–asset ratio (a long-term strength) of these financial institutions and re-establish the market confidence on these financial institutions through the result of the stress test.

On other hand, although the European Union also conducted the stress test in the later phase of the European Debt Crisis, the European banks were not forced or encouraged to take the pain in raising capital before the stress test. As a result, the European banks continued to be weak, with little improvement in their long-term strength, which had in turn contributed to the very weak and slow recovery of the European economy in the subsequently years.

Thus, if the Hong Kong government adopts the proposal of conducting a stress test on banks during the expected crisis, it is important to follow the US strategy of requiring the banks to take the pain to raise sufficient capital before the stress test. Otherwise, the whole economy has to pay for the mistake in terms of extremely weak banks and prolonged recession.

4.5.1.4 *A minor reform in Hong Kong's currency board system to allow for the possibility of a mini QE*

In Chapter 1, the author has explained that there will be drastic decline in the money multiplier (m) during the crisis period. In addition, there will also be a drastic decline in the monetary base (MB) due to substantial net capital outflows during the crisis period. According to the equation

$$M = m \times \text{MB},$$

the drastic decline in m and MB will cause a substantial fall in Hong Kong's money supply (M), which will by itself be large enough to pull the Hong Kong economy into a prolonged depression. To avoid the disastrous outcome, the US experience suggests that it is important for the government to inject a huge amount of monetary base (MB) to offset the above changes so that Hong Kong's money supply (M) could continue to grow at the normal pace without a drastic decline.

Nevertheless, according to the strict interpretation of the Currency Board System in Hong Kong, the amount of monetary base (MB) in Hong

Kong has to be 100% supported by Hong Kong's foreign reserves holding, and the HKMA has to let the market force (such as net capital inflows/ outflows and net current account surplus/deficit) decide the amount of monetary base. A strict following of these requirements would mean that Hong Kong could not implement the QE, which would in turn mean that the end result would be a prolonged depression. Fortunately, the Hong Kong government has, over the past few decades, accumulated a huge amount of foreign reserves that are many times the monetary base in Hong Kong. Thus, it is still possible for Hong Kong to inject a substantial amount of monetary base (through the huge buy back of the Exchange Fund Note) to offset the above negative changes in m and MB without violating the requirement that all monetary bases in Hong Kong have to be 100% backed up by Hong Kong's foreign reserves holding. Of course, the HKMA will still need to accept a domestic interest rate that will be moderately higher than the US interest rate because of the rise in the exchange rate risk premium during the crisis period. With the above possibility of a mini or limited QE, there is a chance that the monetary authority could keep the money supply (M) growing at the normal pace without a drastic decline. If so, the mini QE would be able to help Hong Kong avoid a prolonged depression so that its stock market and economy could gradually recover from crisis level. (*Note*: As it will take quite a few years for Hong Kong's property prices to reach the bottom, the author believes the mini QE could at most help to shorten the expected recession from 7–10 years to 3–6 years.)

4.5.2 Lessons from Singapore's Experience during the Asian Financial Crisis in 1997–1998

The second set of proposed measures are drawn from Singapore's experience during the Asian financial crisis in 1997–1998.

4.5.2.1 *The significant difference in macroeconomic management between Singapore and Hong Kong at that time*

As explained in Section 3.2.9, during and after the 1997 financial crisis, the Singapore government managed to mitigate the recession and avoid massive layoffs during the crisis and post-crisis recession by

(i) a substantial reduction in the employer's Central Provident Fund (CPF) contribution rate to reduce employers' labor costs;

(ii) a substantial depreciation of Singapore's NEER; and

(iii) fiscal relief packages to reduce firms' labor costs, operating costs and rental costs.

As explained in Yip (2005), these curbing measures managed to keep firms' reputation cost of retrenchment high and therefore helped avoid massive layoffs from happening in Singapore. That is, with these supporting measures of meaningful scale (e.g., almost 10% reduction in labor cost through the cyclical reduction of the employer CPF contribution rate, about 12% depreciation of the NEER and substantial fiscal relief package), employers in Singapore found it embarrassing (and damaging in reputation) to make massive layoffs unless their businesses were no longer viable. When the viable firms decided not to make massive layoffs (because of the damage to its reputation and hence much higher recruitment and labor costs in the future), firms' reputation cost of retrenchment was kept high, which could in turn ensure most viable firms would not make massive layoffs in the subsequent stage of crisis and during the post-crisis recession. On the other hand, there was no such rescue package in Hong Kong during the 1997 financial crisis. As a result, some viable firms in Hong Kong did not find it that embarrassing to make massive layoffs during the recession. The act of these firms in turn reduced the other viable firms' reputation cost of retrenchment and hence induced some more viable firms to make massive layoffs. Thus, there was a vicious cycle between the falling reputation cost of retrenchment and more viable firms making massive layoffs. In fact, during the 1997 financial crisis, some viable firms in Hong Kong even retrenched the more expensive senior workers and replaced them by some new recruits of junior staff or cheaper outsourcing. As a result, the Hong Kong economy eventually reached the state where firms' reputation cost of retrenchment fell to zero and almost all the viable firms had made massive layoffs until their labor force was trimmed to the new "optimal size" with respect to the severe recession at that time (i.e., these viable firms could recruit cheaper junior workers when the economy started to recover). Nevertheless, these microeconomic decisions were made without proper consideration of the subsequent macroeconomic spillover effect and vicious cycles, the cyclical nature of the crisis and post-crisis recession, as well as the permanent losses and destruction caused by the massive layoffs.

Thus, the above comparison suggests that there are some policy measures in Singapore that are worth adopting in Hong Kong during and after the expected crisis.

4.5.2.2 Modified policy measures that could be useful to Hong Kong

Firstly, as Hong Kong's exchange rate was pegged with the US dollar under its Currency Board System, Hong Kong could not follow Singapore's practice of using a decent depreciation to offset the negative effect of the crisis.[35] As such, Hong Kong could only adopt a cyclical reduction of employer Mandatory Provident Fund (MPF) contribution rate and the fiscal relief package. Nevertheless, unlike the 16–20% employer CPF contribution rate in Singapore, the employer MPF contribution rate in Hong Kong is only 5%. Thus, one can reasonably believe that a reduction of the employer MPF contribution rate would not be enough to pre-empt the firms from making massive layoffs. Worse still, as there will probably be another Asian financial crisis (triggered by the bursting of Hong Kong's property bubble) at that time, the US dollar is likely to rise due to its safe-haven status. The effect of the rise in the Hong Kong dollar (which is pegged to the US dollar) could substantially (or more than) offset the effect of the 5% reduction in the employer MPF contribution rate.

To pre-empt the massive layoffs, the Hong Kong government has to reply on a far more aggressive fiscal package. For example, the Hong Kong government could consider the following fiscal announcement:

For those firms that do not make any retrenchment[36] during the forthcoming year and in the past one year, each firm will be entitled to a tax rebate (or subsidy) that is equivalent to 15–20% of its total wage bill during the crisis period.[37]

---

[35] As noted in Yip (2005), an unpegging of the fixed exchange rate in Hong Kong Currency Board System could be disastrous during a crisis period. Thus, even if one believes Hong Kong should eventually move toward the Singapore exchange rate system, one should do it during the normal time (and preferably at a time that Hong Kong is experiencing a moderate appreciation pressure).

[36] Note that normal resignation should not be counted as retrenchment.

[37] For those firms that really cannot wait for 1 year, they could apply to the government for special approval of a tax rebate on a quarterly basis.

Hopefully, such an either "zero" or "full-rebate" choice would provide the employers enough incentives not to make massive layoffs right from the beginning. If so, this would avoid the vicious cycle between the reduction in firms' reputation cost of retrenchment and more firms opting for massive retrenchment, which would in turn trigger more vicious cycles such as the multiplier effect (i.e., vicious cycle between falling consumption and falling output), the accelerator effect (i.e., vicious cycle between falling investment and falling output) and the long list of vicious cycles discussed in Section 4.5.1 (e.g., vicious cycle among more asset fire sales, falling asset prices and deeper recession).

It should be emphasized that the percentage of the tax rebate has to be large enough to convince the viable firms not to make lumpy retrenchments. Otherwise, the policy announcement will not be effective. Given that the viable firms also care about their reputation costs (which would affect their recruitment and labor cost in the future) and these firms could also cut their employees' bonus during the crisis and post-crisis recession, the author believes a 15–20% tax rebate should be large enough to preempt widespread massive layoffs in viable firms.

With the huge fiscal surplus accumulated by the curbing measures during the bubble period, there is a reasonable chance that the cumulated fiscal surplus would be enough to help Hong Kong go through the crisis and post-crisis recession without widespread massive layoffs. If so, this would substantially mitigate the depth of the recession at that time. Nevertheless, there is still a chance that the cumulated fiscal surplus could not cover the 15–20% tax rebate for a prolonged post-crisis recession of 5–10 years. If so, the Hong Kong government could consider a 10% tax rebate plus a modification of policy announcement to enact the following:

For those firms that do not make any retrenchment and cut more than 10% (or 5%) in any employees' basic salary during the forthcoming year and in the past one year, each firm will be entitled to a tax rebate (or subsidy) that is equivalent to 10% of its total wage bill during the crisis period.

That is, if reduction in labor cost is unavoidable for the viable firms, it will be better to help them making such a cut by convincing them to cut every workers' salary by a moderate amount (and take the cyclical tax rebate). Without the above facilitation by the government, employers will find it less troublesome to cut the labor cost by lumpy layoffs, while requesting those remaining to work harder. As illustrated by the significant difference between Singapore and Hong Kong during the 1997–1998 crisis and its post-crisis recession, the macroeconomic damages of such type of lumpy layoffs would be far greater. According to Hong Kong's painful experience at that time, the implied widespread massive layoffs would also cause severe social problems to both the retrenched workers and the remaining employed workers. That is, the retrenched workers and their family members would be under enormous psychological pressure and anxiety when they lose their source of income to meet the basic food expenses, education expenses, medical expenses and rental expenses (or mortgage installment). Even for those remaining employed workers, they would also experience severe work pressure with extremely long overtime (OT), and live with fear of not knowing whether they would be in the next batch of massive layoffs. Thus, announcing the proposed tax rebate measures will be important not only to the whole economy but also to the psychological healthiness of most Hong Kong citizens.

Finally, for those unemployed (say, due to the shutting down of the non-viable firms), the Hong Kong government could adopt the policy measures implemented during the post-crisis recession in 1998–2003. One important example is providing retraining and granting qualifying skill certificates to these unemployed workers in new types of skill jobs such as various categories of skilled construction jobs, plumbers, skilled caretakers of mothers during and after the baby delivery and domestic helpers on hourly basis. Given the problem of aging population in Hong Kong, the author believes that there will be enormous job opportunity in the caretaking of old people. Thus, the Hong Kong government should at that time provide substantial amount of retraining courses to help these unemployed workers to enter the industry.

4.5.3 A Summary of the Proposed Policy Measures

As already suggested for the case of Singapore (i.e., Section 3.2.9), the Hong Kong government should first keep the curbing measures until the cumulated fall in the property prices reaches 20–30% (or until the government can no longer resist the political pressure for announcing some supportive measures on the property market). At this stage, it could start to slow down the fall through a few rounds of relaxation of the curbing measures. Although a substantial portion of pent-up demand will disappear during the expected plunge, unwinding the curbing measures could still release a moderate amount of pent-up demand, which will help to slow down the fall in property prices at that time. Nevertheless, the gigantic size of Hong Kong's property bubble would mean that the property prices have to fall by 40–60% before it could reach the long-term sustainable level.[38] The subsequent fall in the property prices after the policy announcement will unavoidably weaken the market's confidence on the government's ability to contain the fall in property prices.[39] Thus, the government has to make it clear at the announcement date that

(i) the unwinding of the policy measures is just a normalization of the market setting;

(ii) potential property buyers should be prudent and careful when making their property investment decisions; and

(iii) for the time being, the government will let the market force search for the equilibrium. The government will implement more serious policy measures if it believes Hong Kong's property prices have fallen too much.

Obviously, Hong Kong's property prices will stabilize for a while before they exhibit another plunge with further bad news from the financial industry, the economy and other areas.

At this stage and before the banking and financial industry make fire sales, the Hong Kong government should start progressively announcing the proposed policy measures outlined in Section 4.5.1, i.e., the Hong Kong version of TARP, the temporary change in the mark-to-market rule,

---

[38] As mentioned in the other sections, the property prices could, in the short term, fall by 60–75% if there are not enough supportive measures from the government.

[39] Note that the confidence issue will be more serious if the government announces the unwinding of the curbing measures too early (say, at the time of just 10% cumulated fall of property prices from the peak).

encouraging the banks to raise capital before the stress test, encouraging the practice of temporarily allowing the distressed mortgagees to pay only the mortgage interest and the mini QE.

Meanwhile, before the firms make the massive layoffs, the government should announce the proposed tax rebate measures outlined in Section 4.5.2.

PART IV

FURTHER DISCUSSIONS ON THE HOUSING POLICIES IN ASIA

CHAPTER 5

FURTHER DISCUSSIONS ON THE PROPERTY MARKETS AND HOUSING POLICIES IN ASIA

In Chapter 1 (and Yip, 2011), the author has provided the basic theoretical framework on the property markets and housing policies in China and the other Asian economies. In this chapter, he will do further follow-up discussions which are not yet addressed. While these discussions could still be preliminary thoughts, they are so important that it is worthwhile for him to write it down for further follow-up research.

5.1 INEQUALITY AND UNEVEN DISTRIBUTION OF PROPERTIES

5.1.1 High Potential Capital Gain of Property Ownership in Asia

In Chapter 1, the author has explained that property prices will rise with inflation, GDP growth, urbanization as well as improvements in transportation and infrastructure. Together with the absence of capital gain tax, this has made property investment extremely profitable and attractive (see Box 5.1. for an illustration). In fact, Asian households who own properties have ended up with substantial growth of wealth over the past few decades. This has in turn (i) made property investment a traditional investment wisdom in these Asian economies and (ii) induced most Asian citizens to spend a lot of time, effort and resources in property investment.

Box 5.1:   Property investment as a highly profitable long-term investment in Asia: An illustration

To appreciate property investment as an attractive long-term investment in Asia, first note that long-term inflation rate in many Asian economies will be in the range of 2–6% per annum. Added to this, economic and population growth could mean another 3–6% per annum potential long-term rise in property prices. These would mean that potential long-term capital gain from property investment in Asia will be in the range of 5–12% per annum, with occasional jumps in capital gain due to improvements in transportation and infrastructure around the related properties. (*Note*: The visibility of the long-term capital gain could be complicated by the short-term volatility of property prices. For example, if the related government does not do a good job in controlling its money supply, inflation or property prices, the short-term capital gain for property investment could be very big (e.g., 10–30% for a few years) until a severe correction of property prices. If an investor bought a property at an overheated price or during the property bubble, he might be forced to sell the property with heavy losses during the crash. Nevertheless, as long as the investor does not buy a property at a highly overheated price or manages to hold the property through the crisis, he should be able to benefit from the long-term capital gain.)

Unfortunately, these have also caused further undesirable effects on these economies. In what follows, the author will discuss some of these undesirable effects.

5.1.2 Property Price will Rise to Such A Level where A Significant Portion of Households Could Not Afford to Own their Homes

In Section 5.1.1, we have seen the huge potential capital gain from property ownership in Asia. Meanwhile, deep inside the Asian culture, there is a strong desire for Asian citizens to own as many properties as possible.[1]

---

[1] Possibly because of the past history of political and economic instability as well as weak social welfare system, the insecure feeling inherent in the Chinese (and East Asians) has made them almost insatiable when it comes to wealth holdings, e.g., eager to hold as many properties as possible. The absence of capital gain tax also provides the Chinese and East Asians a strong incentive to hold as many properties as possible.

Together with the high wealth and permanent income inequality in Asia, these would mean the following strong result:

Free market force will push the property prices to high enough levels so that the more well-off could own many flats (with some rich households owning tens or even hundreds of flats), while a significant portion of households could not afford to own their homes. Even for those who just manage to own one flat, economic pressure to service the mortgage installment will be enormous.[2] In fact, a new term "property slave" was created in China and some Asian economies to describe this group of people.

That is, as long as there is wealth (or permanent income) inequality and the rich people have the desire (or find it beneficial) to own more than one flat, property prices will rise to high enough levels so that the rich people's extra demand for properties would be satisfied at the cost of lower homeownership for the low-to-middle income group and higher property prices for the middle to middle-high income group (see also the simulation results in Chapter 6). Furthermore,

(i) the greater the inequality,
(ii) the greater the cultural desire to own more flats, and
(iii) the greater the benefit of property ownership,

the greater the above problems will be. Given that China and the Asian economies score extremely badly in the above three dimensions, it is important for these Asian governments (a) not to rely on just free market

---

[2]Note that there are two forces acting on the well-being of these property slaves. On one hand, the high property prices, and hence the heavy monthly mortgage installment burden, would make their life very miserable in the first 5–10 years after the purchase of their properties. If they bought it at the wrong time and were subsequently forced to sell during the bursting of property bubble, then life would be even more miserable for them. On the other hand, if they bought the flat at the right time or the normal time, so that they managed to keep their properties, then they would still have a handsome pecuniary gain, which could help to support the households' retirement need when they downgraded their flats to smaller units. Nevertheless, such a capital gain is also obtained at the cost of great hardship in the early years.

force to do the housing allocation and (b) to provide sufficient amount of various types of public housing to eligible households. (Note that the discussion in this section has not included (i) the market structure problem and (ii) the higher likelihood of property bubbles highlighted in the previous chapters, which would mean even stronger reasons for a major role of affordable public flats in these Asian economies.)

5.1.3 Vicious Cycle between Inequality and Uneven Distribution of Properties

Given the high potential capital gain from property ownership, there are now evidences that the uneven distribution of properties to the richer groups in Asia has caused greater wealth and income inequality. There are also evidences that the greater inequality has caused more uneven distribution of properties to the richer group. That is, there is now a vicious cycle between inequality and uneven distribution of properties in China and the other Asian economies. If not rectified or properly controlled, this could eventually cause serious social and political instability or unrest in the future. (*Note*: Again, the provision of sufficient amount of affordable public flats to eligible households could at least mitigate the problem, and imply a limit on such a vicious cycle.)

5.2 IS THE QUANTITY OF HOUSING LESS THAN SOCIAL OPTIMAL?

Given the market structure problem highlighted in the previous chapters, an interesting question is whether the quantity of housing in the Asian economies is less than the social optimal.

The author believes there are two opposing forces working here. Firstly, with the informal cartel and the indicator effect highlighted in the previous chapters, developers in these Asian economies are able to charge a high property price through the "industrial practice" or "common adoption" of high range of gross profit margins for their housing units (e.g., 40–60% in China and Hong Kong, and 30–50% in Singapore). Thus, *ceteris paribus*, the high housing price would tend to result in a quantity of housing far below the social optimal level.

On the other hand, because of the huge potential capital gain from property ownership and the absence of capital gain tax in Asia, there is also a huge investment demand for properties in Asia. *Ceteris paribus*, this would tend to increase the available number of housing units in Asia (i.e., the richer people in Asia will buy more flats and rent them out to those who do not have the wealth or permanent income to buy the flat).

Nevertheless, given that the housing prices in these Asian economies are far above the average total costs and marginal costs, the total quantity of housing in these economies should be far less than the social optimal level, albeit not necessarily in the form of the *total number of housing units* but in the form of *total size of all housing units*. That is, because of the high housing prices, it is highly likely that the total size of all housing units is far below the social optimal, although the total number of housing units may not be that far away from what the Asian citizens want. One clear example is Hong Kong where some flat owners partition a normal flat into 3–5 (and in some cases over 10) partitioned units and rent them out to the lower-income households. As a result, the total number of housing units (i.e., number of normal non-partitioned flats plus the number of partitioned units) may not be too far away from the number of households, but the total living areas of households are definitely far below the social optimal level. In fact, flat size in Hong Kong is squeezed to extremely pressurizing and psychologically unhealthy levels.

While the case in Hong Kong is more on the extreme side, Yip (2011) also noted that developers have managed to keep reducing the flat sizes in China, Singapore and other Asian economies over the past few decades. If left unattended, the flat size in these Asian economies could keep falling to psychologically unhealthy levels.

5.3 NEGATIVE EFFECT ON BUSINESS VENTURES, INNOVATION AND BUSINESS ETHIC

5.3.1 Negative Effect on the Start-up Cost and Risk of New Business Formation

Another important question is whether the high property prices in these Asian economies would substantially increase the risk and start-up cost of new firm formation and business ventures. Although new firms are usually small in size at the beginning, some of them might eventually grow into big firms with significant contribution to the economy. In fact, most existing big private firms started from sizes that were far smaller than their current sizes. Thus, new firm formation and business ventures are important sources of economic development and growth, and an economy with a low rate of new firm formation and business ventures is unlikely to be promising in the distant future.

Similar to the case of residential properties, developers have strong pricing power in new offices, retail premises and flatted factories in urban Asia. (*Note*: as explained in the footnote, factory spaces in rural Asia could behave differently.[3]) As a result, these developers were able to charge very high prices or high rentals for these commercial properties in urban Asia.[4] Meanwhile, the high residential property prices, and hence the high residential rentals, in these Asian economies have also contributed to higher wages and higher costs of living. As wages and rentals for these commercial properties are important costs of business, this would in turn mean high start-up cost and high risk for new firm formation in urban Asia.

Again, Hong Kong is a clear example with such a negative effect, and its experience would provide an important lesson on the potential risk in other Asian economies. In the 1960s–1980s during which rentals and wages were relatively low, Hong Kong was a vibrant economy with the formation of a lot of small businesses. However, after the rapid rise of property prices in the 1990s, Hong Kong's rentals, wages and costs of

---

[3]As there is still plenty of space in rural Asia and local governments in rural Asia would like to attract manufacturers to build their factories there, manufacturers would usually be able to get the required land at a reasonable cost from the local government and build their factories at a decent cost without paying a high price to the developers. Meanwhile, wages and costs of living are cheap in rural Asia. Thus, manufacturers in Asia could still maintain their competitiveness by relocating their production lines to rural areas.

[4]Unlike residential properties, which are direct demand and whose values could be highly subjective, commercial properties are of the derived demand category whose values are derived from the expected rental income. As a result, indicator effect may be weaker for resale commercial properties. Nevertheless, limitation of land in the urban areas and the industrial practice of high gross profit margin for commercial properties could still mean very high prices and very high rentals for commercial properties.

living have become so high that it is no longer a competitive economy. After the hollowing-out of its manufacturing industries to China at that time, there is now basically no manufacturing industry in Hong Kong.[5] Even for the service industry, the high wages and rentals would imply a very high start-up cost and risk for new business. As a result, new small business formation is now much lower than that in the 1960s–1980s. This has in turn resulted in a much lower growth rate in Hong Kong. In fact, Hong Kong is now locked in a vicious cycle of high property prices, high wages, high rentals, high costs of living and lack of growth prospect.

Fortunately, the current situation in China and other Asian economies is far less serious than that in Hong Kong (at least wages and prices of rural factory spaces in these economies are still not that high). Nevertheless, if the prices of their residential units, offices, retailed premises and flatted factories continue to rise at the current pace, these Asian economies would become less and less competitive. In fact, there are early signs in China and some Asian economies that the rapid rise in property prices, rentals and wages was associated with a significant drop in new business formation.

5.3.2 Negative Effect on Business Ventures and Innovation

Because of the attractive return from property investment outlined in Section 5.1.1, many smart Asians found that the best strategy to increase their wealth was through property investment instead of the hard business ventures or innovation.

This could again be illustrated by the following examples in Hong Kong. In order to earn profits amid the high rentals in the late 1990s, restaurant operators in Hong Kong were so innovative that the same restaurant space was used to run business for long hours: on top of the normal lunch and dinner business with standard charges, they also managed to use

---

[5] Unlike the case of Hong Kong, Singapore has managed to upgrade some industries (e.g., from the shipbuilding industry to the oil rig building industry) and develop some new industries (e.g., the pharmaceutical manufacturing industry). As a result, the manufacturing industry still represents about 20–25% of the Singapore economy. Recently, the Singapore government is working to develop the aerospace industry by attracting successful foreign firms to set up their production lines and repair centers in Singapore.

various types of discount or special services to attract large numbers of customers during the early breakfast hours (i.e., 5am–7am), breakfast hours (i.e., 7am–12am), afternoon-tea hours (i.e., 2pm–5pm) and late supper hours (i.e., 9pm–12am).[6] These innovative arrangements had, at the beginning, resulted in an increase in profit for the restaurant operators. For example, a lot of retirees would like to have dim-sum during the afternoon-tea hours and some other citizens would like to have good food with attractive discounts during the late supper hours. Nevertheless, with the jump in their profits, owners of the restaurant premises soon found that they could raise the rentals substantially. When these innovative restaurant practices became new standard practices among the restaurant operators, rentals of restaurant premises also rose to a high enough level that normal restaurant operators could only earn a normal profit,[7] and owners of the restaurant premises were the ones who benefitted the most from the innovative practices.

Similarly, to help the economy to recover from the 1997 financial crisis, the Hong Kong government and the Chinese government have made great effort to encourage Chinese tourists to visit Hong Kong. At the beginning, retailers benefitted a lot from the sharp increase in Chinese tourists. Again, owners of the retailed premises soon found that they could raise the rentals to share a significant part of the rise in profit.[8]

---

[6] In some cases, the restaurant would provide dinner cum mahjong (i.e., a Chinese gambling game) to attract customers interested in playing mahjong with their friends.

[7] Of course, for outstanding restaurant operators whose cooking or services could not be easily copied, they could still earn abnormal profit. Nevertheless, given the competitiveness of, and the large number of, talented cooks in Hong Hong's restaurant industry, it would not be easy to keep the restaurant's food and services unique for too long. As a result, there could only be a moderate percentage of restaurant operators who could earn an abnormal profit.

[8] Unlike the case of restaurant business, retailers for the tourists are more heterogeneous (e.g., the profit margins for selling gold-wares, electrical appliances, baby milk powders, medicine and branded make-up could be very different from each other). Some branded products may also imply that large reputable chain retailers would have an advantage over small retailers. As a result, there could still be some abnormal profit for some of these retailers even if part of it was also "taken away" by the higher rentals of the retail premises.

These two examples illustrate that, instead of doing the hard innovative job or business ventures, owning a commercial property at a good location would ensure that the investor could benefit from any innovative business that is related to his commercial property. Furthermore, as explained in Section 5.1.1, there would also be ongoing capital gain and rental increments due to inflation, economic and population growth, urbanization, improvement in transportation and infrastructure (i.e., continuously "working for" the return of the property owners).[9] While their rental income would be taxed, capital gain was never taxed because of the absence of capital gain tax in Asia.[10]

Because of the huge potential long-term capital gain from property investment, a lot of smart and talented people have put in much attention, effort and resources into property investment. Nevertheless, their successes would only mean a transfer of wealth and incomes (among citizens of the same or different generations), instead of creating value-added or growth prospect for the economy. In other words, because of the huge potential capital gain form property investment, a lot of talent, human effort, funds and resources were diverted (and wasted) into property investment. Without this, these more talented people would spend their effort, attention, funds and resources in business ventures and innovation, which would be growth-enhancing. Among these successful cases, some could even keep growing into huge corporations of national and international significance.

5.3.3 Negative Effect on Business Ethic

High property prices could also cause a significant negative effect on business ethics, which would further damage the well-being of its citizens. For

---

[9]Of course, developers could also share part of the profit by building new retail malls in various tourist areas. Nevertheless, given the limitation of space for more retail malls in the tourist areas, rentals of these retail premises still rose a lot. In fact, Hong Kong developers are so smart that most of them usually rent out the retail premises instead of selling them.

[10]While commercial property investors could experience much bigger capital gain than residential property investors, they could also lose heavily if they buy the commercial properties during the bubble period and are then forced (say, because of overleveraging) to sell during the crisis after the bursting of the bubble.

example, with high property prices, some private-sector doctors could recommend their patients to undergo unnecessary operations simply because they have to earn enough money to pay the mortgages of their few expensive flats. In fact, the author has seen a case in Hong Kong where a private sector doctor recommended a 95-year old woman to undergo an operation by claiming that she could live beyond the age of 100 years if she did the operation. The end result was that the 95-year old woman died soon after the operation. (*Note*: Many doctors in Hong Kong, especially those working in the government hospital, are devoted doctors. However, given that the high real property prices in Hong Kong and many other Asian economies, there is a reasonable chance that some private sector doctors in these economies recommend their patients to undergo unnecessary operations or medical procedures. For example, it is rather common for private sector doctors in Hong Kong and Singapore to recommend pregnant women to have the birth delivery through operations instead of natural delivery. In fact, because of this principal–agent problem, the author will only go to the government hospitals in both Hong Kong and Singapore.) Another malpractice is that private hospitals in Hong Kong try to hide the charges to the clients before the medical treatments or operations, and then send very expensive bills to clients after the medical treatments or operations. During the property bubble period in 1996–1997, the author also saw a case in which a middle-class partially subsidized hospital managed to use a trick to collect HK$2.7 million from a professional (i.e., by putting his mother in an intensive-care room (with a daily charge of HK$30,000) instead of a normal room for 90 days, while knowing that his mother had zero chance of survival).

Such type of malpractice is not only limited to the medical industry, but also the other industries in Hong Kong. For example, with the heavy losses of many male property investors since the plunge of Hong Kong's property bubble in 1997–2003, some beauty-care operators found that it was a good business to mislead their female clients to undergo expensive and probably not effective beauty-care procedures. Some big companies, such as cable TV, also tried to attract clients to use credit cards to autopay for the scheme at the beginning and then make it extremely difficult for the clients to cancel the scheme while automatically deducting the charge from the clients' credit card every year.

In the case of China, it is an open secret that doctors in both the private and public hospitals will recommend to their patients expensive medicines whose suppliers will provide a handsome rebate or commission to the related hospitals and doctors. As a result, the real cost of having medical treatment in China is extremely high. Behind these medical malpractices are rising property prices, rising rentals and rising costs of living. Without a proper control on the rising and high property prices, it is hard for the hospitals and doctors in China to give up these malpractices: even if some really devoted doctors want to give it up, it will be very difficult to go against the enormous vested interests behind the malpractices.

Again, such kind of malpractice does not only happen in the medical industry. Because of the rising costs of living created by the rising property prices and rising rentals, widespread malpractice was also seen in the education, finance, banking, media, food, agriculture and many other industries in China. The damages of these deteriorations of business ethics are so enormous that it is affecting most citizens in China, leading to huge living pressure and low health safety standards.

5.4 FURTHER DISCUSSIONS ON THE ROLE OF PUBLIC FLATS

In May 2015 and then in March 2016, in view that China has difficulty in achieving the 7% target growth rate, the author published a policy article recommending the Chinese government to supply and sell a huge number of public flats to eligible households. As Chinese households' demand for these public flats are enormous, the article highlighted that such a policy proposal could help China reachieve at least 8% GDP growth for at least the next 1–2 decades. Meanwhile, the proposal would help hundred millions of Chinese households fulfill their dreams of owning their homes at affordable prices, and therefore enable them to share the benefit of the economic growth in China.

The article first noted that the anti-corruption campaign implemented by President Xi Jinping and Mr. Wang Qishan would be recorded down in Chinese history with good comments and appreciation. If they could adopt the above proposal to help Chinese households to own their homes and be free from the enormous economic pain caused by the high real property price, their historical status would be comparable to great former Chinese leaders such as Mr. Deng Xiao Peng. On the other hand, if they continued to be misled by the badly trained (or corrupted) economic officials and think-tanks to use the rise in share prices to maintain China's economic growth, there would soon be a stock market bubble, which would eventually burst. The severe recession during the bursting would then weaken their authority of ruling and leave them a black mark in Chinese history. The article also suggested them to urge the Chinese central bank to correct the exchange rate policy mistake at that time. Otherwise, the policy mistake would drag China's export and GDP growth further down in the subsequent years. Worse still, the mistake could make the Chinese economy vulnerable to a currency attack, and even a financial crisis in the subsequent years.

5.4.1 Core Design of the Proposal Made in 2007

Regarding the details of the proposal, the article first recalled the author's following core design proposed in 2007.[11] The government should provide the following types of public flats with the following recommended percentages in China's *new housing supply* per year:

(a) 10% in low rental flats for the lowest income group;
(b) 15% in economy flats (i.e., flats with zero or negligible profit to the government) for sales to the low to middle-low income groups;
(c) 45% in a few classes of sandwich-class flats (i.e., flats with reasonable profit to the government and yet at affordable prices to eligible citizens) for sales to the middle-low to middle-high income groups;
(d) 30% in private flats for the middle-high to high income groups.

With the support of former President Hu Jintao, China had thereafter decided to build a large number of economy flats, two-limit flats and low-rental flats and set up a new ministry (i.e., the Ministry of Housing and Urban–Rural Development) to implement the housing plan. In the second year, the Chinese government also set the 5-year public housing targets and included them in the 12th 5-year plan.

---

[11] The proposal was subsequently included in Yip (2011, Chapters 9 and 10).

5.4.2 Good Proposal Wasted by Ignorant and Corrupted Officials

Unfortunately, that very good plan was wasted by some ignorant officials at the senior levels and some corrupted officials at the junior levels. For example, with the wrong belief that the government should not earn profit from the public flats, these senior officials mistakenly deleted the proposed sandwich-class flats (i.e., the core part of the author's proposal) from the public housing plan at that time. As a result, the mistake has at the same time destroyed the following important design in the author's proposal:

The new public housing authority could allow eligible applicants to buy the planned sandwich-class flats through a 15–20% downpayment and an 80–85% bank loans. Once the planned sandwich-class housing estate is fully (or 90%) subscribed, the housing authority could use the downpayment to support the first phase of construction. When the first phase construction is completed, the housing authority would ask the banks to do the necessary progress inspection and then release the first batch of bank loans to support the second phase construction. When the second phase construction is completed, the housing authority would again ask the bank to do the necessary progress inspection and then release the second batch of bank loans to support the third phase construction. This procedure would be repeated until the construction is completed and the housing authority collects the profit from the sandwich-class flats.

The core of the design is that it does not require any fiscal support from the central and local governments. Thus, China could immediately and simultaneously start a large number of sandwich-class housing estates *in each district*. (In fact, the above design could also be used to start a decent number of economy flats in each district.) Thereafter, part of the profit collected from the sandwich-class flat scheme could be used to support the whole construction cost of low-rental flats and other reforms.

Unfortunately, once the above design was destroyed because of the cancellation of the sandwich-class flat scheme, the initial construction cost of the economy flats and the whole construction cost of the low-rental flats have to be financed by the limited fiscal budget. Because of the limit of the fiscal budget, the actual construction scale of these public flats was drastically reduced to *not meaningful enough levels*. Worse still, the change had (i) removed the local governments' incentives to support the public flat schemes (i.e., they could no longer have additional fiscal revenue through the sharing of profit from the sandwich-class scheme) and (ii) created strong disincentives for the local governments to implement the proposed schemes (i.e., the whole construction cost of the low-rental flats will increase their fiscal burden, and the initial construction cost of the economy flats would increase their initial fiscal burden). As a result, the local governments had used various types of tricks to scale down and delay the construction of the public flats, thus leading to further reduction of the actual construction of the public flats to even less meaningful levels. Because of this mistake, many Chinese households are still suffering from the enormous pain of high real property price.

5.4.3 Further Details of the Design

After explaining the above mistakes committed by some Chinese senior officials, the article recommended the Chinese government to restart the housing schemes according to the proposed design. As Chinese households' demand for the public flats at affordable prices is enormous, the proposal could actually help China to achieve not only 7% GDP growth in the near future, but at least 8% GDP growth *for the next 1–2 decades*.

With the profit from the sandwich-class flats, the whole public housing scheme could be permanently sustainable without any fiscal support from the government. Furthermore, because of the huge potential demand for the sandwich-class flats, even a fair gross profit margin of, say, 15–20% could mean enormous amount of total profit. Thus, the government could use part of this enormous profit to support the low-rental flat scheme and other reforms such as the medical reform or the education reform. Thereafter, the government could invest the remaining part of the enormous profit overseas so that (i) during the normal time, it could help China to earn normal investment return and (ii) in case of an economic crisis in China, it could be repatriated back to help China to survive through, and recover from, a crisis. Furthermore, as the local governments could share part of the profit from the sandwich-class flats, there would be strong incentives for them to support at least the sandwich-class flat scheme.[12]

The article also recommended the following progressive profit margin (above the construction cost and land cost) for the economy and sand-wich-class flats: a 5–10% profit margin for the economy flats (with only basic quality, basic decoration, basic facilities and basic sizes at less-convenient location); a 10–15% profit margin for the lowest class of sandwich-class flats (with quality, facilities, decoration and location slightly better than the economy flats); a 15–20% profit margin for the medium class sandwich-class flats and a 20–25% profit margin for the highest class of sandwich-class flats (with quality, decoration, facilities and location comparable to mass-market private flats, but with 8–10-year resale restriction, an income ceiling for eligible applicants and sublet restriction). With the restriction that each eligible household could only apply for one public flat, the government could let the applicants choose the type of public flats they want to apply, and start the construction once the public flats are fully (or 90%) subscribed. As most citizens believe the class of their flats would reflect their social status, they would tend to choose the higher class of flats as long as they can afford it. This would in turn minimize the incentives for corruption at the origin — of course, the government still needs to (i) ensure that each household (including the corrupted officials) could at most be allocated one and only one public flat and (ii) stick to the 8–10-year resale restriction for the public flats.[13]

Furthermore, as explained in Yip (2011), the profit from the public flats is in fact a tax. In fact, it is a tax with the least economic distortion, and is the only tax in the world that the citizens are willing to queue over-night to pay the tax (i.e., queue overnight to buy the public flat). Finally,

---

[12] For the economy flats, a 5–10% profit on top of the construction cost and land cost, plus the presale arrangement outlined in Section 5.4.2, will help to remove the disincentives and create moderate incentives for the local governments to support and implement the econ-omy flat scheme. To ensure some low-rental flats would be built by the local governments, the central government could, at the beginning, set a certain mandatory, but subsequently adjustable, ratio (e.g., 9:2 or 5:1) between the sandwich-class flats and low-rental flats.

[13] If the government follows the resale restriction strictly, corrupted officials may not dare to hold a lot of public flats for 8–10 years, as the risk of being discovered within such a long period would make them extremely restless during the 8–10-year resale restrictions.

the 7:3 recommended ratio between the public flats and the private flats (the actual ratio in Singapore is 8:2) is meant to create a healthy competition between public and private flats: private flats will give incentives and pressure for the housing development authority to improve the quality of its public flats, while the price of the public flats will help to contain the level (and future rise) of private flat prices. In fact, as explained in Yip (2011), appropriate setting of public flat prices could (i) in the short run help pull down the private flat prices with high controllability (i.e., the prices of mass-market private flats would not fall below the price of the highest-class sandwich-class flats) and (ii) in the long run reduce the likelihood of property bubble.

Finally, the article highlights that the best way for China to keep its high GDP growth for the next 1–2 decades is to do the hard and real job of building the public flats to fulfill the Chinese households' housing dream. This would also give China 1–2 decades of stable property prices. During this period, Chinese citizens would turn their attention back to real businesses and innovations, which would in turn help China to discover and cultivate new areas of economic growth and development.

On the other hand, using the rise of share price to achieve China's GDP growth target would eventually lead to a stock market bubble, whose bursting will be just a matter of time. Worse still, the damage of the bursting would be far more serious and damaging than the bursting in 2007–2008, as China has already developed highly leveraged margin trading, short selling facilities and stock futures. When a lot of individual investors get their hand burnt, and other innocent people also get hurt by the recession triggered by the bursting of stock market bubble, the Chinese leaders' (and the Chinese Communist Party's) reputation, public image and moral authority would be seriously damaged. Thus, the Chinese leaders have to be cautious with the risk that the corrupted officials could earn a lot of money from the stock market and then "disappear", while leaving the leaders' and the Party's public rating seriously damaged. More importantly, public rating could be a very fragile and sophisticated thing. That is, once the public rating falls because of the mistake, it will be very difficult for it to rise back. Worse still, once the rating falls beyond an acceptable threshold, a lot of people (e.g., political enemies or even neutral third parties) would be tempted to criticize the leaders, which would in turn trigger further reduction in the public rating and induce more criticism and challenges. (*Postscript*: As predicted by the articles, a stock market bubble did emerge in 2014–2015 and burst in 2015–2016. The Chairman of the Securities Regulatory Commission was also transferred out from the post because of the mistake.)

5.4.4 Final Comment: Scale Matters

Finally, it should be noted that scale matters in China's housing issue. That is, the number of public flats, especially the number of the proposed sandwich-class public flats, has to be big enough to

(1) help contain the rise in private property prices;
(2) help the poor households to stay in the low-rental flats and enable each low to middle-high income household to own a public flat that corresponds to its preference and affordability;
(3) help keep China's annual GDP growth at around 8% for at least another 1–2 decades (so that China would have the extra time to sort out the appropriate growth strategy in the future).

Unfortunately, because of the sensitivity of the discussion, the author's published article (in the major Hong Kong financial newspaper)

(a) had only limited citations in China at that time;
(b) was not used as an internal report to the Chinese leaders through the Xinhua News Agency.

As a result, the Chinese government had thereafter continued to

(i) use the wrong policies to stimulate growth (e.g., attempting to use the rise in share prices and even a stock market bubble to achieve higher growth);
(ii) adopt the wrong exchange rate policy (e.g., keeping renminbi stable against the rising US dollar at that time instead of keeping a stable NEER), which had in turn dragged China's export and GDP growth and made renminbi vulnerable to a speculative attack in the more distant future.

More importantly, there is no significant increase in the public housing and no discussion on the proposed sandwich-class flats. Until such a mistake is corrected, it could be anticipated that China's growth would continue to be weak for a prolonged period, with the possibility of a bursting of the stock market bubble and a speculative attack or loss in confidence on the exchange value of renminbi. (*Postscript*: As predicted by these articles, (i) China's stock market bubble did burst in August 2015; (ii) the exchange rate policy mistake eventually caused a loss of confidence on renminbi, a capital flight from China and a speculative attack on renminbi in the offshore renminbi futures market and huge losses in China's foreign reserves; (iii) China's GDP growth continued to be weak at the range of 6–7% per annum.)

CHAPTER 6

SOME NEW RESEARCH RESULTS ON LONG-TERM HOUSING POLICIES IN ASIA

by G. S. Teo* and P. S. L. Yip

In this chapter, we will present some of our latest simulation results related to long-term housing polices in Asia. In particular, we will show that

(a) the market structure problem in the Asian property markets could result in high real property prices and a significant portion of house-holds who cannot afford to own their homes;

(b) the high wealth (or permanent income) inequality in these economies would further increase the proportion of households who cannot afford to own their home.

Thereafter, we will show that government's direct supply and sale of "affordable public flats" to eligible households could substantially mitigate the above problems. Nevertheless, there will still be a portion of households who cannot afford to buy the affordable public flats, and provision of "low-rental flats" to this group is necessary. The simulation results also show that

(i) by providing these public flats at less convenient locations, of basic quality and/or of basic size, the government could enable more

---

* Dr. Ernie Teo Gin Swee, Sim Kee Boon Institute of Financial Economics, Singapore Management University.

households to own their homes and reduce the required subsidies to the low-rental flats;

(ii) by charging a slightly higher price for the affordable public flats and using the profit to subsidize the low-rental flats, the combined public housing scheme (i.e., affordable public flat scheme and low-rental flat scheme) would be self-budget-balanced and fiscally sustainable.

6.1 THE ROLE OF INEQUALITY AND MARKET STRUCTURE PROBLEM IN ASIA'S PROPERTY MARKETS

In Chapter 1, the author has provided the basic theoretical framework for the housing market in urban Asia. In particular, he has explained that the market structure of urban Asian property markets is very different from that in the Western world[1]: To satisfy the huge housing demand with the limited land in urban Asia, the related governments have to opt for a large proportion of high-rise apartments, which would involve a high fixed development cost and hence implies a barrier of entry (i.e., barrier of scale) in the property market in urban Asia. In addition, there is an additional barrier of entry due to dynamic cumulated efficiency. With the barriers of entry, the differentiated characteristics among various housing estates and the limited amount of auctioned land at each period, each developer in Asia is in fact facing a downward sloping, instead of a horizontal, demand curve for the housing units in his housing estate. As a result, these developers are able to set the prices of their housing units somewhat different from the market price. Thus, in sharp contrast to what is assumed in the simple supply and demand analysis and the latest housing models in the Western world, developers in Asia are *price setters*, instead of price takers, of their housing units. Worse still, the Asian property markets have thereafter developed the following practices and culture

---

[1] Chapter 1 also explains that, because of the unique market structure problem in the Asian property markets, (i) the simple supply and demand analysis and the latest housing models (i.e., the first generation and second-generation models) in the Western world could not be the right model for the Asian property markets and (ii) a mechanical application of these models for the analysis of the Asian property market could lead to very wrong assessments of the markets and highly misleading housing policies in Asia.

that would substantially augment the developers' market (pricing) power not only in the market of new properties but also in the market of all properties (i.e., both the new and resale properties):

(a) Asian developers were able to form an informal cartel through the common adoption of an industrial practice or "norm" of a *high, wide* and *adjustable* range of gross profit margin for their housing units (e.g., 30–50% for Singapore and 40–60% for China during the boom period, and 20–40% for Singapore and 30–50% for China during the consolidation period); and

(b) A culture where there is a strong indicator effect from new property prices and resale property prices.[2]

As a result, Asian developers could collectively set the average property price at a level well above the social optimal, which would in turn imply (i) the quantity of housing would be well below the social optimal level and (ii) the real housing prices will be painfully high for the low to middle-high income earners. Worse still, as explained in Chapter 1, because of the high wealth (and income) inequality in Asia, market force would only allocate the limited (i.e., the less than social-optimal) quantity of housing to those who are "rich" instead of those who "need" the flats for accommodation.

To analyze the impacts of the above market structure problem and wealth inequality on the *price level* and *affordability* of housing in Asia, we (i.e., Yip and Teo, 2014) built a simple model that captured the unique market structure problem and wealth inequality in these Asian property markets. With the new model, we run a large number of simulation exercises and find the following results:

---

[2]Without the indicator effect (i.e., no rise in resale property prices with the rise in new property price), developers in Asia would be less able to collectively set high prices for new properties, as their pricing power would be constrained by the competition from the "relatively stable" prices of the much bigger pool of resale properties. However, with the indicator effect (i.e., the prices of the much bigger pool of resale properties will follow the rise of the price of the smaller pool of new properties), developers would be able to collectively set high prices for the new properties, as such actions would be able to pull up the prices of resale properties through the indicator effect.

(1) As expected, the market structure problem (i.e., the price setting powers of developers through the informal cartel and the indicator effect) would result in (i) a very high real property price and (ii) a significant proportion of households who cannot afford to own their homes. Furthermore, the simulation results demonstrate that the market structure problem is the most important cause of the high property price and hence the huge economic pains experienced by the Asian households. To solve or mitigate the problem, it is important to design policies or new housing systems that could remove, or offset the above effects of, the market structure problem.

(2) As expected, higher wealth (or permanent income) inequality would also result in a greater proportion of households who cannot afford to own their homes.

(3) However, in sharp contrast to our initial expectation, higher wealth inequality would tend to reduce the real property price. Tracing back the logic within the model, we found that higher inequality would *ceteris paribus* reduce the effective demand for housing, which would in turn reduce the market price of housing. Thus, in sharp contrast to many people's impression, developers also dislike inequality, although their market (pricing) power is the main source of the problem.

(4) Economic growth will benefit the developers the most, but could only cause a second-order improvement in homeownership.

(5) On top of the sub-optimal amount of private properties allocated by the (distorted) market force, government's provision and sale of affordable public flats to eligible citizens could help a substantial proportion of households to own their homes.

(6) For any smooth distribution of wealth starting from zero or low enough wealth, there will always be a certain proportion of households who cannot afford to own their homes even if the government offers affordable public flats to eligible citizens at cost. Thus, on top of the proposed affordable public flat scheme, it is also important to provide low-rental flats for the very poor group of households.

To provide a better understanding of the above results and their policy implications, this section and Section 6.2 will reproduce some of the simulation results reported in Yip and Teo (2014).

6.1.1 Results for the Case of a Collectively Profit-maximizing Price

As explained in Chapter 1, the ranges of the commonly adopted industrial "norm" of gross profit margin in the Asian property markets are wide and adjustable (e.g., 40–60% in China and 30–50% in Singapore during the normal period, and 30–50% in China and 20–40% in Singapore during the consolidation period). Thus, it is possible that these Asian developers' profit-maximizing gross profit margin (or profit-maximizing price) would lie within the wide and adjustable range. In such a case, these Asian developers would usually be able to charge the profit-maximizing price for their housing units. To cater for such a possibility, we will report the simulation results for the following two cases:

(a) Section 6.1.1 will report the case in which the developers could through the informal cartel collectively set a profit-maximizing price for their housing units; and
(b) Section 6.1.2 will report the case in which the developers could collectively set a high, but not profit-maximizing, price for their housing units.

6.1.1.1 Simulation results for the benchmark case: Different inequality but same mean of wealth

Our first exercise is to analyze the effect of wealth inequality on the level of property price and homeownership. To single out the effect of wealth inequality, we will compare economies with different wealth inequalities but the same mean of wealth.[3] Table 6.1 reports the case of different

---

[3] In this chapter, we assume the following functional form of wealth distribution:

$$f(w_{it}) = (2 + \alpha_t)(3 + \alpha_t) \, (\beta_t - w_{it})^{1+\alpha_t} w_{it},$$

where w_{it} is household i's wealth at time t, and α_t and β_t are parameters that could change over time.

We also assume (i) flats of different characteristics could be measured and compared by the "characteristics-adjusted size"; (ii) the minimum available size of flat (measured in characteristics-adjusted size) is s and flats in the markets are measured in continuous multiple of s (e.g., $1.1s$ or $3.9s$) and (iii) the average total unit cost (i.e. total average cost for

Table 6.1:   Results for the Benchmark Case (rising inequality but same mean of wealth)

(α, β)	Mean	Gini	p*	Profit	m*	CAH
1.0, 0.9462	1/3	0.247	0.297	0.183	66.3%	36.2%
1.2, 0.97286	1/3	0.258	0.291	0.180	65.6%	37.3%
1.4, 0.98068	1/3	0.269	0.286	0.176	65.0%	38.7%
1.6, 0.98776	1/3	0.281	0.281	0.173	64.4%	39.3%
1.8, 0.99417	1/3	0.292	0.276	0.170	63.8%	40.3%
2.0, 1.0	1/3	0.303	0.271	0.167	63.1%	41.2%
2.2, 1.0053	1/3	0.314	0.267	0.165	62.5%	42.2%
2.4, 1.0101	1/3	0.325	0.263	0.162	62.0%	43.1%
2.6, 1.0145	1/3	0.337	0.259	0.186	61.4%	43.9%
2.8, 1.0186	1/3	0.348	0.255	0.156	60.8%	44.8%
3.0, 1.0223	1/3	0.359	0.251	0.154	60.2%	45.7%

Note: p^* = profit-max price; m^* = profit-max gross profit margin; CAH = cannot afford housing (%).

combinations of the wealth distribution parameters (α, β) so that all the sub-cases have different Gini coefficients (i.e., the third column) but the same mean of wealth (i.e., the second column).

As we can see from the table, *even for the case of moderate inequality (e.g., (α, β) = (1,0.9642) with a Gini coefficient of 0.247), there is quite a large proportion (e.g., 36.2%) of households who cannot afford to own their homes. For the case of higher inequality (e.g., (α, β) = (3,1.0223) with a Gini coefficient of 0.359), there will be quite a large increase in the proportion of households who cannot afford property (e.g., a 11.5 percentage points rise to 45.7%).* That is, *ceteris paribus*, a rise in inequality will mean fewer households can afford to own their homes. Such a result implies the following corollary: *if we compare two economies with the same mean but different inequality of wealth, the economy with higher inequality will ceteris paribus have fewer households who can afford to own their homes.*

---

flats of the minimum available size s) is c. By appropriate choice of dollar unit, we can set $c = 0.1$ (which will be $0.1 million if the dollar unit is $1 million, or $0.5 million if the dollar unit is $5 million). In other words, the price of flats expressed in the tables should be multiplied by the dollar unit.

With the large number of simulation results similar to that reported in Table 6.1, we can make the following conjecture:

Conjecture 1. Given any continuous and single-peaked wealth distribution and assuming that property developers act as an informal cartel, the higher the inequality (Gini coefficient),

1. the greater the proportion of households who cannot afford to own their homes;
2. the lower the profit-maximizing price (and hence the market price) per unit of property;
3. the lower the developers' gross profit margin.

While the first result in Conjecture 1 (i.e., higher inequality implies greater proportion of households who cannot afford to own their homes) is what we expect, the second and third results are surprisingly interesting. Tracing back the logics from our model, we found that the greater the inequality, the lower the effective housing demand for the same mean of wealth, and therefore the lower the profit-maximizing price of housing and lower the developers' gross profit margin. Thus, given the same mean of the distribution, developers also dislike inequality. However, as will be explained in Section 6.1.1.2, given any level of inequality, developers' pricing power does contribute to worse outcomes (e.g., higher market price for property and greater proportion of households who cannot afford to own their homes). In China and some Asian economies, there is now a popular criticism that "developers only build flats for the rich". If developers have the pricing power as assumed in Yip and Teo (2014) and this book, it is more than natural that they will only be interested in serving those who can afford to buy property (i.e., the "rich" in the above criticism). In view of this problem, Section 6.2 will explain why government provision and sales of affordable public flats (at lower price and profit margin) to the poorer groups is important.

6.1.1.2 Simulation results for the case of Asia over time: Economic growth with rising inequality and rising mean of wealth

Table 6.2 reports the case that is similar to the case of China and many Asian economies over the past few decades: economic growth resulted in rising inequality and rising mean of wealth, e.g., (α, β) take the values in column 1

Table 6.2:   Results for the Case of Asian Growth (rising inequality and rising mean of wealth)

(α, β)	Mean	Gini	p^*	Profit	m^*	CAH
1.0, 0.9462	1/3	0.247	0.297	0.183	66.3%	36.2%
1.2, 0.9802	(1/3)×104%	0.267	0.293	0.187	65.9%	37.1%
1.4, 0.9948	(1/3)×108%	0.287	0.288	0.192	65.3%	38.0%
1.6, 1.0079	(1/3)×112%	0.308	0.284	0.196	64.8%	38.9%
1.8, 1.0199	(1/3)×116%	0.330	0.280	0.200	64.3%	39.7%
2.0, 1.0309	(1/3)×120%	0.353	0.277	0.205	63.9%	40.5%
2.2, 1.0408	(1/3)×124%	0.376	0.273	0.208	63.4%	41.4%
2.4, 1.0499	(1/3)×118%	0.401	0.269	0.212	62.8%	42.2%
2.6, 1.0581	(1/3)×132%	0.426	0.265	0.215	62.3%	43.0%
2.8, 1.0657	(1/3)×136%	0.452	0.262	0.219	61.8%	43.7%
3.0, 1.0726	(1/3)×140%	0.479	0.259	0.222	61.4%	44.5%

Note: p^* = profit-max price; m^* = profit-max gross profit margin; CAH = cannot afford housing (%).

so that there is a gradual rise in the mean of wealth by up to 40% (i.e., the second column) and a rise in the Gini coefficient from 0.247 to 0.479 (i.e., the third column).[4]

As we can see from the table, with the additional rise in β on top of the same rise in α, developers' gross profit margins (i.e., the sixth column) will be higher when compared with the corresponding cases in Table 6.1. The profit-maximizing price (i.e., the fourth column) and hence the market price of housing will also be higher when compared with the corresponding cases in Table 6.1. Nevertheless, as shown in the fifth columns of Tables 6.1 and 6.2, the developers' collective profit could rise by 44% from 0.154 units to 0.222 units, mainly because the rise in wealth has caused a substantial increase in the effective demand for housing. Meanwhile, the rise in the market price is much more moderate than the rise in the wealth (i.e., the second column). As a result, the proportion of households who cannot afford property (i.e., the last column) is moderately lower than the corresponding cases in Table 6.1, even if there is a sharper rise in the Gini coefficient (i.e.,

---

[4]Note that β is actually the maximum of the wealth distribution. The rise in the mean wealth and Gini coefficient here are due to a rise in β and the rise in the shape parameter (α) of the distribution.

the third column) due to the change in the shape of distribution amid the economic growth. Thus, from the point of view of home-ownership, the rise in the wealth due to economic growth could still be good, even though it could cause a sharper rise in the Gini coefficient. Nevertheless, as illustrated in the last rows of Table 6.2 and Table 6.1, the increase in the home-ownership due to a 40% increase in the mean wealth is only of the order of 1.2 percentage points (=45.7–44.5%). Such a minor improvement suggests that it might not be a good idea to rely on the general rise in wealth or permanent income (i.e., economic growth) as a promising strategy to increase home-ownership. In Section 6.2, we will discuss more promising ways to increase homeownership.

Finally, with the above results of a substantial increase in the developers' collective profits and a relatively mild change in $p*$ and %CAH (percentage of households who cannot afford housing (CAH)), developers are likely to be the group that benefit the most from the above type of economic growth.

6.1.2 Results for the Case with Other Gross Profit Margins

While we are open to the possibility that developers could, through the informal cartel and the indicator effect, collectively set a profit-maximizing price for each period, it is also possible that the selected price corresponds to only a high, but not profit-maximizing, price. To allow for such a possibility, this section will report the simulation results in which the developers could collectively set (i) a high, but not profit-maximizing, gross profit margin of 50% and (ii) a moderately high gross profit margin of 30%. To allow for the possibility that the related government could find ways to reduce the gross profit margin to more reasonable levels, we also consider the case of a more reasonable gross profit margin of 10%. In particular, we are interested in the level of property price and the proportion of households who CAH in these scenarios.

As we can see from columns 4–7 of Table 6.3, for any given pair of (α, β), the higher the gross profit margin the developers could collectively charge (say, because of insufficient competition or the formation of the informal cartel), the higher the property price[5] and the greater the

---

[5] The large number of simulation results also confirm that the higher the general price (i.e., higher nominal levels of c and w_{ij}, the higher the nominal level of $p*$. Thus, one can infer that the greater the market structure problem, the higher the real property price.

Table 6.3:   Percentage of Households who Cannot Afford Housing (same mean of wealth)

(α, β)	Mean	Gini	$m = m^*$ %CAH (p^*)	$m = 50\%$ %CAH	$m = 30\%$ %CAH	$m = 10\%$ %CAH
1.0, 0.9462	1/3	0.247	36.2% (0.297)	19.2%	10.7%	6.8%
1.2, 0.97286	1/3	0.258	37.3% (0.291)	20.6%	11.6%	7.4%
1.4, 0.98068	1/3	0.269	38.7% (0.286)	22.0%	12.5%	8.0%
1.6, 0.98776	1/3	0.281	39.3% (0.281)	23.4%	13.3%	8.6%
1.8, 0.99417	1/3	0.292	40.3% (0.276)	24.8%	14.3%	9.2%
2.0, 1.0	1/3	0.303	41.2% (0.271)	26.3%	15.2%	9.8%
2.2, 1.0053	1/3	0.314	42.2% (0.267)	27.7%	16.1%	10.5%
2.4, 1.0101	1/3	0.325	43.1% (0.263)	29.1%	17.1%	11.1%
2.6, 1.0145	1/3	0.337	43.9% (0.259)	30.6%	18.0%	11.8%
2.8, 1.0186	1/3	0.348	44.8% (0.255)	32.0%	19.0%	12.5%
3.0, 1.0223	1/3	0.359	45.7% (0.251)	33.4%	20.0%	13.2%

proportion of households who cannot afford to own their homes. For example, if the developers could collectively charge a profit-maximizing m^*, the level of property price will be in the range of 0.251–0.297. On the other hand, for the cases of $m = 50\%$ and $m = 30\%$, the level of property price will be lower at 0.2 and 0.143, respectively. For the case where the government can find ways to reduce the market structure problem so that $m = 10\%$, the level of property price will fall further to 0.11. In fact, the level of property price in the case of $m = m^*$ is 2.3–2.7 times that in the case of $m = 10\%$. Because of the difference in the levels of property price, the proportion of households who CAH is also the highest for the case of $m = m^*$. This proportion is lower for the case of $m = 50\%$ and $m = 30\%$. If the government can find ways to reduce the market structure problem so that $m = 10\%$, it can substantially reduce the CAH by 29.8–32.5 percentage points to 6.8–13.2%. In Section 6.2, we will discuss one such way to help more households to own their homes.

6.1.2.1 *Combinations of high gross profit margin and high inequality*

Table 6.3 also suggests that the combination of high gross profit margins and high inequality would result in a large proportion of households who cannot afford property. For example, when the gross profit margin is at the profit-maximizing level and (α, β) takes the value of (3, 1.0223) so that the Gini coefficient is 0.359, the proportion of households who cannot afford property will be the highest (i.e., 45.7%) when compared with the other cases in the table. On the other hand, when the gross profit margin is at 10% and (α, β) take the values (1, 0.9462) so that the Gini coefficient is 0.247, the proportion of households who cannot afford property will be the lowest (i.e., 6.8%) when compared with the other cases in the table.

6.1.2.2 *Impacts of the inequality problem*

On top of these, Table 6.3 also suggests that inequality will, in general, have a moderately large effect on the proportion of households who cannot afford to own their homes. For example, when (α, β) takes the value of the first row of the table, i.e., (1, 0.9462) so that the Gini coefficient is 0.247, the proportion of households who could afford property for the four cases from profit-maximization to 10% gross profit margin will be 36.2%, 19.2%, 10.7% and 6.8%, respectively. On the other hand, when (α, β) takes the value of the last row of the table, i.e., (3, 1.0223) so that the Gini coefficient is 0.359, the corresponding proportions of households who cannot afford property will rise by 6.4–14.2 percentage points to 45.7%, 33.4%, 20.0% and 13.2%, respectively.

6.1.2.3 *Impacts of the market structure problem*

However, what is most striking is that Table 6.3 suggests the impacts of the market structure problem could be far greater than the impacts of inequality. For example, if there is sufficient competition in the Asian property market or there is sufficient government supply of affordable public flats so that the gross profit margin is only 10%, the proportion of households who CAH for the various levels of (α, β) and inequality in the table will only be 6.8–13.2%. On the other hand, if there is a market structure problem so that developers could charge a high gross profit margin of 50%, the proportion of households who cannot afford to own their homes will jump by 12.4–20.2 percentage points to 19.2–33.4%. If developers could collectively charge the profit-maximizing gross profit margin through the informal cartel, the jump in the proportion will be even greater (i.e., by 29.4–32.5 percentage points to 36.2–45.7%).

6.1.2.4 *Impacts of economic growth*

In the profit-maximizing case discussed in Section 6.1.1, we have seen that the increase in wealth will (i) help decrease the proportion of households who cannot afford to own their homes but (ii) the reduction in the proportion is relatively mild (e.g., of the order of only 1.2 percentage points). Tables 6.3 and 6.4 confirm that such results also apply to the cases of other gross profit margins. For example, when (α, β) take the value of (3, 1.0726) instead of (3, 1.0223), i.e., the last row of Table 6.4 instead of the last row of Table 6.3 so that there is a 40% rise instead of no rise in the mean wealth, there is only a moderate reduction of the proportion of households who cannot afford property by 1.1–2.1 percentage points (i.e., 1.2 (= 45.7–44.5), 2.1 (= 33.4–31.3), 1.5 (= 20.0–18.5) and 1.1 (=13.2–12.1) percentage points for the cases of $m = m^*$, 50%, 30% and 10%, respectively).

Table 6.4: Percentage of Household who Cannot Afford Housing (rising mean of wealth)

(α, β)	Mean	Gini	$m = m^*$ %CAH (p^*)	$m = 50\%$ %CAH	$m = 30\%$ %CAH	$m = 10\%$ %CAH
1.0, 0.9462	1/3	0.247	36.2% (0.297)	19.2%	10.7%	6.8%
1.2, 0.9802	(1/3)×104%	0.267	37.1% (0.293)	20.4%	11.4%	7.3%
1.4, 0.9948	(1/3)×108%	0.287	38.0% (0.288)	21.5%	12.1%	7.8%
1.6, 1.0079	(1/3)×112%	0.308	38.9% (0.284)	22.7%	12.9%	8.3%
1.8, 1.0199	(1/3)×116%	0.330	39.7% (0.280)	23.9%	13.6%	8.8%
2.0, 1.0309	(1/3)×120%	0.353	40.5% (0.277)	25.0%	14.4%	9.3%
2.2, 1.0408	(1/3)×124%	0.376	41.4% (0.273)	26.3%	15.2%	9.8%
2.4, 1.0499	(1/3)×128%	0.401	42.2% (0.269)	27.5%	16.0%	10.4%
2.6, 1.0581	(1/3)×132%	0.426	43.0% (0.265)	28.7%	16.8%	11.0%
2.8, 1.0657	(1/3)×136%	0.452	43.7% (0.262)	29.9%	17.6%	11.6%
3.0, 1.0726	(1/3)×140%	0.479	44.5% (0.259)	31.3%	18.5%	12.1%

6.1.2.5 *Always a certain percentage of very poor households who cannot afford housing: Need for low-rental housing*

Finally, Tables 6.3 and 6.4 suggest that, as long as we assume a smooth distribution of wealth starting from zero or a low enough wealth, there will always be a certain percentage of very poor households who cannot afford to own their homes even if the government manages to use some policies to achieve affordable housing with just 10% (or even 0%) gross profit margin. For example, as shown by the last column of Table 6.3 (Table 6.4), even if the government managed to reduce the gross profit margin of property development to 10%, there is still 6.8–13.2% (6.8–12.1%) of households who cannot afford to own their homes. Repeating the exercise for 0% gross profit margin, there is still 5.6–11.0% (5.6–10.1%) who cannot afford to own their homes. These results suggest that, on top of the normal scheme of providing affordable public flats to help eligible households to own their homes, it is also important to provide low-rental flats for the very poor group of households. In Section 6.2, we will discuss how an affordable public flat scheme and a low-rental flat scheme could be integrated together to help mitigate the housing problems in these Asian economies.

6.1.2.6 *Policy implications*

The above results suggest that, while the increase in wealth due to economic growth could help reduce the proportion of households who cannot afford property, the reduction is so mild that the related government should not put too much hope on it. Efforts to reduce inequality and to rectify the market structure problem in the Asian property markets would have a far greater effect and are therefore more promising. Among the two, reducing inequality will have a moderately large effect, while rectifying the market structure problem will have a substantial effect. Given that reducing inequality is much more difficult to achieve in the short and medium terms while rectifying the market structure problem (e.g., through substantial government supply of affordable public flats to eligible households) could be done more quickly, we believe the best strategy is to have heavy emphasis on the latter policy option while working hard on the former policy option with a medium- and long-term policy horizon. Parallel with the above affordable public flat scheme, the discussion in Section 6.1.2.5 also suggests that it is important to provide low-rental flats to the poorest group of households. In Section 6.2, we will discuss how the government could play a significant role in (i) reducing the proportion of households who cannot afford to own their homes, and (ii) helping the very poor group of households who cannot even afford to buy a public flat at cost.

6.2 LONG-TERM POLICY PROPOSAL: THE CASE FOR AFFORDABLE PUBLIC FLATS AND LOW-RENTAL FLATS

In Section 6.1, we have shown that in an economy where property developers enjoy high market power will result in high real property price and a significant proportion of households who cannot afford to own their homes. These results suggest that there may be room for government intervention. In this section, we will discuss how the government's

(i)   provision and sales of "affordable public flats" to eligible households; and

(ii) provision of "low-rental flats" to the poorest group of households

could substantially mitigate the housing problems in China and many Asian economies.

6.2.1 The Case with no Profit from the Affordable Public Flats to Subsidize the Low-rental Flats

6.2.1.1 *The simple case in which the minimum characteristic-adjusted sizes of public flats are the same as that of private flats*

Table 6.5 shows the simulation results for the case where (i) the (α, β) combinations are the same as those in Table 6.3 and (ii) the government will

(a)   provide and sell the "affordable public flats" at cost to only those households who cannot afford private properties; and

(b)   provide "low-rental flats" to those households who cannot even afford to buy the affordable public flats.

As we can see from the last row of Table 6.5, only 54.3% of the households could own (private) property if there is no government provision of public flats. With the "affordable public flat" scheme, there will be another 34.7% of households who can afford to own the affordable public flats, thus substantially raising the home-ownership from 54.3% to 89%. With the "low-rental flat" scheme, the remaining (poorest) 11% households would be able to live in the low-rental flats.[7]

Table 6.5:   Percentage of Households in Various Types of Housing ($c = c_g = c_r = 0.1$)[6]

(α, β)	Mean	Gini	Private flat	Affordable public flat	Low-rental flat	Subsidy
1.0, 0.9462	1/3	0.247	63.8%	30.6%	5.6%	0.00560
1.2, 0.97286	1/3	0.258	62.7%	31.2%	6.1%	0.00608
1.4, 0.98068	1/3	0.269	61.7%	31.7%	6.6%	0.00658
1.6, 0.98776	1/3	0.281	60.7%	32.2%	7.1%	0.00709
1.8, 0.99417	1/3	0.292	59.7%	32.7%	7.6%	0.00761
2.0, 1.0	1/3	0.303	58.8%	33.1%	8.1%	0.00815
2.2, 1.0053	1/3	0.314	57.8%	33.5%	8.7%	0.00870
2.4, 1.0101	1/3	0.325	56.9%	33.8%	9.3%	0.00926
2.6, 1.0145	1/3	0.337	56.1%	34.1%	9.8%	0.00983
2.8, 1.0186	1/3	0.348	55.2%	34.4%	10.4%	0.01041
3.0, 1.0223	1/3	0.359	54.3%	34.7%	11.0%	0.01100

---

[6] In this section, we will assume the minimum characteristics-adjusted sizes of private flats (s), affordable public flats (s_g) and low-rental flats (s_r) are the same (i.e., $s = s_g = s_r$) so that $c = c_g = c_r = 0.1$, where c, c_g and c_r are, respectively, the average total cost per unit of private flats of size s, affordable public flats of size s_g and low-rental flats of size s_r. In Section 6.2.1.2, we will consider the case in which the government could choose a lower s_g and s_r (i.e., $s_r < s_g < s$) by providing the public flats with only basic quality at less convenient location.

[7] Here, we assume those who cannot even pay the rental of the low-rental flats would be covered by a social welfare scheme for their basic consumption and housing needs.

In other words, unlike the case of free market force where only 54.3% households could afford to own their homes, the "affordable public flat" scheme and the "low-rental flat" scheme could also help the remaining 45.7% households to either own their homes or to stay in the low-rental flats.

Table 6.5 also shows the numerical simulation result for the (α, β) combinations with the same mean wealth but rising inequality. As we can see from the table, *the greater the inequality, the more important the two public housing schemes in helping people to own their homes or to stay in the low-rental flats.* For example, when (α, β) takes the values in the first row of Table 6.5 so that the Gini coefficient is 0.247, the affordable public flat scheme will help 30.6% of households to own their homes and the low-rental flat scheme will help the poorest 5.6 households to stay in the low-rental flats. On the other hand, when (α, β) take the values in the last row of Table 6.5 so that the Gini coefficient is 0.359, the affordable public flat scheme will help 34.7% (i.e., another 3.1 percentage points) of households to own their homes and the low-rental flat scheme will help 11% (i.e., another 4.4 percentage points) households to stay in low-rental flats.

Thus, the potential benefits of these two schemes on social welfare improvement could be substantial.[8] Moreover, the two public housing schemes will be more important for economies with greater inequality (e.g., China and many Asian economies). Furthermore, as "having a flat as shelter" is one of the top priorities in the Chinese and many Asian culture, the schemes could lay a solid foundation of social and political stability in the related economies. Given the pervasive corruption and cronyism in China and some Asian economies, the potential contribution of the latter would be particularly important.

Nevertheless, these could only be achieved if the related government is able, and willing, to provide a substantial subsidy for the low-rental flat scheme (e.g., paying the building cost for the low-rental flats while charging a rental just sufficient to cover the maintenance cost of the low-rental housing estate).[9] To allow for the case in which the related government is

---

[8]Assessment of the social welfare improvement could be done if one can specify the related social welfare function. However, as will be explained in Section 6.3, we will leave such an extension to follow-up research.

[9]As shown in Table 6.5, the amount of subsidy for the benchmark case will be 0.00560–0.01100 units.

not able, or not willing, to provide the subsidy for the public housing schemes, Section 6.2.2 will consider the case in which the government could choose a higher price (p_g) for the affordable public flats so that the profit from the affordable public flats could be used to subsidize the low-rental flat scheme. Before doing so, we will first investigate in the next section whether it would help if the government chooses to reduce the minimum characteristics-adjusted size of low-rental flats and affordable public flats, say, by providing these public flats with only basic quality and at less convenient locations than those of private flats. (One good example is in Singapore where private flats usually contain standard luxurious facilities such as private condominium swimming pools, barbecue pits, tennis courts, gymnasium, function rooms, car parks and guard services. On the other hand, HDB flats (i.e., a form of affordable public flats in Singapore) only contain basic common facilities such as common car parks, common children playgrounds and common leisure areas. Besides, the public flats are usually less well-located than private flats.)

6.2.1.2 *The potential benefits of offering affordable public flats and low-rental flats of smaller minimum characteristics-adjusted sizes*

In Section 6.2.1.1, we have assumed the minimum characteristics-adjusted sizes of low-rental flats (s_r), affordable public flats (s_g) and private flats (s) are the same so that their cost per unit of flat are the same (i.e., $s = s_g = s_r$ so that $c = c_g = c_r = 0.1$). An interesting question is whether it would help if the government chooses to provide some affordable public flats and low-rental flats at less convenient location with only basic quality so that $s_r' \leq s_g' \leq s$ and $c_r' \leq c_g' \leq c = 0.1$, where c_r' is the cost for each unit of low-rental flats of size s_r' and c_g' is the cost for each unit of affordable public of size s_g'. Table 6.6 shows the simulation results for one such case (i.e., $c_r' = 0.05$, $c_g' = 0.08$ and $c = 0.1$).

As shown in the last row of Table 6.6, with the choice of allowing some less well-off households to buy an affordable public flat of a smaller characteristics-adjusted size (i.e., $s_g' \leq s_g$ so that $c_g' = 0.8c_g = 0.08$), we can see that

(i) the characteristics-adjusted sizes of flats purchased by those households with $w_i \geq 0.1$ will remain the same; while

Table 6.6: Percentage of Households in Various Types of Housing ($c = 0.1$, $c_g' = 0.08$ and $c_r' = 0.05$)

(α, β)	Mean	Gini	Private flat	Affordable public flat	Low-rental flat	Subsidy
1.0, 0.9462	1/3	0.247	63.8%	32.5%	3.7%	0.00369
1.2, 0.97286	1/3	0.258	62.7%	33.3%	4.0%	0.00402
1.4, 0.98068	1/3	0.269	61.7%	34.0%	4.4%	0.00436
1.6, 0.98776	1/3	0.281	60.7%	34.6%	4.7%	0.00471
1.8, 0.99417	1/3	0.292	59.7%	35.2%	5.1%	0.00507
2.0, 1.0	1/3	0.303	58.8%	35.8%	5.4%	0.00544
2.2, 1.0053	1/3	0.314	57.8%	36.3%	5.8%	0.00582
2.4, 1.0101	1/3	0.325	56.9%	36.8%	6.2%	0.00621
2.6, 1.0145	1/3	0.337	56.1%	37.3%	6.6%	0.00661
2.8, 1.0186	1/3	0.348	55.2%	37.8%	7.0%	0.00701
3.0, 1.0223	1/3	0.359	54.3%	38.2%	7.4%	0.00743

(ii) for those less well-off households with $0.08 \leq w_i < 0.1$, they can now afford to buy and own the affordable public flats, albeit of smaller characteristics-adjusted sizes between the lower s_g' and the original s_g.

That is, the choice would help another 3.6 percentage points of households to own their homes. On top of this, the choice of a lower s_g' would reduce the number of households in the low-rental flat scheme by 3.6 percentage points (= 11.0–7.4%). This would in turn reduce the total amount of subsidy the government needs to pay for the low-rental flat scheme. With the additional choice of a lower s_r' so that $c_r' = 0.5c_r = 0.05$, the total amount of subsidy could be further reduced to 0.00743 units, which is 32.5% lower than the corresponding case shown in the last row Table 6.5.[10]

6.2.2 The Case with Profits from the Affordable Public Flats to Subsidize the Low-rental Flats

If the related government is not able, or not willing, to provide a subsidy to the two public housing schemes, what the related government could do

---

[10]Comparison of the other rows between Tables 6.5 and 6.6 also show similar results.

Table 6.7: Percentage of Households in Various Types of Housing ($c = c_g = c_r = 0.1$)

(α, β)	Gini	p_g	Private flat	Affordable public flat	Low-rental flat	Subsidy
1.0, 0.9462	0.247	0.1127	63.8%	29.2%	7.0%	0
1.2, 0.97286	0.258	0.1151	62.7%	29.4%	7.9%	0
1.4, 0.98068	0.269	0.1175	61.7%	29.5%	8.8%	0
1.6, 0.98776	0.281	0.1194	60.7%	29.6%	9.7%	0
1.8, 0.99417	0.292	0.1226	59.7%	29.4%	10.9%	0
2.0, 1.0	0.303	0.1274	58.8%	28.7%	12.5%	0
2.2, 1.0053	0.314	0.1408	57.8%	26.5%	15.7%	0
2.4, 1.0101	0.325	0.1401	56.9%	26.54%	16.5%	0.00121
2.6, 1.0145	0.337	0.1380	56.1%	26.9%	17.0%	0.00245
2.8, 1.0186	0.348	0.1362	55.2%	27.2%	17.6%	0.00374
3.0, 1.0223	0.359	0.1340	54.3%	27.6%	18.1%	0.00508

is to sell the "affordable public flats" at a slightly higher price so that its profit could be used to offset the required subsidy for the low-rentals flat scheme.[11] Tables 6.7 and 6.8 show the results if the government attempts to do so.

As shown in the last column of Table 6.7, for the case of lower inequality (i.e., the 1st to 7th cells of that column with the corresponding Gini coefficient at the range of 0.247–0.314), the government would be able to achieve the aim of using the profit from the affordable public flat scheme to offset the required subsidy for the low-rental flat scheme. However, when the inequality is higher (i.e., the 8th to 11th cells of the last column with the corresponding Gini coefficient at the range of 0.325–0.359), the net revenue from the two public flat schemes have to be negative even if the government tries to charge an optimal p_g^* to maximize the net revenue from the two schemes. That is, even if the mean of wealth remains unchanged (at 1/3), higher inequality would mean lower

---

[11]Again, for simplicity sake, we will continue to assume the related government will charge a rental just sufficient to cover the maintenance cost of the low-rental flat housing estates. As the model could be easily applied to the case where the government charges a different rental for the low-rental flat, interested readers could easily do it on their own if they ever find such kind of exercise is useful to them.

effective demand for housing and hence more households have to be covered by the low-rental flat scheme. When the inequality reaches the level shown in the 8th to 11th rows of Table 6.7, the profit from the affordable public flat scheme can never be enough to offset the required subsidy for the low-rental flat scheme. Nevertheless, as we will show later, there are still ways to help economies with high inequality to provide the two public flat schemes without any deficit (or required subsidy from the government).

The third, the fifth, and the sixth columns of Table 6.7 are also interesting. For the case of the 1st to 4th rows where the Gini coefficients are at the lower range of 0.247–0.281, the government only needs to charge a p_g that is 12.7–19.4% higher than the cost (i.e., $c = 0.1$). With the moderate increase in p_g, the government could, on one hand, avoid any subsidy to the two public flat schemes and could, on the other hand, help 29.2–29.6% households to own their affordable public flats and help the remaining poorest 7.0–9.7% households to live in the low-rental flats. For the case of the 5th to 7th rows where the Gini coefficients are at the medium range of 0.292–0.314, the government would need to charge a much higher p_g (i.e., 22.6–40.8% higher than the cost) before the two public flat schemes could be self-balanced. Because of the higher p_g and the higher inequality, the government can only help 26.5–29.4% households to own the affordable public flats. In addition, a much larger proportion (i.e., 10.9–15.7%) of households cannot afford to own their homes and have to be covered by the low-rental flat schemes. For the case of the 8th to 11th rows where the Gini coefficients are at the higher range of 0.325–0.359, we have already explained that, even if the government tries to charge an optimal $p_g{}^*$ to maximize the net revenue from the two public flat schemes, the profit from the affordable public flat scheme would still be less than the required subsidy for the low-rental flat scheme. Worse still, to minimize the deficit from the two public flat schemes, the related government has to charge a $p_g{}^*$ that is 34.0–40.1% higher than the cost. With the higher $p_g{}^*$ and the higher inequality, the government could only help 26.5–27.5% households to own the affordable public flats. In addition, a relatively high proportion (i.e., 16.5–18.1%) of households cannot afford to own their homes and have to be covered by the low-rental flat schemes.

To help more households to own their homes and to help the two public flat schemes to be self-balanced even in the higher inequality case, we suggest that the related government consider the following simultaneous policy designs:

1. charging a slightly higher p_g so that the profit from the affordable public flat scheme could be used to offset some or all of the required subsidy for the low-rental flat scheme; and
2. the government can also reduce the minimum characteristics-adjusted size of the public flats, say, by providing these public flats at less convenient location with only basic quality.

Table 6.8 shows the results for one such case (i.e., $c_r' = 0.05$, $c_g' = 0.08$ and $c = 0.1$). As shown in the last column of the table, the two public flat schemes can now be self-balanced, even for the higher inequality cases. The fifth column also shows that the government can now help 32.4–37.3% households to own their homes. That is, when compared with the corresponding cases in Table 6.7, the design could help another 3.2–9.7 percentage points of households to own their homes. As a result, only the poorest 3.8–8.4% of households have to be covered by the low-rental flat

Table 6.8:   Percentage of Households in Various Types of Housing ($c = 0.1$, $c_g' = 0.08$ and $c_r' = 0.05$)

(α, β)	Gini	P_g'	Private flat	Affordable public flat	Low-rental flat	Subsidy
1.0, 0.9462	0.247	0.0825	63.8%	32.4%	3.8%	0
1.2, 0.97286	0.258	0.0828	62.7%	33.0%	4.3%	0
1.4, 0.98068	0.269	0.0831	61.7%	33.6%	4.7%	0
1.6, 0.98776	0.281	0.0834	60.7%	34.2%	5.1%	0
1.8, 0.99417	0.292	0.0836	59.7%	34.8%	5.5%	0
2.0, 1.0	0.303	0.0838	58.8%	35.3%	5.9%	0
2.2, 1.0053	0.314	0.0842	57.8%	35.8%	6.4%	0
2.4, 1.0101	0.325	0.0845	56.9%	36.2%	6.9%	0
2.6, 1.0145	0.337	0.0848	56.1%	36.6%	7.3%	0
2.8, 1.0186	0.348	0.0853	55.2%	36.9%	7.9%	0
3.0, 1.0223	0.359	0.0856	54.3%	37.3%	8.4%	0

scheme (i.e., the sixth column of the table). Moreover, the required profit margin between p_g' and c_g' is now 3.0–6.5%,[12] which is much lower than the 12.7–40.8% in Table 6.7. That is, even for those households who can afford to buy the affordable public flats under the case of Table 6.7 (i.e., those with wealth w_i greater than p_g in Table 6.7), they can still benefit from the new policy design as they can now use the same wealth to buy an affordable flat of bigger characteristics-adjusted size.[13] In other words, the new policy design could help not only another 3.2–9.7% households to own an affordable public flat (of characteristics-adjusted size greater than the new s_g' but smaller than the original s_g), but could also help the original 27.6–29.2% households to own an affordable public flat of bigger characteristics-adjusted size.

6.3 DIRECTIONS FOR FURTHER RESEARCH

As we can see from Sections 6.1 and 6.2, our study has a lot of important policy implications. Yet, there are a few potentially promising extensions that could be done in the future. One promising extension is to build a model, and show that the following three public flat schemes suggested by Yip (2011) could be better than the two public flat schemes analyzed in this chapter:

1. a low-rental flat scheme to help the poorest group of households;
2. an affordable public flat scheme (or economy flat scheme) to help the next group of households to buy these flats at cost;
3. a sandwich-class flat scheme to help the next group of households to buy public flats with price, quality and location somewhere between the private flats and affordable public flats (and use the profit from the sandwich-class flat scheme to support the low-rental flat scheme, and

---

[12] For example, the profit margin for the first cell of the third column will be $(p_g'-c_g')/p_g' = (0.0825-0.08)/0.0825 = 3.03\%$.

[13] For example, the affordable public flat can now be much bigger in total area, so that the benefit from the increase in total area can be more than enough to compensate the disadvantage of a less well-located public flat with only basic standard quality. This explains why some Singaporean households could stay in relatively big public flats of size around 150–200 square meters.

other important reforms such as the medical reform and the education reform in China).

While such an extension is definitely interesting, it will be beyond the scope of this chapter. It would involve a two-stage game where the government first announces prices (of affordable flats and sandwich class flats) and the income ceiling for eligibility; property developers then decide how much to charge for private properties. Marginal home-buyer would need to decide between different classes of properties. The government's welfare function in such an extension will involve many variables such as net revenue from the three types of public flats, the percentage of homeownership, and the levels of private and public property prices. As specifying the functional form of such a welfare function is highly debatable and limitation of space has made such an extension beyond the scope of this chapter, we will leave such an extension as follow-up research.

Finally, extending the model to include public rental flats[14] will be interesting. However, modeling this would be even more complicated. Our preliminary thought is that the public rental flats, the economy flats and the other two types of public flats have their own strengths in different areas of potential contribution. That is, it is better to have all these types of flats coexisting in the economy. If our preliminary thought is subsequently supported by the results of the subsequent model extension, China's latest discussion of discarding the economy flat scheme, and replacing it by the public rental flat scheme would be highly misleading.

6.4 CONCLUSIONS AND REMARKS ON LONG-TERM HOUSING POLICIES

In Chapter 1, the author has explained that the market structure problem in the Chinese and many Asian property markets could enable developers to collectively charge a high gross profit margin. In Section 6.1, we have shown that the higher gross profit margin developers could collectively

---

[14]Public rental flats are meant for normal working class with a rental higher than that of low-rental flats.

charge, the higher the property price and the greater the proportion of households who cannot afford to own their homes.

We also show that, *ceteris paribus*, a rise in inequality will increase the %CAH. That is, economies with higher inequality will tend to have a higher proportion of households who cannot afford to own their homes. Meanwhile, for economies with the same mean of wealth, higher inequality will mean lower effective demand for housing, which will in turn reduce the gross profit margin and hence the real price of property that developers could charge. This gives us a moderately surprising result: developers also dislike inequality, although their market power is the most important source of the problems of high real property price and high proportion of households who cannot afford to own their homes.

For the case where economic growth causes both a general rise in wealth and a rise in wealth inequality, such as the case in China and many Asian economies over the past two decades, there could be an improvement in homeownership even if there is a significant rise in the Gini coefficient. Nevertheless, our numerical simulation suggests the improvement would be very minor, while the developers' profit would surge substantially. That is, developers are likely to be those who benefit the most from the economic growth, and policymakers should avoid hoping that general economic growth could help much in reducing real property price and the %CAH in China and many Asian economies. In view of this, we proceed to investigate whether it will help if the policymakers try to address the above market structure problem and the inequality problem.

Using the theoretical model and numerical simulation, we demonstrate the following:

1. The market structure problem is the one with the greatest impacts on the level of property price and the %CAH. For example, comparing the cases between $m = m^*$ and $m = 10\%$, the property price in the former case will be 2.3–2.7 times that in the latter case, and the %CAH in the former case will be 29.4–32.5 percentage points higher than that in the latter case.

2. The inequality problem is the one with the second largest impact on the %CAH, although it will cause a mild reduction in property price through the above-mentioned impact of a lower effective demand for housing. For example, comparing the first row and the last row of Table 6.3 where

the Gini coefficients are 0.247 and 0.359, respectively, the %CAH will rise by 9.5, 14.2, 9.3 and 6.4 percentage points for the cases of $m = m^*$, $m = 50\%$, $m = 30\%$ and $m = 10\%$, respectively.

As China and many Asian economies have the worst combinations in the above two dimensions (i.e., both the market structure problem and high inequality), it is not surprising that the %CAH in these economies are high. In fact, the difference between the two extreme cases shown in Table 6.3 is as high as 38.9 percentage points (= 45.7–6.8%).

These simulation results suggest that tackling the market structure problem in the Chinese and many Asian property markets is the most promising strategy to mitigate the problems of high real property price and high %CAH in these economies. In addition, reducing inequality could also help. That is, even though it is not easy to reduce inequality in the short and medium term, it is still worthwhile to try reducing inequality with a medium- and long-term policy horizon.

Our simulation results also suggest that, as long as we assume a distribution of wealth w_i starting from zero, or any distribution with some $w_i < c$, there will always be a group of very poor households who cannot afford to own their homes. While this will be more severe for economies with the above market structure problem and high inequality, there will still be a certain %CAH even for economies without the above market structure problem and with a reasonably low level of inequality. Thus, there is still a need for low-rental flats even if the related government could find ways to mitigate the above market structure problem and bring its inequality to a reasonably low level.

The numerical simulation in Section 6.2.1 also shows that the government's provision of affordable public flat at cost and provision of low-rental flats to eligible households could help a large proportion (e.g., 30.6–38.2%) of households to own their flats and the remaining proportion of households to stay in the low-rental flats. If the government is not able, or not willing, to provide the required subsidy to the low-rental flat scheme, it could consider the following measures:

1. reduce the minimum characteristics-adjusted size of the two public flat schemes, by providing these flats at less convenient location with only basic quality; and

2. raise the price of affordable public flats slightly so that its profit could be used to offset the required subsidy for the low-rental flat scheme.

Our simulation results in Section 6.2.2 suggest that the two additional measures could make the two public flat schemes self-balanced and yet help 32.4–37.3% households to own their homes and the remaining poorest 3.8–8.4% households to live in the low-rental flats. Thus, the potential benefit of the two public flat schemes on social welfare improvement could be substantial. In addition, as "having a flat as a shelter" is one of the top priorities in the Chinese (and many Asian) culture, the schemes could lay a solid foundation of social and political stability in the related economies. Given the pervasive corruption and cronyism in China and some Asian economies, the potential contribution of the latter would be particularly important.

PART V

THE NEED FOR A PROPER SELECTION PROCEDURE AND A NEW DISCIPLINE ON MACROECONOMIC MANAGEMENT

CHAPTER 7

SELECTING THE RIGHT OFFICIALS AND THE NEED FOR A NEW DISCIPLINE ON MACROECONOMIC MANAGEMENT

In this chapter, the author will first explain (i) why most developing economies and some advanced economies failed to select the right people in the key macroeconomic positions, (ii) how heavy such mistakes had cost these economies and (iii) how a proper selection procedure could help avoid these heavy costs. Thereafter, he will discuss some more lessons for macroeconomic management, and explain why it is necessary and important to develop macroeconomic management as a new discipline in economics.

7.1 IMPORTANCE OF HAVING THE RIGHT PEOPLE IN KEY MACROECONOMIC POSITIONS

In this section, the author will first point out that, except a few advanced economies such as the US and the UK, most developing economies and some advanced economies had failed to select well-trained economists with outstanding policy insight to take up the key monetary and economic positions within their governments. This had in turn cost them heavily, especially during the asset inflation era and the subsequent crises. Therefore, the author will, in the later part of this section, propose a proper and rigorous procedure in selecting the potential candidates, which could help these economies avoid these types of costs in the future.

7.1.1 Importance of Selecting Well-trained Economists with Outstanding Policy Insight in Key Economic Positions

Before and during the Great Depression in the 1930s, the Federal Reserve did not have the right theoretical framework to make the right and important decision (e.g., ultra-expansionary monetary policy) to pre-empt the stock market crash at that time from triggering the Great Depression. Similarly, before and after the crash of the property bubble and stock market bubble in Japan in the late 1980s, cronyism and economic ignorance within the Japanese political circle had made Japan's key monetary and economic positions being occupied by insufficiently trained and far from suitable people (see Yip, 2011). Because of these far from qualified officials and the lack of right curbing policies at the seeding stage, the property bubble and stock market bubble had the chance to emerge and then grow into gigantic bubbles. Even after the crash, Japanese politicians did not learn from the mistake and did not recognize the importance of selecting the right monetary chief and economic chief to manage the after-crash economy. This mistake had in turn cost Japan the "lost two decades" after the crash.

Nevertheless, prominent academic economists had drawn important lessons from the mistakes of "the Federal Reserve in the 1930s" and "the Japanese government during the lost two decades", and suggested that ultra-expansionary monetary policy might be able to help an after-crash economy from entering into a depression. Meanwhile, the US had also selected well-trained academic economists like Ben Bernanke, Janet Yellen, Federic Mishkin and many other outstanding economists into the Federal Reserve before the outbreak of the subprime crisis. Thus, when the subprime crisis triggered the global financial tsunami, these well-trained central bankers were able to appreciate the importance of having an ultra-expansionary monetary policy (i.e., the QEs) to pre-empt the US, and hence the global economy, from entering a depression similar to that in the 1930s.

In Europe, before the outbreak of the sovereign debt crisis in 2010, Jean-Claude Trichet was selected as the President of the European Central Bank (ECB) mainly because of political consideration. Although Trichet was an economics professor, the author believed he was not knowledge-able enough to judge the importance, and be able to select the right policy, to pre-empt the debt crisis from triggering a severe recession or depres-sion in the whole Europe and the global economy. The author also believed that there were a lot of potential candidates in Europe who were much more knowledgeable, devoted and suitable for the post. Because of such a mistake, the sovereign debt crisis in Europe had the chance to trig-ger a few vicious cycles and downward spirals, which had in turn pushed the European economy into a severe recession. Fortunately, Mario Draghi was later selected as the President of the ECB. Although Draghi was not as well trained as Ben Bernanke and Janet Yellen, he was at least an M.I.T. Ph.D. graduate with extensive central banking and financial experiences. As such, with the observed success of the QEs pioneered by Ben Bernanke and Janet Yellen, he still had the knowledge to judge that Europe needed at least a modified version of QE to stop the sovereign debt crisis and its vicious cycles from pushing the whole Europe into a depression. Meanwhile, he was politically skillful enough to persuade the then German Chancellor, Angela Merkel, to adopt the Long Term Refinancing Operations (LTRO) and then the Outright Monetary Transactions (OMTs). This was not easy as Germany's Bundesbank President, Jens Weidmann, was strongly against these policies. As a matter of fact, the LTROs did mitigate the adverse impacts of the debt crisis, and the subsequent OMTs had successfully ended the European Debt Crisis.[1] Thus, the author believed Draghi and his supporting specialists within the ECB should be credited for such an important success. The author also believed future research would further confirm Trichet and Weidmann were wrong in their approaches to the debt crisis.

---

[1] Note that there remains a debate on whether it would be better for the ECB to adopt the outright QEs similar to those in the US and the UK. Nevertheless, given the constraints imposed by Germany and other northern EU members at that time, the LTROs and the OMTs were the maximum that Mario Draghi could ask for at that time.

From a wider perspective, the above incidences and results in the US, Japan and Europe suggested that having poor or well-trained monetary and economic officials in the key positions could mean two different worlds, especially if there is an asset bubble or an outbreak of crisis. In fact, the latest formation of the property bubbles and the expected collapse of property prices in some Asian economies are further examples reflecting the importance of selecting well-trained officials in key central banking and economic positions.

As explained in Chapters 2 and 4, Hong Kong's failure to have well-trained monetary and economic officials to monitor its economy had allowed the QEs in the US and other major economies to cause the formation of a huge property bubble. If Hong Kong had selected well-trained officials in these key positions, they would have the knowledge to appreciate the author's numerous warnings since 2009. These well-trained officials would also be knowledgeable and devoted enough to appreciate the authors' proposals to (i) adopt sufficient curbing measures between mid-2009 and mid-2010 so as to pre-empt the bubble at its seeding stage; or (ii) adopt much stronger curbing measures after mid-2010 so as to stop the bubble from growing further at the development stage.

In sharp contrast to the case in Hong Kong, monetary and economic officials in Singapore were reasonably well trained. Although they still did not have strong enough theoretical foundation and policy insight to sort out the unique characteristics of the Asian and Singapore property markets, the characteristics of various stages of an asset bubble and the high likelihood of property bubble formation after the US's QEs (see Chapter 3 for the detailed discussion), they did have the knowledge to understand the author's warnings, new theoretical framework and policy proposals. Thus, although they failed to pre-empt the bubble with sufficient curbing measures at the seeding stage, they eventually managed to use the fifth and the seventh rounds of curbing to stop the bubble from growing and then used the eighth round of curbing to squeeze part of the bubble. As a result, the property bubble in Singapore in 2017 was much smaller than that in Hong Kong. Furthermore, when the Singapore private property market entered a new seeding stage of bubble in 2018H1, the well-trained monetary officials at that time had learned from the mistake of their predecessors in 2009H2–2010H2. As such, they introduced the ninth round of curbing measures to stop the private property market from moving into the development stage of bubble. Although it is still too early to tell what will happen in Singapore's property market, the effort had at least pre-empted a rapid rise of private property prices at that time.

Thus, even if Singapore's property prices would still plunge due to the contagion effect originated from the expected bursting of property bubble in Hong Kong or another Asian economy, the total amount of the expected fall in property prices and hence the implied damages would be at least substantially mitigated by its previous and existing curbing measures. Of course, it is the author's hope that Singapore could further upgrade its macroeconomic management ability so that they could in the future pre-empt a potential bubble even at the seeding stage.

Because of Hong Kong's poor performance in tackling its property bubble, the author had highlighted in his policy articles that it was already impossible for Hong Kong to avoid the eventual bursting of its property bubble. The author's only hope was that Hong Kong citizens and the next Hong Kong government could learn from the mistake during the "could-be-anticipated" crisis, and would thereafter select more well-trained officials to monitor their economy. Otherwise, there would be further crises in the future.

While Hong Kong had performed badly in its macroeconomic management, this was in fact quite common in many Asian and developing economies. As explained in Chapter 2, India, Malaysia and many other Asian economies had also performed badly in tackling their property bubbles. For the other Asian economies, the problem was less acute, not because they had well-trained monetary and economic officials, but because it took a longer time for the US's QEs to cause the formation of property bubbles in these economies. In Chapter 1, the author has also highlighted that there could be an emergent market crisis,[2] partly because the key monetary and economic positions in these emergent markets were occupied by unsuitable people who managed to get their positions through cronyism, political relation and even corruption. Thus, the author would

---

[2]This would probably happen after the expected plunges of property prices in Asia, although there is a moderate chance that it would happen before the expected plunges in Asia.

like to warn the readers that it is quite likely and in general the case that key monetary and economic officials in many Asian and developing economies are actually not qualified and not suitable for the posts, and these economies would pay heavily (e.g., in terms of crisis, severe recession, massive layoffs and poor economic development performance) for this horrible negligence.

Finally, although many central bankers in the US, the UK and Europe are of top quality, fiscal and economic officials in these economies are not that well trained for and devoted to the job, i.e., they got their positions mainly because of political reasons. It is thus important to start a debate on how to guarantee the selected fiscal and economic officials are well trained and devoted enough for the job, while allowing the related president or prime minister to choose an expert that could support his vision on the fiscal and economic front.

7.1.2 Importance of a Proper Selection Procedure

7.1.2.1 *The adverse selection and moral hazard problems in macroeconomic management*

Other than cronyism, political consideration and corruption, another important reason for many economies' failure to select the right people in the key macroeconomic positions (e.g., central bank governor, finance minister and economics minister) is the *adverse selection problem.* That is, as the potential personal benefits from occupying the key macroeconomic positions are substantial, a huge number of far from qualified or even unsuitable candidates would have the incentives to fight for the positions through various means. If the related presidents, premiers or chief executives of the economies do not have the economic knowledge to identify the right candidates whose number would be outnumbered by the large number of unsuitable candidates, the chance for them to select the right candidates for the key macroeconomic positions would be extremely slim.

Worse still, once these unsuitable candidates are selected, there will also be a severe *moral hazard problem* in the macroeconomic management in these economies. That is, as these unsuitable candidates do not have the knowledge and ability to solve the economic problem, they will try to refrain from their responsibility (e.g., defer the treatment of the problem until it is too late), or take risky bets without a viable plan when they are at the edge of losing their job.

For example, as explained in Chapter 4, in view of the high likelihood of further enlargement of Hong Kong's property bubble before the eventual collapse, the author had written articles in the press and sent letters to the key monetary and economic officials in Hong Kong throughout the seeding stage, the development stage and the final stage of the bubble. In particular, during the development stage of the bubble, he kept on urging these monetary and economic officials pre-empt further enlargement of Hong Kong's property bubble by implementing further curbing measures (e.g., substantial reduction in the mortgage period for non-first-time homebuyers) and at the same time start a discussion on the possibility of prepaid mortgage rate. Unfortunately, because of personal consideration and lack of the necessary knowledge, these officials chose to refrain from their responsibility (i.e., refrained from any treatment of the problem). As a result, the author had to declare in the press articles that it would be almost certain that Hong Kong's property bubble would eventually burst, and all the citizens in Hong Kong would pay heavily for the above adverse selection and moral hazard problems. In particular, the articles warned that Hong Kong could experience a disastrous plunge in its property prices by 60–75%, a severe recession of 5–8 years and a surge in the unemployment rate to 8–12%. Noting that the related Hong Kong officials lacked both knowledge and sense of responsibility to tackle the bubble and pre-empt the subsequent crisis, the articles admitted that the author's only hope at that time was that Hong Kong citizens could at least learn from the mistake after the "could-be-anticipated" bursting of bubble.[3]

---

[3] The example cited here only refers to Hong Kong's mistake since mid-2013. While the Financial Secretary of the Hong Kong government (i.e., Mr. John C. W. Tsang) and the Chief Executive of the Hong Kong Monetary Authority (i.e., Mr. Norman T. L. Chan) should be condemned for this mistake and irresponsible attitude, the author has explained in Chapter 4 that the person most responsible for the "could-be-anticipated" disaster should be Mr. Donald Y. K. Tsang, the then Chief Executive of Hong Kong. Mr. Donald Tsang was unsuitably (and perhaps intentionally) chosen by the former British government as the Finance Secretary of Hong Kong despite the fact that he did not even have a

Similarly, before the 1997 Asian Financial Crisis, the far from suitable key monetary and economic senior officials in Thailand and South Korea first made the mistakes of opting for a quasi-fixed exchange rate while allowing sustained accumulation of internal weaknesses (e.g., rapid credit growth and substantial rise in current account deficit due to sustained capital inflows, asset inflation, weak supervision of banks, etc.). With the sustained building up of these internal weaknesses to hopeless levels and hence the subsequent speculative attack by numerous hedge funds, these unsuitable central bankers chose to bet heavily with the hedge funds in the currency futures market. Subsequent evidence showed that even though they reached the stage where it was clear that they would not be able to defend the currency around the quasi-fixed rate, they chose to commit a moral hazard activity by using the remaining foreign reserve in the betting, instead of keeping the remaining reserve to reduce the subsequent overcorrection of the currency. As a result, when they lost the betting in the currency futures market, there was no remaining reserve to reduce the subsequent plunge in the currency, and the exchange value of the currency had to nosedive to an ultra-undervalued level, which in turn caused more chaos and harm to the economy. Because of their moral hazard activities, many of these central bankers were subsequently sued and jailed for the misconduct.

Furthermore, with the outbreak of the European Debt Crisis and the success of unconventional monetary policy in the US, former ECB president Trichet should seriously consider a European form of unconventional monetary policy to stop the debt crisis from triggering a banking crisis, severe recession and then further deterioration of the debt crisis to the verge of a full-blown crisis. Fortunately, his term in the ECB was soon over and Draghi was later selected as the new ECB president — as explained in Section 7.1.1, Draghi's subsequent LTROs and OMTs had rescued the European economy from a full-blown crisis. Otherwise, it would be quite doubtful that Trichet would be (i) knowledgeable enough to sort out the necessary rescue package (e.g., the LTROs and OMTs or the US-type QE) and (ii) devoted and skillful enough to convince the then

---

university degree, not to mention this book's suggested basic requirement of at least a Master degree in economics for the post.

German Chancellor, Angela Merkel, to support the rescue packages. If there was no powerful enough rescue package because of any one of the above reasons, the European economy would have to go through a full-blown crisis and be trapped in the subsequent depression.

In addition to the above examples, there are numerous examples that many developing economies and some advanced economies had paid heavily because of the adverse selection and moral hazard problems in selecting the right candidates for the key macroeconomic positions.[4] Thus, it is important to establish a formal and proper procedure to solve the above adverse selection and moral hazard problems.

7.1.2.2 *A proper selection procedure to solve the adverse selection problem and mitigate the moral hazard problem*

To solve the adverse selection and moral hazard problems, and hence avoid the huge macroeconomic mismanagement costs, it is important to establish a formal and proper selection procedure to choose the right candidates for the key economic positions. Along this line of thought, the author would like to propose the following standards or requirements for the selection procedure. The potential candidates must have the following characteristics:

1. solid theoretical foundation in the related economics discipline[5]; and
2. proven record of good policy insight.

---

[4]Another problem of having unsuitable candidates is that it would mean substantial deterioration of macroeconomic management standard to extremely low levels.

[5]Actually, the author would like to add the third requirement: the potential candidate should have the devotion to help the economy and its citizens. However, as (i) it is difficult to set up procedures to ensure that without undesirable effect and (ii) the requirement for solid theoretical foundation would mean the candidates have spent at least 1–2 decades in a related economics discipline, and a devotion to serve the economy and its citizens should have been developed during the process, the author thinks that it should be good enough to state only the requirement of solid theoretical foundation in the proposed procedure. Nevertheless, if in the future we could sort out a procedure that would ensure the devotion requirement would be met without risk of being abused, it would better to revise the proposed procedure to include the devotion requirement.

To ensure these two important standards or requirements would be met, I would like to propose the following selection procedures:

(a) All shortlisted candidates should have at least a Ph.D. degree[6] in the relevant economics discipline with at least 5 years of experience demonstrating that they do have good policy insight.[7]

(b) The shortlisted candidates should be interviewed by a panel in which the internal and external members are outstanding academic economists with good publication records. Other than ranking the candidates on their suitability for the job, the panel should also explicitly state with detailed reasons whether the candidates pass or fail the minimum requirement on the theoretical foundation in the related economics discipline.

(c) The shortlisted candidates should also be interviewed by another panel in which the internal and external members have a proven record of good policy insight. This panel would then rank the candidates' policy insight and suitability for the job with detailed reasons for their ranking.

(d) The successful candidate has to (i) *pass the first panel's minimum standard on the theoretical foundation in the related economics discipline* and (ii) *be recommended by both panels for the appointment.* If more than one candidate meets these requirements, the candidate with the highest average score in the two panels will be the successful candidate. In case no candidate meets the minimum requirement of the theoretical foundation and is recommended by both panels, a new search and recruitment process should be made until there is a candidate that could meet all the above requirements.

---

[6] For less-developed economies, the author is open to a temporary standard of at least a Master degree in economics (from a reputable university) with at least 10 years of policy-related experience. Nevertheless, it should be emphasized that the less-developed economy should aim to the long-term standard (i.e., a Ph.D. degree with at least 5 years of experience) in the second or third appointment.

[7] Such experience could be actual policy implementation experience or policy research experience. The important point is that the candidate and the selection panels have to explain how such experience demonstrates that the candidate does have a good policy insight.

To reduce the chance that the above selection procedure gets manipulated, there should at least be two (and preferably three) external members in both panels. In fact, for developing or less-advanced economies, there may be no, or not enough, expert(s) who could qualify as internal panel members. In such a case, reputable external panel members from the advanced economies could fill this very important role until the related economy has built up its pool of qualified policymakers over time. For example, if former central bankers and academia such as Professor Ben Bernanke, Professor Janet Yellen, Professor Federic Mishkin or Professor Randall Kronzer in the US, or Professor Charles Bean in the UK are invited to be the external members of the panels, I believe they would be very willing to take up the one-off but very meaningful responsibility. For the case of Hong Kong and Singapore, the author would also be more than willing to help as an internal panel member.

Once such a selection procedure is in place, the related economy could avoid its key macroeconomic positions being occupied by unsuitable candidates, and could therefore save the economy from the huge macroeconomic management costs such as those highlighted in Section 7.1.1. (See also Box 7.1 on the implicit standard in the US).

Box 7.1:   The implicit standard in the US and other advanced economies

Note that although the above proposed procedures are not found in the US and other advanced economies, there is however an implicit norm in the selection of the Chairman, Deputy Chairman and Regional Presidents in the US Federal Reserve: the selected person should have a reasonably good theoretical foundation in the related discipline with impressive experience or good policy insight. In fact, before Professor Ben Bernanke, Professor Janet Yellen, Professor Federic Mishkin and Professor Randall Krozner joined the Federal Reserve, they were economics professors with substantial policy experience and/or policy insight in the relevant disciplines. In the UK, before Professor Mervyn King and Professor Charles Bean joined the Bank of England, they were economics professors with impressive experience. Nevertheless, as the norm is not as formal as the proposed procedure, there is a risk of deteriorating standard if the US President violates the norm by appointing a less-qualified candidate. For example, while Donald Trump's

---

(Continued)

Box 7.1:   (*Continued*)

appointment of Mr. Jerome Powell as the Federal Reserve Chairman is not too much a deviation from the usual norm in the US, the author is concerned with the possibility that Powell might not be well trained enough to deal with new sophisticated challenges, although the other more well-trained members of the FoMC should be able to help him if such new sophisticated challenge appears in the future. In addition, there is a risk that the next US President thinks that the lower norm adopted by Donald Trump is good enough.

7.2 SOME MORE LESSONS FOR MACROECONOMIC MANAGEMENT

In this section, the author will discuss some more lessons drawn from the macroeconomic management cases discussed in this book and his publications over the past two decades.

7.2.1 Importance of Further Theoretical Development and Practical Studies on Asset Inflation, Bubbles and Crises

Firstly, the author will highlight in this section that

(a)   the *strategy, dose* and *timing* of the policies used during the asset inflation era, bubble period and crisis period should be very different from those used during the normal period; and

(b)   if one classifies the asset inflation era, bubble period and crisis period as "abnormal periods" that are not well covered by standard textbooks, the lengths of these abnormal periods relative to that of normal period are in fact much longer than the general perception.

Thus, it is important for us to go beyond the standard textbook cases of macroeconomic fine-tuning, and put more research effort on the strategy, dose and timing of policies that should be used during the asset inflation era, bubble period and crisis period. In Sections 7.2.1.1 and 7.2.1.2, the author will take the first steps along this line by summarizing a few important lessons drawn from the macroeconomic management cases discussed in this book and his publications over the past two decades.

7.2.1.1 Policies used during the bubble and crisis periods should be qualitatively different from those used during the normal period

Here, the author will summarize a few discussed examples to illustrate that policies used during the asset inflation era, the bubble period and the crisis period should be qualitatively different from those used during the "normal period". Firstly, as explained in Chapter 1,

(1) It is always the best to use curbing measures to pre-empt any potential asset inflation era or asset bubble at the seeding stage. Unlike the simple textbook case and the usual belief of most economic commentators in Asia, such a result suggests that the best *strategy* and the best *timing* to pre-empt an asset inflation and the subsequent curbing costs is *doing the curbing at the seeding stage.* If the related government fails to do so, the subsequent cost of curbing the asset inflation or asset bubble would be substantial. In case the related government fails to curb or squeeze the potential bubble at the development stage, the economic costs of the subsequent crisis would be even more substantial. That is, with the possibility that a sustained rebound of asset prices (e.g., from a trough for a few months) could cause an expectation of further rises in asset prices which could in turn (i) trigger enormous investment demand, panic demand and speculative demand for the assets and (ii) bring the asset bubble into the development stage where there would be a series of changes in economic behaviors, vicious cycles and upward spirals that would fuel the growth of the asset bubble, it would be better and less costly to pre-empt the potential bubble at the seeding stage.

(2) If the government fails to pre-empt the potential asset bubble at the seeding stage and an expectation of rampant asset inflation has been formed, an extra *dose* of curbing measures is needed to offset the effects of the above changes in economic behaviors, vicious cycles

and upward spirals. Such a result suggests that the dose of curbing measures during the development stage of an asset bubble would be much greater than that during the normal period.

If the related government treats the strategy, timing and dose of policy measures during the above abnormal periods as the same as those during the normal period, it would not be able to pre-empt the bubble at the seeding stage and stop the bubble from growing at the development stage. This would mean the related economy would eventually need to pay a high cost during the "could-be-expected" bursting of asset bubble and the after-crisis recession. Similarly, as explained in Chapter 1, during the bursting of the asset bubble and the subsequent crisis period, there would be herding behaviors and other changes in economic behaviors, vicious cycles and changes in expectation in the downward direction. Thus, it would be important to have further rigorous theoretical development and practical studies on the appropriate strategy, timing and dose of stimulation measures during the crisis periods. For example, to mitigate the crisis and its impacts, the government might need to unwind its previous curbing measures and implement the necessary stimulation process in big steps and good timing.[8]

7.2.1.2 *The bubble and crisis periods are much longer and more common than the general perception*

Another important reason for further rigorous theoretical development and practical studies on macroeconomic management during the above abnormal periods is that these abnormal periods are in fact much longer and more common than the general perception.[9]

---

[8] It would be interesting to compare the effectiveness of the stimulation measures between the following two possible timings: (1) at the time the asset price falls to a level that is around the long-run equilibrium level; or (2) at the time the asset price is overcorrect by a moderate percentage (e.g., 10%) below the long-run equilibrium level. The author believes the second option could be a more effective choice unless the stimulation measure is of very large or unlimited scale. For the case of stimulation measure of virtually unlimited scale, such as the QEs in the US, the first option could imply a lower disruption cost than the second option.

[9] This is especially the case for developing economies in which macroeconomic misman-agement has resulted in bubbles and crises in these economies. Nevertheless, in the

For example, as well documented in the literature on the asset bubbles and then the lost two decades in Japan, Japan has gone through a prolonged asset inflation before the bursting of its asset bubbles in the late 1980s. After the bursting of the asset bubbles, the Japanese economy was trapped in a prolonged stagnation for more than two decades. Thus, the length of the "abnormal periods" (i.e., the asset inflation era and the two decades of stagnation) was much longer than the normal period in the standard textbook. As explained in Section 7.2.1.1, the strategy, timing and dose of policy measures during the asset inflation era and the post-crisis period should be very different from those during the normal period. Should there be formal and rigorous studies on the appropriate strategy of policies for the two abnormal periods, Japan could have avoided the huge bubble formation in the 1980s and substantially reduced the length of the post-crisis recession from more than two decades to 5–6 years (Yip, 2011, p. 377).

Next, consider the asset inflation era before the 1997 Asian Financial Crisis. As documented in the literature on the 1997 Asian financial crisis, the pre-crisis asset inflation era in Thailand, Malaysia, Indonesia, Singapore, South Korea, Taiwan and Hong Kong was about 11 years (i.e., from 1986 to 1997).[10] Even for a late comer such as the Philippines, the pre-crisis asset inflation era was about 7 years (i.e., from 1990 to 1997). On the length of the post-crisis recession, with the help of the substantial overcorrections of exchange rate during the crisis period, many of these economies were lucky enough to have a post-crisis recession of about 2–3 years. (Note that without the help of the very low exchange rate inherited from the crisis (and the open nature of these economies), it is quite doubtful whether all the key monetary and economic officials in these economies could judge that drastic change in the related key policy variable(s) was necessary to push each of these economies from the post-crisis recession to a recovery path.) On the other hand, without the help of any correction of its exchange rate during the crisis, Hong Kong had to go

---

subsequent discussion, we will see examples showing that this would also be the case for advanced economies such as Japan and the US.

[10] For the case of Hong Kong, the asset inflation era was between 1986 and 1997 with a temporary consolation in 1989–1990 due to China's 6–4 massacre in 1989.

through a post-crisis recession of 7 years with a very slow and painful deflation of 1–3% per annum. The difference in the length of the post-crisis recession between Hong Kong and the other crisis-hit economies illustrated that drastic change in the related key policy variable(s) is necessary to push the economy from the post-crisis recession to a recovery path.

Similarly, as explained in Chapter 2, the lengths of the seeding stage and development stage of the property bubbles in Hong Kong, India, Taiwan, Malaysia, Singapore and other Asian economies were of the order of at least 8–9 years.

Furthermore, before the outbreak of the subprime crisis, the US home price index rose at the rampant pace of 10.2% per annum between 1997Q3 and 2006Q1, a pace that is unlikely to be sustainable and was much faster than the 3.1% annual rise between 1987Q1 and 1997Q3. Thus, even for the US, the property inflation era before the subprime crisis was 9.5 years. Should there be rigorous theoretical development and practical studies on the appropriate strategy of policies for the asset inflation era, Alan Greenspan, the then Federal Reserve Chairman, might have been able to pre-empt the occurrence of the global financial tsunami at the very beginning. With the outbreak of the financial crisis, the length of the pre-crisis period, the crisis period and the post-crisis recession was also very long, i.e., at least 8–9 years between 2006Q2 and 2014/2015. Similarly, if one adds the length of the crisis period and post-crisis recession during and after the European Debt Crisis, one would recognize the length of the abnormal periods are long enough to justify further rigorous theoretical development and practical studies on these "abnormal periods".

Thus, the above examples suggest that the so-called "abnormal periods" are in fact much longer and more common than generally perceived and it is important to push for further rigorous theoretical development and practical studies on these abnormal periods through the development of "macroeconomic management" as a new discipline in economics.

7.2.2 Many Crises and Bubbles Could be Anticipated Well before Their Occurrence

In Section 7.2.1, the author has explained that it is important to go beyond the standard textbook cases of macroeconomic fine-tuning, and put more research effort on the strategy, timing and dose of polices during the asset inflation era, bubble period, crisis period and post-crisis recession. From this section onwards, he will take the first step along this line by summarizing a few important lessons drawn from the macroeconomic management cases discussed in this book and his publications over the past two decades.

First of all, in most cases discussed in this book, the bubbles and the subsequent crises could be anticipated before its occurrence. Even if one fails to anticipate this at the early stage of these major events, a reasonably well-trained policymaker should sooner or later get enough signals from the subsequent data to judge whether there would be a high likelihood that (a) the sustained rebound in the asset price would end up as an asset bubble and (b) the initial plunge in an asset price (say, from an overvalued level amid substantial internal weaknesses) would mean further deterioration into a deeper crisis or a full-blown crisis.

For example, as explained in Chapter 2, with the new theoretical framework outlined in Chapter 1 and sufficient policy insight accumulated over the past 35 years, the author was able to judge in 2009 that, with

(i) the ending of global financial tsunami and the QEs in the US;
(ii) the market structure problem in the Asian property markets; and
(iii) the characteristics of the seeding stage, the development stage and the final stage of property bubble,

the rebound of property prices in Hong Kong, Singapore and some other Asian economies had a high chance of ending up with a property bubble. Without the new theoretical framework outlined in Chapter 1, policymakers in these economies were not able to anticipate the risk of the bubble formation.

Fortunately, after seeing the author's warnings and new theoretical framework, monetary and economic officials in Singapore were well trained enough to see the implied danger of an eventual bursting of the bubble, and were devoted enough to implement severe curbing measures to stop the growth of, and then squeeze, the bubble. On the other hand, monetary and economic officials in Hong Kong were neither well trained enough to appreciate the importance of the author's warnings, nor devoted enough to take the pain to stop and then squeeze the bubble. For the case of India and Malaysia, the monetary and economic officials were not equipped with the new (or other appropriate) theoretical framework, and therefore did not even know the appropriate way to deal with the bubble. As a result, the property bubbles in these economies have grown to highly vulnerable sizes. The above examples suggest that

(i)   sufficient academic research capacity; and
(ii) properly trained monetary and economic officials in the related economies could make substantial differences.

Similarly, with the outbreak of the subprime crisis in the US, economists or policymakers equipped with the appropriate theoretical framework should be able to anticipate the high likelihood of further deterioration of the financial markets and economic activities in the US. Thus, even though Bernanke had underestimated the risk of further deepening of the crisis at the early stage, he soon recognized that it was necessary to implement quantitative easing (QE) to stop the US economy, and hence the global economy, from entering a great depression. During the three rounds of QEs, quite a number of Wall Street participants were either skeptical about the effectiveness of the QEs or worried about an immediate inflation risk. Nevertheless, these skeptics were eventually proved to be very wrong. As a matter of fact, with the QEs and other supplementary policies, the US was able to avoid a great depression similar to that in the 1930s. On the other hand, with the economic slack between 2009 and 2014–2015, inflation in the US was also low during that period of recovery. While the debate in the media at that time was between the Federal Reserve and some of these "theoretically less well trained" Wall Street participants, the author believes the more meaningful debate should be between Ben Bernanke and Paul Krugman.[11]

Similar examples also happened in China during the early stage of the global financial tsunami: with the proper theoretical framework and policy insight accumulated over the past 35 years, the author was able to judge that the subprime crisis and the anticipated deterioration in the US would

---

[11]Professor Paul Krugman, a Nobel Prize winner, was arguing for more stimulation on both the fiscal and monetary sides.

affect the Chinese economy. Thus, in his hot debate with the then Chinese central bank governor and most other Chinese economists at that time, the author urged the Chinese government to implement ultra-expansionary fiscal and monetary policies at the early stage of the global financial tsunami, i.e., before China's domestic demand being substantially weakened, which could trigger financial deleveraging and financial disintermediation, which would in turn deepen the potential recession (see Yip, 2011 for further details).

As a matter of fact, the 4 trillion yuan fiscal expenditure, drastic reduction in China's interest rate and then the ultra-expansionary monetary policy had pre-empted China from the very costly financial deleveraging and financial disintermediation that occurred in the US at that time. As a result, China only experienced a mild recession during the most turbulent period of the global financial tsunami, and such an achievement was well regarded by the international community. Unfortunately, because of the debate with the then Chinese central bank governor and other reasons, the author was both less able and less eager to submit policy recommendations to the Chinese central bank and to the Chinese leaders through the Xinhua News Agency. Without such type of assistance, the Chinese central bank did not seem to be aware of the need to mop up the excess liquidity after the turbulent period of the global financial tsunami. Such an excess liquidity had in turn contributed to an unnecessary surge in China's property prices in the subsequent period.

7.2.3 The Importance of Clearing Internal Weaknesses before It is Too Late

Another lesson for macroeconomic management is the importance of avoiding the accumulation of, or clearing existing, internal weaknesses before it is too late. While the US had managed to use the QEs to pre-empt the global financial tsunami from pushing the US economy into a depression, there was still a Great Recession with huge output loss, substantial rise in unemployment and disruptive plunges in asset prices. As well documented in the literature, the underlying cause for this very costly tsunami was prolonged and substantial accumulation of internal weaknesses in terms of rapid and prolonged rises in property prices, huge rises in risky loans, gigantic issues of toxic assets such as collateralized debt obligations (CDOs) and so on. If the US had avoided the building up of these internal weaknesses at the early stage, it could have pre-empted the costly tsunami at the beginning.

Similarly, if the government of Greece and some other peripheral European economies were willing to control their budget deficit (and avoid the related cheating) at the beginning, there would not be continuous accumulation of sovereign debts to unsustainable levels, and there would not be a European Debt Crisis right from the beginning. In other words, although the LTROs and OMTs had stopped the sovereign debt crisis from pushing the European economy into a depression, the debt crisis still resulted in a huge cost to Europe and the global economy (in terms of output losses, rises in unemployment rates and financial disruption), which could be avoided from the beginning.

On the Asian side, if Thailand and the other crisis-hit economies were able to avoid the accumulation of internal weaknesses (such as rapid and prolonged rises in asset prices, excessive loans and weak banking supervision, sustained rises in external debts through capital inflows and substantial surge of current account deficit) between the mid-1980s and 1997, there would have been no Asian financial crisis in 1997. Similarly, if Hong Kong, India, Malaysia and some other Asian economies were able to pre-empt the current property bubbles at the seeding stage or stop the gigantic enlargement of the bubbles at the development stage, the author would not need to issue the assessment of an unavoidable bursting of bubble in the subsequent years.

Thus, ability to identify internal weaknesses, pre-empt such kind of accumulation and clear (or reduce) these weaknesses at the early stage would be able to help the economy to avoid a costly crisis, and should be an important area of theoretical and practical development in macroeconomic management. For example, if there was sufficient theoretical development along this line, government economists and banks should by now know their "mortgage brokers" was one of the underlying causes of the Global Financial Tsunami, and should no longer allow the banks to make loans through mortgage brokers. Unfortunately, because of insufficient understanding of this among policymakers (and the greedy bank CEOs), Australian banks were still using mortgage brokers to approve a lot of risky housing loans for the banks. This had, in turn, contributed to a property bubble in Australia. If continued to be unchecked, this would eventually cause a bursting a property bubble and financial crisis in Australia.

As another example, based on previous literature on economic and financial crises, one could at least identify that there are currently a large number of internal weaknesses in many emerging markets (e.g., huge current account deficit financed by capital inflows, sustained accumulation of external debts and substantial rise in bank loans, rapid and prolonged rises in asset prices, and extensive moral hazard activities in the banking and financial sectors), and therefore be able to judge the high likelihood of an emergent market crisis during the later phase of interest rate hike in the US. If these emergent markets are able to select well-trained monetary and economic officials, these officials would be able to identify the major internal weaknesses of their economies, and clear (or reduce) some of these weaknesses before it is too late. Unfortunately, the author believes most, if not all, governments of these emergent economies are not aware of the importance of selecting well-trained officials who are capable of doing the hard job. Even in the very fortunate case that one or two of these emergent market government(s) managed to select the right officials, most emerging market governments would not be able to do so. Thus, as long as one such emergent market has an outbreak of crisis during the later phase of interest rate hike in the US, it will, through the contagion effect, trigger crises in other emergent markets with similar internal weaknesses. Therefore, one can easily judge that the likelihood of an emergent market crisis during the later phase of US interest rate hike would be extremely high. (*Postscript*: While the above comments were written in 2014, there were occasional emergent market crises happening in 2018. The author believes this is just the beginning, and more serious emergent market crises will appear in the subsequent years.)

7.2.4 Macroeconomic Management Requires a Proper Forward-looking Assessment of the Subsequent Economic Condition

Unlike the existing practice in economics which puts a lot or emphasis on empirical evidence or mathematical proofs, the proposed new discipline of macroeconomic management requires a forward-looking assessment of the subsequent economic condition, which would in turn affect the *scale* and *timing* of the adopted policies.

On the scale aspect, a serious assessment error could mean the adoption of insufficient or excessive measures, which could in turn make the policy virtually ineffective or result in an overcorrection of the target variables. For example, as explained in Chapter 1, if a property market has already built up an expectation of further rises in property prices which would trigger various changes in economic behaviors, vicious cycles and upward spirals that would fuel further rises in property prices, the unawareness (or an under-assessment) of these powerful changes would make the adopted curbing measures virtually ineffective (i.e., effects of the "far from sufficient curbing measures" being much smaller than the effects of these powerful changes, giving market participants the wrong impression that curbing measures during the asset inflation period would be ineffective). Similarly, a substantial plunge in property prices would also cause a reversal of expectation and trigger changes in economic behaviors, various vicious cycles (including the financial deleveraging, the financial disintermediation and the massive scale of fire sales highlighted in Chapter 1) and herding behavior in the downward direction. Failure to anticipate (or an under-assessment of) these powerful changes would make the adopted stimulation measures virtually ineffective (i.e., effects of the "far from sufficient stimulation measures" being much smaller than the effects of the powerful changes, thus unable to stop the crisis from deteriorating further). On the other hand, an overassessment error could also imply excessive curbing or stimulation measures. Nevertheless, as policymakers are more aware of standard economics than the new theoretical framework outlined in Chapter 1, this type of error is now less common. One such example was Charles Plosser's and Richard Fischer's opposition of the scale and length of QE2 and QE3 due to their overassessment of the pace of US economic recovery and inflation threat at that time. In Section 7.2.5, the author will discuss useful ways to avoid or reduce the consequence of such type of assessment errors.

On the timing aspect, an assessment error on the timing of economic prospect would mean a wrong timing of the adopted measures, which could be counter-productive and could create unnecessary volatility or even chaos. The cases discussed in Section 7.2.3 are some of the good examples on the time aspect. That is,

(1) Clearing the internal weakness at the early stage could help the economy avoid the potential crisis, while failure to clear the internal weakness at the early stage had cost (i) the US substantially during the global financial tsunami; (ii) the EU substantially during the European Debt Crisis and (iii) many Asian economies during the financial crisis in 1997. The author also believes similar failure would cost (i) Hong Kong and many Asian economies substantially during the expected bursting of the Asian property bubbles and the new round of Asian financial crisis and (ii) another emergent market crisis during the later phase of the interest rate hike in the US.

(2) On the other hand, China's good timing in its ultra-expansionary policies at the early stage of the global financial tsunami had pre-empted the financial deleveraging and financial disintermediation from happening in China. Without these good timing stimulations, there would be much deeper recession even if the Chinese govern-ment was able to perform a much bigger stimulation at the middle stage of the global financial tsunami.

7.2.5 Ways to Avoid or Reduce the Consequences of Assessment Error

In this section, the author will discuss some ways to avoid or reduce the consequence of the assessment errors outlined in Section 7.2.4. One pos-sible way is to *implement the measures* (e.g., curbing measures against overheating or asset inflation) *by phases from the early stage, with the pos-sibility of revising the doses and the timing of the measures with new data.* Such a strategy would help the government to search for the right dose of measures, and hence avoid unnecessary overdose or underdose of the measure. In fact, this was the spirit of Greenspan's strategy to achieve a softening of the US economy when he was the Federal Reserve Chairman. While recognizing the risk of an overheating of the US economy with insufficient information on the potential scale of the overheating and hence the necessary doses of interest rate hike, Greenspan adopted the strategy of increasing the interest rate hike step by step. With the feedback data on the subsequent US money supply and economic activities, Greenspan adjusted the subsequent dose and timing of the next interest rate increment.

The advantage of such a strategy is that it could help the related authority to search for the right dose and length of measures even though there could be unexpected major economic events. In fact, Ben Bernanke's and Janet Yellen's *state-dependent strategy* to

(i) end the government bond purchasing program in the US's QE; and
(ii) start the gradual increases in US interest rate back to the normal level,

could be considered as a modified version of Greenspan's strategy.

With this *state-dependent, forward-looking and adjustable strategy*, Bernanke and Yellen were able to avoid major negative events (such as further deterioration of the European debt crisis, concerns on the European, the Chinese and the global economic activities, as well as the drastic drop in oil price between late 2014 and early 2016) from stopping the gradual recovery of the US economy. In addition, if there is evidence of an overheating or slower trend in the subsequent recovery of the US economy, the Federal Reserve could adjust the dose and pace of its subsequent interest rate hike.

Similarly, the bubble-squeezing strategy against Hong Kong's property bubble proposed in Chapter 4 was another useful example inspired by Greenspan's strategy of doing the curbing by phases. That is, while

(i) recognizing that it was necessary to squeeze Hong Kong's property bubble before the eventual bursting of the bubble,
(ii) being unsure about the required dose of the prepaid mortgage installment and
(iii) recognizing the need to contain the correction of property price within the acceptable range,

the author tried to partition the effect of the whole policy into may parts, i.e., the unanticipated part versus the anticipated part, and then more subparts within the later stage.

While the strategy of implementing the measures by forward-looking and adjustable phases could be very useful, policymakers should avoid dogmatic adoption of the strategy without proper assessment of the suitability of the strategy for the particular circumstance. For example, in case there is a rapid deterioration of the situation (e.g., a crisis), the policymaker should implement stimulation measures in much bigger steps. For example, instead of the standard 0.25% interest rate cut, Bernanke chose to reduce US interest rate by 0.5% and then another unexpected 0.75% amid the rapid deterioration of the subprime crisis in early 2008. Subsequent outcome suggested even such a drastic pace of interest rate cut was at most enough to cause a temporary slowdown of the deterioration. If Bernanke were still sticking with the standard 0.25% gradual cut in interest rate, it would be highly likely that the US economy would dip into a crisis at a much earlier time (i.e., in early 2008). In short, while the strategy of implementing the measure by phases could be useful to search for the right doses of the measure, there are situations in which very bold measures should be adopted.

7.3 THE NEED FOR A NEW DISCIPLINE ON MACROECONOMIC MANAGEMENT

In short, good macroeconomic management requires deep theoretical foundation in economics (especially international macroeconomics and macroeconomics) as well as good policy insight and practical skill. As the consequences of macroeconomic mismanagement are huge, it is important to set up a new discipline on macroeconomic management.

Such a step would allow further knowledge accumulation on both the theoretical side and practical side. With further development of the new discipline, the author believes many of the painful outcomes (such as asset bubbles, financial crisis, exchange rate crisis, severe recession, hyperinflation and stagnation) could be avoided.

SHORT REFERENCES

Mishkin, F. S. (2012), *The Economics of Money, Banking Financial markets*, 10th edition, Addison-Wesley: Boston.

Shliefer, A. and Vishny, R. (2011), "Fire sales in finance and macroeconomics", *Journal of Economic Perspectives*, 25, 29–48.

Yip, P. S. L. (2005), *The Exchange Rate Systems in Hong Kong and Singapore: Currency Board vs Monitoring Band*, Prentice Hall: Singapore.

Yip, P. S. L. (2011), *China's Exchange Rate System Reform: Lessons for Macroeconomic Policy Management*, World Scientific: Singapore.

Yip, P. S. L. (2014), "The risk of property bubbles in Hong Kong and Singapore: Another aftershock crisis of the global financial tsunami?", *Singapore Economic Review*, 59, Article ID: 1450026.

Yip, P. S. L. and Teo, G. S. (2014), "A simple model on the Asian housing market and its policy implications", Working Paper, Economics Division, Nanyang Technological University.

Yip, P. S. L. (2018), "Some important characteristics of asset bubbles and financial crises", *Modern Economy*, 9, 1173–1168. www.scrip.org/journal/me.

Printed in the United States
By Bookmasters